Vertical Control of Markets

Vertical Control of Markets

Business and Labor Practices

Frederick R. Warren-Boulton
Washington University in St. Louis

Ballinger Publishing Company • Cambridge, Massachusetts
A Subsidiary of J.B. Lippincott Company

This book is printed on recycled paper.

International Standard Book Number: 0-88410-040-5

Library of Contress Catalog Card Number: 77-9618

Printed in the United States of America

Library of Congress Cataloging in Publication Data

Warren-Boulton, Frederick R
Vertical control of markets.

1. Restraint of trade. 2. Trusts, Industrial. 3. Restrictive practices in industrial relations. I. Title.

HD2731.W37 338.8 77-9618
ISBN 0-88410-040-5

To Mimi

Contents

List of Figures and Tables

FIGURES

TABLES

Preface

The incentives for economic units to exert some form of control over multiple stages of production are examined in this book. The goal is to help explain the vertical dimensions within which economic organizations such as firms and unions choose to operate, and the economic effects of that choice. An understanding of vertical relationships is essential both for explaining the existing economic structure and for formulating desirable public policy.

As a policy issue, vertical control has an extensive history in both the economic and legal fields. Forms of vertical control as diverse as vertical integration, resale price maintenance, franchising, and union work rules have all come under attack in legislatures and in the courts, and the use of most forms of vertical control has been declared illegal in at least some situations.

At this writing the vertical structures in two major industries—petroleum and telecommunications—have become major policy issues. Largely in response to the energy crisis, several bills have been presented in Congress that would require vertical divestiture by the major oil companies, and divestiture is also a likely goal of the Federal Trade Commission's proceedings against the major oil companies. In telecommunications, the Justice Department is once again attempting to separate AT&T from its equipment manufacturing subsidiary, Western Electric. The assets that could be affected by these actions alone total literally in the hundreds of billions of dollars.

The recent heightening of policy interest in vertical integration has stimulated an already significant amount of theoretical work done in this area over the past few years. In particular the transaction cost approach, and the introduction of variable-proportions models that allow substitution between inputs, have significantly increased our understanding of the incentives for vertical control and its effects. While most of this work has dealt with vertical control by firms, there is a growing interest in applying the analysis to explaining and evaluating labor union behavior.

To the extent possible in a rapidly growing area, this book tries to present both the traditional and the more recent developments in the vertical control area, although an overemphasis on my own work is perhaps inevitable. It is hoped that this attempt at completeness will make what follows of interest not only to economists working in the area but also to policymakers with either legal or economic backgrounds. Some understanding of basic microeconomics is assumed throughout, although an attempt has been made to segregate sections that require a stronger background in economics, especially in mathematical terms. In particular the analysis of vertical control is enormously simplified if production with fixed proportions between inputs is assumed. For many incentives, this assumption is not crucial. The discussion of the variable-proportions case for firms is thus deferred until Chapter 5. The reader impatient with seemingly endless equations or who is willing simply to accept their validity will probably wish to read in detail only the very beginning and the final section of Chapter 5. Chapter 6, dealing with vertical control by labor unions, does assume variable proportions. Most of the analysis, however, deals with the Cobb-Douglas case (constant unitary elasticity of substitution), which makes this chapter less dense than Chapter 5. Chapters 5 and 6 are expanded versions of two previously published papers: "Vertical Control with Variable Proportions," *Journal of Political Economy*, vol. 82, July/August 1974 (© 1974 by the University of Chicago Press, all rights reserved); and "Vertical Control by Labor Unions," *American Economic Review*, vol. 67, June 1977 (© American Economic Association 1977).

Acknowledgments

A major reward to any author is the chance to thank those who have been of assistance along the way. This book is a grandson of my Princeton Ph.D. dissertation, and my greatest debt is to Professor Charles Berry, the chairman of my committee. For better or worse, this book would never have been written without his continued encouragement, assistance, and remarkable patience. David Bradford, Laura Tyson, and Alan Blinder also provided a number of helpful criticisms. I owe a large debt to my colleagues at Washington University in St. Louis, both for their comments and for their restraint in asking when this book would be completed. In particular, Edward Kalachek, Robert Parks, Lee Benham, and Trout Rader read parts of the manuscript and gave numerous helpful comments. By definition, any errors are in sections on which they did not comment. Thanks are also due to Mark McBride for his valuable work as a research assistant, to Mrs. Gloria Lucy for her always cheerful typing of revisions and mathematical appendixes, and to Karl Oelgeschlager at Ballinger for his suggestions and patience. Financial support from the Center for the Study of American Business at Washington University, as well as the encouragement of its director, Murray Weidenbaum, are also gratefully acknowledged.

Vertical Control of Markets

Chapter 1

Introduction

Industrial organization theory has always been more advanced in its analysis of horizontal market structure than in its analysis of vertical market structure. The incentives and effects of horizontal control appear theoretically clearer and more susceptible to empirical testing than do the incentives and effects of vertical control. As a result, economic analysis has provided a firm basis for public policy toward horizontal mergers or horizontal price-fixing agreements, while providing far less guidance for public policy toward efforts to exert vertical control. This failure has been stressed in a recent review of the theory of vertical integration (vertical control through ownership):

> The study of vertical integration has presented difficulties at both theoretical and policy levels of analysis. That vertical integration has never enjoyed a secure place in value theory is attributable to the fact that, under conventional assumptions, it is an anomaly: if the costs of operating competitive markets are zero, "as is usually assumed in our theoretical analysis" (Arrow, 1969, p. 48), why integrate?
>
> Policy interest in vertical integration has been concerned mainly with the possibility that integration can be used strategically to achieve anticompetitive effects. In the absence of a more substantial theoretical foundation, vertical integration, as a public policy matter, is typically regarded as having dubious if not outright antisocial properties. [Williamson, 1971, p.112]

In the absence of a better model, the courts have evaluated vertical control in terms of its foreclosure effects,[1] although the exclusion of competitors from certain markets is only one of numerous possible motivations or effects of vertical control. In addition, the various forms of vertical control have generally been analyzed separately. Vertical control can take several forms, as listed below. Examples include:

1. *Vertical integration*: Two or more separable stages of production are combined under common ownership.[2] Integration can result either from the merger of previously independent firms at different stages or by de novo entry by a firm operating at one stage into production at another stage. "Downstream" or "forward" integration (integration into stages closer to the final consumer) is usually distinguished from "upstream" or "backward" integration (integration into production of inputs previously supplied by independent firms).[3]

2. *Tying arrangements*: The seller agrees to sell one product (the tying good) to the buyer only if the buyer also agrees to purchase another product or service (the tied good) from the seller.

3. *Exclusive dealing*: The buyer is required not to deal in the products of some other producers.

4. *Requirements contracts*: The buyer is required to purchase all of his requirements from the seller.

5. *Full-line forcing*: The buyer must purchase the seller's entire line of products as a condition of purchase of any one product.

6. *Royalty arrangements:* Payment to the supplier of an input such as labor or technology is based on the quantity of output of the final product rather than on the quantity of the input.

7. *Profit-sharing agreements*: Payment for one input is based on the profits made in the final-product market, or on the return to another input such as capital.

8. *Resale price setting*: The producer or wholesaler of a product, as a condition of sale, sets a minimum or maximum price for resale.

9. *Work rules*: The supplier of an input requires the purchaser to use the input in a given proportion either to output or to some other input. While usually imposed by labor unions, a fixed input-output ratio can also be imposed by firms, either by agreement or by designing the product so as to prevent its use in different proportions.

For analytical purposes, the distinction between price and nonprice forms of control is often relevant. For example, work rules and (generally) vertical integration permit direct control over vertically related levels, while tying or royalty arrangements utilize the price mechanism. Different forms of vertical control can be close substitutes for achieving a given end, and the choice between forms will often depend on the relative costs of market and hierarchical operations.

For public policy, however, it is not the form of vertical control chosen that is critical, but rather the rationale and effect of control.

For example, both vertical integration and tying contracts can be used to achieve price discrimination. If price discrimination is deemed undesirable, then vertical integration and tying arrangements should be treated identically when they are utilized to achieve price discrimination. On the same principle, vertical integration undertaken in order to achieve price discrimination should be treated differently from vertical integration undertaken in order to eliminate monopoly payments to suppliers. Indeed, in certain circumstances horizontal and vertical control can be shown to have identical motives and effects, a situation that calls for the harmonization of public policies between vertical and horizontal control.

In addition, an economic model of vertical control should be applicable to all users of vertical control. Unions and firms, for example, may have different goals, and society may choose to evaluate the effects of their actions differently. Nevertheless, an economic model of vertical control should be able to explain the motivation and effect of vertical control undertaken both by firms and by unions.

The economic analysis of vertical control should thus take the approach of analyzing the particular motivations for vertical control and their effects, whatever the form of control used or the economic units involved. For public policy purposes, these incentives can be placed in three general classifications:

1. Incentives for vertical control that exist under competitive conditions in all markets.
2. Incentives for vertical control that are created as a result of certain governmental actions.
3. Incentives for vertical control that are created as a result of horizontal market power.

The basic reason for all vertical control is the absence of a "perfect" intermediate market—a market with zero transactions costs, perfect information, and competitive pricing. To the extent that these conditions do not exist, the use of vertical control becomes more attractive relative to reliance on markets.

When market costs reflect the social opportunity cost of using markets, public policy can remain neutral toward the degree of vertical control chosen. However, if markets are imperfect due to government policies or market power, there is a case for public intervention. In general the "first-best" solution would be improvement of the market mechanism through the elimination of market power and through the redesign of government policies to make them "neutral" toward the degree of vertical control. If this is not done, however, then restriction of the resulting degree of vertical control may be a feasible "second-best" solution.

Of the above three classifications of vertical control, only vertical control resulting from horizontal market power and government policies are of major public-policy interest. For three reasons, however, it is still necessary to examine briefly the motivations for vertical control under competitive conditions. First, it provides an understanding of much of existing market structure. Second, it enables identification of cases of vertical control where public policy is not required; by elimination, this assists in determining those cases where public action is desirable. Third, vertical control in any particular case may occur for several reasons—some desirable and some undesirable—and policies to restrict vertical control may prevent the realization of socially desirable aims as well as undesirable ones.

Chapter 2 is therefore devoted to a discussion of the incentives for vertical control that can exist under competitive conditions in all markets. Vertical control due to government policies is examined in Chapter 3. Vertical control resulting from market power is treated in Chapter 4, assuming a fixed-proportions technology. Chapter 5 deals with the variable-proportions incentive for vertical control, for the case where an input monopolist is a profit-maximizing firm. Chapter 6 examines the variable-proportions incentive when the input monopolist is a utility-maximizing labor union, with particular reference to vertical control by the United Mine Workers. Finally, Chapter 7 provides a summary of the analysis and some conclusions for public policy.

NOTES

1. The primary vice of a vertical merger . . . is that, by foreclosing the competitors of either party from a segment of the market otherwise open to them, the arrangement may act as a "clog on competition," which "deprives rivals of a fair opportunity to compete." Every extended vertical arrangement by its very nature, for at least a time, denies to competitors of the supplier the opportunity to compete for part or all the trade of the customer party to the vertical arrangement.

Opinion of Chief Justice Warren in *Brown Shoe Co.* v *United States*, 370 U.S. 323, 324 (1962).

2. Like a camel, vertical integration is easier to recognize than to define. The problem is to define a "stage of production," since "within every establishment, the same productive functions may be conceived as a continuous process or, alternatively, subdivided into a vast number of separate operations, each of which may be identified as a separate stage of production" (Gort, 1962, pp. 11-12).

Every productive unit (including households) is vertically integrated to some degree. Vertical integration is thus often defined in economic rather than technological terms—for example, as the "[transmission] from one of [a firm's] departments to another [of] a good or service which could, without major adaptation, be sold in the market" (Adelman, 1949, p. 27). In practice, however, we do not know if stages are economically separable unless we actually observe successful separate production by at least some firms.

One operational "solution" to this problem is simply to define economically separable stages as successive 4-digit SIC industries (Gort, 1962). Alternatively, production can be divided into intuitively reasonable stages—for example, extraction, refining, semifinished manufacturing, finished manufacturing, transportation, wholesale distribution, and retail distribution (Livesay and Porter, 1969). Even if there is no clear absolute definition of vertical integration, however, we can still compare the degree of vertical integration between firms (Gort, 1962; Rusin and Atwood, 1976) or over time (Livesay and Porter, 1969; Laffer, 1969) using such measures as the ratio of value-added to sales; the ratio of employment in all "auxiliary" activities to aggregate employment (Gort, 1962); (inversely) the ratio of corporate sales to gross corporate product (Laffer, 1969); the number of "stages" (Livesay and Porter, 1969); or the ratio of value added by the firm to the "final product value" of the firm's output (the value of all final products incorporating any of the firm's output) (Rusin and Atwood, 1976).

3. This distinction is not always clear or useful. Vertical integration may be simultaneously upstream and downstream. For example (see Oi and Hurter, 1965), a firm may use its own trucks both to distribute its final products (downstream integration) and to transport inputs to its factory (upstream integration). As another example, suppose that an automobile assembler integrates into parts production (see Crandall, 1968). The same part may be used either as an original part in assembly (in which case this is clearly upstream integration) or sold as a repair part (in which case we could regard parts production as either horizontal integration or, if time is the distinction, as downstream vertical integration).

Chapter 2

Vertical Control Under Competition

The motivations for vertical control under competitive conditions can be listed under five headings. While this particular taxonomy is somewhat arbitrary and can result in some overlapping, vertical control under competitive conditions can be discussed in terms of technological interdependencies, information costs, control effectiveness, externalities, and risk aversion.

Since vertical integration enables complete vertical control, only vertical integration can be used in every case to achieve all the aims of vertical control. Where partial forms of vertical control can achieve the particular goal, the choice depends on the relative costs and effectiveness of the possible forms. Thus the general discussion of each motivation will be in terms of vertical integration, with alternative forms of vertical control introduced and evaluated when applicable.

TECHNOLOGICAL INTERDEPENDENCIES

Some production sequences must be carried out in immediate order and in the same place in order to minimize costs. These are usually flow processes, the classic example of which is iron and steel manufacture, where steady flow reduces reheating costs and provides use of the by-products of one stage, such as burnable gases, as inputs in other stages. Major technological interdependencies have also been asserted to exist between the equipment manufacturing and the operating levels in telecommunications.[1]

Strictly speaking, the technology itself does not require vertical integration. It is quite possible for two stages of production that must be closely coordinated in time and place to be under different ownership and separated by a market. Such a technology would, however, place particularly heavy demands on the market. First, considerable detailed information and exact control may have to be provided by a price mechanism. Second, externalities may well arise. Third, efficient production may dictate a single plant at each level, and competitive behavior may not be possible with such a market structure. Technological interdependencies can thus be broken down into problems of information, control, externalities, and market-power.

INFORMATION COSTS

In many cases vertical integration may enable the acquisition or transfer of information at lower cost than would a market. A market system is simply one way of transferring information (notably in the form of prices) and controlling behavior. If markets fail to provide accurate and complete information about a transaction, however, alternative systems may be preferred. It has been argued that markets have particular difficulties with information transfer in three situations: first, where the good transferred is information itself, usually technological in nature; second, where information about future market price and quality is desired, but small numbers of participants in the market can be expected and considerable uncertainty or complexity is present; and third, where information costs lead to price inflexibility.

Information as a Commodity

The arguments that the market for information is inherently imperfect are well known (see Arrow, 1962). The difficulty with specifying property rights in information is that the benefits from its use cannot be completely appropriated even when patent or other legal devices can be used. There is a "fundamental paradox in the determination of demand for information; its value to the purchaser is not known until he has the information, but then he has in effect acquired it without cost" (Arrow, 1962, p. 615). In other words, it is difficult to provide information about information without giving it away. Transferring information through a market can thus involve high contracting, monitoring, exclusion, and enforcement costs. If the internalization of the transfer would reduce these costs, firms may integrate backward into production of information or downstream into applications of information.[2]

As Hirshleifer (1971, 1973) points out, however, the problems raised by imperfect appropriability may be significantly reduced if new information results in pecuniary effects (wealth redistributions due to price revaluations) in addition to any technological effects (improvements in production functions). Through speculation or sale of the information, the original possessor may be able to capture some of these pecuniary effects. This observation has some very interesting implications for the traditional argument that imperfect appropriability leads, from a social viewpoint, to underinvestment in inventive activity.[3] If capturable pecuniary effects are significant, the private gain from information acquisition may be greater than the social gain, information acquisition may be profitable even when information cannot affect action so no social gains are present, and the privately optimal price (that is, the profit-maximizing price) for information may be zero or negative (advertising, for example).

If capturable pecuniary effects are significant, the incentives for vertical control become more complex. In particular, vertical integration may no longer be necessary or even desirable. Since extensive dissemination of the information magnifies any pecuniary effects, the privately optimal price for the information will tend to fall. Contracting, monitoring, exclusion, and enforcement costs also fall as a result, ultimately to zero as the price approaches zero. In addition, integration often involves the acquisition of factors whose rents may either rise or fall as the result of new information. Ownership of these factors would be clearly undesirable if the new information would reduce the value of these factors. Even if their value increased, it may be much less expensive to capture these pecuniary effects through mechanisms such as futures markets than through ownership of factors.

Market Information

The problem of information transfer in narrow markets has been extensively analyzed, notably by Williamson (1975). Williamson sees the choice between market and hierarchical (internal) transactions as explained by a set of environmental and human factors. The environmental factors are complexity compounded by uncertainty, and small numbers of transactors. The human factors are bounded rationality (the limited capacity of the human mind to deal with very complex real-world problems) and opportunism (strategic manipulation of information, or misrepresentation, for personal gain). If information relevant to a transaction is known by one or more parties, but cannot be discerned by or displayed for others without cost ("information impactedness") because of bounded rationality and complexity, opportunistic behavior may result unless checked by large-numbers competition. Unfortunately, even if the number of potential participants to a transaction is large, the "winners of initial contracts acquire, in a learning-by-doing fashion, nontrivial information advantages over nonwinners. Consequently, even though large-numbers competition may have been feasible at the time the initial award was made, parity no longer holds at the contract renewal interval. . . . Small-numbers bargaining situations thus evolve" (Williamson, 1975, pp. 34-35).

In such situations the information supplied by market prices will be incomplete or inaccurate. If hierarchical organization can reduce the conditions giving rise to transaction difficulties, internal transfer in a hierarchical organization becomes correspondingly more attractive. In particular, "hierarchy extends the bounds on rationality by permitting the specialization of decision-making and economizing on communication expense, . . . permits additional incentive and control techniques to be brought to bear in a more selective manner, thereby serving to curb small-numbers opportunism, . . . permits interdependent units to adapt to unforeseen contingencies in a coordinated way and furthermore serves to 'absorb' uncertainty, . . . permits small-numbers bargaining indeterminacies to be resolved by fiat, . . . extends the constitutional powers to perform an audit, thereby narrowing the information gap; . . . [and] provides, for some purposes at least, a less calculative exchange atmosphere" (Williamson, 1975, pp. 257-58).

Although information considerations may lead to vertical integration, the connection should not be overstated. To begin with, vertical integration is not a perfect solution to information-transfer problems. Opportunistic behavior often leads to information distortions within firms, especially if information distortion can affect pecuniary rents to subgroups.[4] Integration does not eliminate the need for accurate internal prices at each production level, or the need to investigate alternative external sources of supply. Vertical integration does not guarantee that information becomes less expensive or more reliable.

In addition to any such defects in internal organization, there are two other points worth some discussion, which restrict the role of information as an incentive for vertical integration. First, for a very wide range of cases, use of the market will not result in information problems. Where large markets for standardized commodities exist, prices provide accurate and sufficient information. But even when transfer of nonprice, complex, and individual information is necessary, markets may still provide incentives for supplying accurate and sufficient information. Second, even where markets fail, forms of vertical control other than integration may be chosen or, if integration is chosen, it may only be partial.

Opportunistic behavior may be unprofitable in the long run, even if temporary gains can be made. Deliberate distortions can result in a loss of goodwill or reputation, which can be expensive in future transactions, as well as possibly inviting legal sanctions or punitive retaliation.[5] This deterrent to deliberate distortion usually requires, however, both that the "true" information will eventually become apparent and that future transactions are anticipated that would be endangered by the discovery that inaccurate or incomplete information had been supplied. Since integration is not likely unless a continuing relationship is expected, integration is mainly likely to have a comparative advantage over informal sanctions in cases where true information does not become increasingly evident or where discrete transactions are large and discount rates high.

Supplying incorrect or insufficient information, however, may not be profitable behavior even in the absence of sanctions. Supplying accurate information to other production levels can be expected to reduce costs and, in the long run, reduce prices charged by those levels. If, as would generally be the case, inputs at different levels are complementary, lower prices at other levels will increase the derived demand for the output of the information-supplying level. Integration to reduce intentional information distortion is thus unlikely to the extent that levels are complementary and, ceteris paribus, lower costs at any level can be expected to reduce prices charged by that level.

In addition, even though such information is valuable to other levels, the optimal supply price may well be zero or negative. For example, Arrow (1975) examines the case where output by upstream firms is a random variable, but each upstream firm has some information about its supply one period in advance. This information is valuable to downstream firms, since their capital decision must also be made one period in advance of output. While the acquisition of this information could provide an incentive for upstream integration, the problem is that "the upstream industry can appropriate the benefits of better information by *giving* the information to the downstream industry. Thus while vertical integration is sufficient, it is apparently not necessary" (Spence, 1975, p. 168).

Integration will be a possible result, however, if for some reason the provision of correct information by one level would lead to non-optimal behavior (from the viewpoint of the information-supplying level) by other levels. Crandall (1968b, pp. 32-43), for example, has examined a case very similar to that posed by Arrow (1975), in the context of the automobile industry. Assemblers are assumed to have superior but limited information about future demand for automotive parts, information that would be of considerable value to suppliers in reducing uncertainty, and could thus be expected to reduce the cost of parts to assemblers. In large-numbers situations, this information could be transferred either directly or through futures contracts. Assemblers are unwilling to enter into long-term contracts, however, because "since assemblers can never be absolutely certain of future [upstream] cost conditions, annual contracts permit constant re-evaluation of transaction price which allows the supplier no more than a competitive rate of return. Moreover, this allows the assemblers to wield the potent threat of entry in the bargaining with consequent effects on the final transaction. . . . In short, far from entering into futures contracts with suppliers, assemblers act to engender uncertainty in these upstream firms" (Crandall, 1968b, pp. 33-34).

This control over suppliers is, however, achieved at a real cost. Increased uncertainty upstream can be expected to result in both increased risk and, given lags in adjusting fixed assets upstream to optimal levels, real production inefficiencies. These costs must eventually be passed on to assemblers. In addition, even if suppliers had the best information available, their incentives to adjust output rapidly to new conditions—either by holding inventories, maintaining excess capacity, or by rapidly adjusting fixed capital—will be sub-optimal from the point of view of assemblers, since supply shortages may result in assemblers losing not only present but also future sales.

While backward vertical integration would be one possible solution, Crandall argues that assemblers have found a superior alternative. Since the problem is the level and speed of adjustment of fixed capital used upstream, assemblers need only "quasi-integrate" by providing all special tools, dies, and fixtures used by suppliers, thus directly controlling these inputs. Such quasi-integration is but one example of a preference for the scalpel over the meat axe. If markets are imperfect only in certain aspects, the degree of vertical control required may be correspondingly limited. Partial forms of vertical control such as franchising, dealerships, requirements contracts,[6] tying arrangements, profit-sharing, or royalty arrangements may facilitate information transfer. Access to internal information of suppliers or customers may even be demanded as a condition for market transactions (Blois, 1972).

Even if ownership is necessary, the information provided by integration may not be proportional to the amount of internalized production. Partial or "tapered" integration, where only part of the supply or market is controlled, may then be chosen, especially if there are diminishing returns to information or if information from the controlled segment is applicable to independent producers. Ownership of one source of supply of a particular input (or of one of the users of the firm's output) can provide information for bargaining with the independent firms, for assessing investment opportunities at vertically related levels, or for predicting future conditions at those levels, If there are costs to integration, a limited sampling approach may be optimal.[7]

Information Costs and Price Inflexibility

Finally, if integration improves communication between levels, an integrated structure may allow a more rapid adjustment to changing demand or cost conditions that would use of a market. A major symptom of market failure in such circumstances would be price inflexibility, giving rise to an extended period of disequilibrium during which markets may not clear. In such situations, integration may affect both the new equilibrium position and the disequilibrium path.

The effect of communication failure on the new equilibrium position following a single initial disturbance has been of particular concern to writers on economic development. If investment in one industry leads to price changes, the profitability of other industries may be affected. For these "pecuniary external economies" (Scitovsky, 1954) to be significant requires, first, that investment indivisibilities prevent continuous output and price adjustment in the investing industry and, second, that these price changes are not accurately anticipated at other levels. Markets may fail to accurately signal future prices because they "reflect the economic situation as it is and not as it will be. For this reason, they are more useful for co-ordinating current production decisions, which are immediately effective and guided by short-run considerations, than they are for co-ordinating investment decisions, . . ." (Scitovsky, 1953, p. 150). Such coordination could be provided by futures markets or by centralized planning. In many situations, however, vertical integration may be the efficient solution, especially if, as can be expected, pecuniary externalities occur mainly at vertically related levels. If there is some lag in the reaction of the unintegrated firm's customers to an expansion of output or a reduction in price, the expansion may cause temporary losses to the firm. As a result, an investment and the corresponding price change which would be profitable for an integrated firm with better communication between levels may not be profitable for a unintegrated firm (see Wolfe, 1961). Thus the final equilibrium position may depend on the vertical market structure.

More recent interest, however, has centered on analyzing competitive behavior in situations of continuous disequilibrium due to stochastic demand fluctuations. Firms and their customers can respond to demand uncertainty in a large number of ways. Firms facing unanticipated demand increases, for example, can respond by running down inventories (either of output or of factors which are sufficiently variable to be useable within the excess demand period), by increased search for additional variable inputs, by raising prices, or by nonprice rationing mechanisms such as queuing. If inventories were costless to hold, or if instantaneous production at constant cost was possible, these responses would clearly dominate price or non-price rationing. However for many products such as perishable agricultural commodities, holding inventories can be very expensive, and decisions affecting production levels must be made considerably in advance of output availability. The relevant short-run choice is then between price and non-price rationing. In some cases, prices may be rigid because of administrative costs of price changes or because of government regulations or private contracts which impose legal or quasi-legal restrictions on price changes. A more general explanation for price rigidities, however, can be based on information costs. Unanticipated price changes may induce costly additional search by buyers and sellers (Alchian, 1970). Alternatively if transactions must occur at discrete points in time because of commodity indivisibilities or economies of scale in transacting, an extended period may be required before the new demand conditions are accurately determined (Gordon and Hynes, 1970).

To simplify the analysis, let us assume a non-storable intermediate good which is fixed in supply, and rigid in price, over the relevant period. The good is produced and demanded by competitive firms that face either demand or production uncertainties. Several alternative rationing mechanisms can then be introduced to deal with the resulting temporary shortages and surpluses in the intermediate market. Turnovsky (1971) for example, assumes that firms must order inputs before availability is known, with actual availability fluctuating around the level ordered. The rather surprising result of this model is that firms plan to produce the same quantity and to use the same factor mix as they would under certainty. Firms do, however, increase their orders for uncertain inputs above the amount desired under certainty, thus providing a safety margin which increases the probability of obtaining the desired amount of the input. Turnovsky does not examine the effects of integration in this situation. One result of his model, however, is that firms will never wish to purchase more than the planned level of the input at the given (rigid) price. If the quantity available is greater than the planned level but less than the amount ordered, the firm is committed to purchase the available amount. However the firm will never purchase more than the amount ordered, and any excess over ordered levels is wasted, even if the marginal product of such extra units is positive. If upstream suppliers could sell such extra quantities at their reservation prices, a lower price for ordered quantities would be possible, which would lead to increased planned usage. It appears, therefore, that Turnovsky's result that uncertainty does not alter planned usage is critically dependent on the assumption that uncertainty does not increase the (rigid) price set by suppliers before availability is known. Similarly, even if integration does not reduce uncertainty, integration would be both profitable and desirable if internal transfer would facilitate usage of periodic excess quantities. The resulting reduction in the costs of uncertainty would lead to a reduction in the internal shadow price for the input and an increase in planned usage by the integrated firm.

By contrast, Green (1974) assumes a fixed-proportions technology downstream, so excess quantities above planned levels cannot be used. With a rigid intermediate-good price, stochastic fluctuations in demand from outside users of the intermediate good lead to rationing of one side of the market or the other. Suppliers or customers are randomly chosen for all-or-nothing rationing. Firms which rely on the market cannot affect their probability of being rationed out. Integrated firms, however, can transfer the intermediate good between levels without running the risk of being rationed. Since this implies that all firms would gain from integration, Green assumes that integrated firms are technically less efficient than unintegrated firms. With fixed proportions and constant returns to scale, both the inefficiency cost per-unit from integration and the rationing-induced cost per-unit from use of the market are independent of the degree of integration chosen by the individual firm. Thus if a firm does choose to integrate, integration will be balanced, with no participation in the intermediate market. Integration by any one firm, however, will reduce both demand and supply in the market. In most situations, we would expect this withdrawal to amplify the effect on the market of given fluctuations in demand from outside users, and thus to increase the remaining unintegrated firms' probability of being rationed. Integration by one firm will therefore increase the cost of using the market and tend to induce integration by other firms, while vertical divestiture by one firm will decrease the cost of using the market and tend to induce voluntary vertical divestiture by other firms. Thus the only potential stable equilibria are the two extremes of either industry-wide integration or industry-wide use of the intermediate market. If both extremes are stable equilibria, a public policy which forces vertical divestiture on an industry to above some critical proportion will induce a wave of voluntary divestiture by the remaining firms. Furthermore, changes in the inefficiency cost of integration or in the size of exogenous demand fluctuations will either not affect industry structure or else will induce a discontinuous industry-wide shift from one extreme to the other. Thus both the initial equilibrium position and the timing of any changes in that equilibrium may be non-optimal. While this implies a role for public policy toward integration, three qualifications are immediately apparant. First, the information requirements for a correct policy decision appear to be large and probably beyond the practical ability of policymakers. Second, the required decision-making level is the industry rather than government. Although the externalities from integration are real, they appear to be confined to the industry. Finally, the rationing mechanism assumed in this model is rather drastic. If the cost of being rationed is high, firms can be expected to negotiate contracts specifying both price and availability. Integration can be viewed as one way of facilitating such contracts. But if the cost of integration is high, alternative market mechanisms such as long-term contracts may be used. Since certainty benefits both suppliers and customers, a premium for certainty is not necessarily implied. The transaction cost of the least expensive market mechanism provides an upper bound to the incentive for integration. Furthermore, these transaction costs may well be independent of the degree of integration in the industry, thus eliminating the externalities rationale for public intervention.

In a closely related article, Carlton (1976) argues that final-demand uncertainty can induce competitive firms to control part of their anticipated input requirements through either upstream integration or long-term supply contracts. A fixed-proportions production function with constant returns to scale is assumed for downstream firms. Each downstream firm must determine both its final-product price and the level of at least one input before the firm's final demand is known. Once demand is known, each unintegrated downstream firm can turn to only one unintegrated upstream firm for its variable input needs. Since upstream price and production decisions must also be made by each upstream firm before their demand is known, upstream firms face some probability of being left with unsold and unstorable output. The expected cost of such unsold quantities is reflected in a market price for the input which is higher than the unit cost of production. Under these conditions, upstream integration or long-term contracts involve both potential benefits and potential costs to downstream firms. On the one hand, it is assumed that controlled inputs cannot be sold on the open market. Thus if a downstream firm's input demand is less than its controlled amount, the cost of the resulting excess supply is born directly by the downstream firm. On the other hand, the firm can now frequent two sources of supply, since if the desired quantity is greater than the controlled supply, the firm can still turn to one independent supplier for any additional requirements. The implicit assumption is that internal search is costless, or at least significantly less expensive or time-consuming than external search. If there is a high probability that at least some amount of the input will be desired by the downstream firm, there is a clear incentive for the downstream firm to internally produce or contract for this high-probability demand. Since there is a correspondingly low probability that such quantities will be utilized and wasted, the internal cost of such quantities will be less than the market price, which must reflect the average, rather than marginal, probability of excess supply. Furthermore, since two supply sources can be frequented, it would appear that the integrated firm faces a lower probability of being unable to purchase the desired amount of its input than does the unintegrated firm.

As in Green's model, however, integration by any one firm imposes costs on other firms. With the relatively high-probability demand removed from the market, the risk of unsold quantities increases for upstream suppliers and the market price rises to compensate. Partial integration by all downstream firms will thus reduce their cost of acquiring high-probability quantities while increasing the price paid for residual amounts. Carlton then argues that such risk-shifting is necessarily inefficient since unintegrated upstream firms can serve several downstream firms and can thus pool risks. Since upstream firms are more efficient absorbers of risk, aggregate welfare is always higher with no integration than with either partial or total integration. Carlton also shows, however, that in this situation, the introduction of a new technology that would benefit society is more likely to occur in a market with vertical integration than in a market without vertical integration.

The welfare implications of integration caused by price inflexibility are therefore ambiguous and may be extremely difficult to sign in any particular instance. One possible indication of negative welfare effects would be statements by firms in an industry that upstream vertical control is profitable for any single firm, but unprofitable for the industry as a whole. Even if the social desirability of vertical control can be determined, however, several forms of vertical control—notably integration, long-term supply contracts, or even holding larger inventories—may be close substitutes. In practice, it may be impossible to prevent the use of some of these alternative forms, and thus little or nothing may be gained from intervention.

The models discussed in this section do, however, provide a significant contribution in the analysis of what is probably the most frequently given reason for upstream integration—the need for "assured" or "dependable" supplies when considerable uncertainty is present. We should distinguish, however, between several possible situations where such an explanation for integration might be given. First, if prices are flexible and markets clear, the problem is uncertainty about price rather than about supplies. In this case, the underlying incentive for integration is risk aversion, discussed later in this chapter. Alternatively, prices may be held consistently below the equilibrium level, giving rise to continued shortages. Such cases are usually due to government intervention, and are discussed in Chapter 3 in the section on price controls. Third, prices may be held consistently above the competitive level due to market power upstream. The incentive for upstream integration is then clear. Finally, there are situations where temporary (that is, intra-period rather than inter-period) price inflexibility in a competitive market leads to temporary shortages or supluses. It is such situations which are relevant for the models presented by Turnovsky (1971), Green (1974), and Carlton (1976), as well as for models (discussed in the "Control" section of this chapter) which examine the decision to vertically integrate as a decision to use quantities rather than prices as a planning instrument.

CONTROL

Vertical integration permits decisions to be made by fiat rather than through a process of bargaining. In complex and dynamic situations, where continual revision in specifications and prices is necessary or where immediate decisions are required, the cost of control through fiat may be much less than through bargaining or litigation (see Williamson, 1964; 1972). Control by ownership may also be desired if a firm is critically dependent on a supplier. An upstream strike, for example, may impose heavy costs on both the downstream firm and downstream labor suppliers. Firm vertical integration, especially if followed by union vertical integration, should thus reduce conflict by increasing both labor and managements' incentives to settle rapidly.[8]

One useful approach to the control issue when significant uncertainty is present is to translate the choice between control through markets and control through ownership into a choice between planning instruments. Markets rely mainly on prices as planning instruments, although many market transactions specify non-price aspects. In contrast, internal transactions tend to rely heavily on quantities as planning instruments. If common ownership facilitates the use of quantities as planning instruments, then we should tend to observe integration in situations where users of an intermediate good find that it is more efficient to specify that a certain amount of the intermediate good be supplied at an uncertain mininum cost than to specify a price for the intermediate good, with the resulting quantity uncertain. This choice has been rigorously modeled as a planning problem by Weitzman (1974). He finds that uncertainty in the benefit function (the derived demand for the intermediate good) has a roughly equal effect on the efficiency of price and quantity instruments. Uncertainty about the true cost function, however, can lead to a clear preference between instruments. With uncertain cost functions, quantities become a superior instrument as either the benefit function is more sharply concave to the origin or as the cost function is more elastic. Integration thus appears especially likely when an unstorable intermediate good must be used in fixed proportions with other inputs, so that shortfalls in supply impose large costs from unutilized complementary inputs, while additional amounts of the intermediate good are of little or no value once these complementary inputs are fully utilized. In such situations, specifying price could lead to large losses, especially if the unknown cost function is highly elastic so that small deviations from the optimum price would lead to large deviations of the supplied quantity from the optimum quantity. By contrast, use of the market is relatively efficient when substitutability between inputs is relatively high, when quantities of complementary inputs can be adjusted easily, when inventories are inexpensive to hold, or when alternative sources of input supply are present.

Integration does not necessitate hierarchical control of all aspects. The firm has the option of decentralization—using a price mechanism to coordinate certain functions or divisions while using direct control to modify these internal prices. At the limit, ownership may involve no direct control and be essentially a portfolio investment. Thus with optimal decentralization it would appear that the effectiveness of control could only be increased by integration.

This argument for integration is, however, subject to the same two qualifications as was the argument that integration improves information flow. First, control problems do not disappear after integration.

Second, complete control through integration may not be necessary, and thus any one of a variety of partial control mechanisms may be preferred to integration.

It is clear that the unitary firm suffers from increasing loss of control as size increases. Limited spans of control imply an increase in the number of hierarchical levels as the firm expands. As information is transmitted through these levels, and as commands are passed down, distortions accumulate, reaction time increases, and there is a loss of control. Opportunities for discretionary behavior at lower levels increase, and incentives become a problem. These difficulties can be reduced by a multidivisional organization form that separates out natural decisionmaking units and coordinates these units with the rest of the firm by use of a quasi-market mechanism. But even with decentralization, such a process cannot continue indefinitely without difficulties.[9] In addition, the establishment of common ownership involves costs. Bargaining over transfer prices and quality is replaced by bargaining over terms for merger. Even if a saving in unit transactions costs can be achieved by common ownership, the present value of these savings must be greater than the fixed costs incurred during merger or entry.

The second qualification of the control incentive for integration is that there exists a spectrum of possible formal and informal control mechanisms, with full integration at one extreme and completely impersonal markets at the other. If control by ownership is chosen, effective control can be gained by simple majority share ownership. Minority ownership may suffice if the remaining shares are sufficiently dispersed, or if severe conflicts of interest between levels, and hence between shareholding groups, are not present. Even partial ownership may be unnecessary if control is desired over only a narrow and well-specified range of decisions at another level. The ownership by automobile assemblers of specialized equipment used by parts manufacturers is one example. Manufacturers of durable goods can retain control over their output by pricing policies that make rental more attractive than purchase. Franchise or licensing agreements can be used to impose legally binding controls over operations at other levels. In effect, complex agreements on property rights at different levels can be made between independently owned firms.

The close coordination of independent levels can also be achieved by interfirm cooperation. Richardson (1972), in particular, has argued that while the complementary nature of activities at different levels may necessitate close coordination, integration may be inefficient if these activities require different specialized capabilities. In such situations, complex patterns of voluntary cooperation can arise that effectively coordinate levels without unified control. If one of the parties is clearly dominant, such "cooperation" may come close to direct control. For example, a large customer of a firm whose product is market or firm specific may be able to use the threat of obtaining supplies elsewhere to exert a degree of control over the supplier, and this can closely approximate the control achievable through integration. Blois (1972) has listed a number of special requirements that have been imposed on suppliers in such situations. In addition to price and quality concessions, suppliers have been effectively required to maintain large inventories, provide technical service or credit, end strikes rapidly by accepting otherwise unacceptable terms, provide access to plants and records, disclose internal cost data, and even alter their management.

EXTERNALITIES

In the absence of transaction costs, all externalities would be eliminated by bargaining, since the existence of externalities implies that bargains could be made that would improve the welfare of all concerned. By internalizing externalities, integration may achieve the same result. "Surely the reason that we see so few instances in the real world of 'technical external economies' is that the most obvious of them have been perceived by businessmen who have internalized them"[10] (Malmgren, 1961, p. 142).

Integration does not eliminate the information costs of computing the value of externalities at the margin, since "correct" internal prices or quantities must still be calculated. Integration may, however, reduce the costs of implementing these correct prices if implementation by fiat is less expensive than implementation through bargaining. Using Bator's (1958) classification of externalities, we can examine separately the effect of integration in the presence of ownership, technical, and public-good externalities. In Bator's terminology, ownership externalities are cases of "unpaid factors," where certain "goods" or "bads," with determinate non-zero shadow prices, are not attributed. Technical externalities are cases of increasing returns to scale. Public-good externalities are cases where each individual's consumption of the good leads to no subtractions from any other individual's consumption of that good.

Ownership Externalities

For integration to be preferable to use of the market in the presence of ownership externalities (the unpaid-factor type) requires either that the difficulty lies in the negotiation and enforcement costs of using the market, or that government regulation or standards of legal liability prevent bargains from being made between independent parties that would lead to an efficient solution.[11]

For many cases of ownership externalities, less complete forms of vertical control than integration may be sufficient. For example, where the manner of use of a product by purchasers may affect the reputation and future sales of the producer, the producer may want users to uphold certain standards in the use or maintenance of the product. While the producer could simply reward adherence to such standards, the information and control costs of doing so may be high. Complete control through vertical integration over all aspects of the purchasing firm may also be expensive. The producer may therefore choose simply to tie the sale of the product to a maintenance contract,[12] either explicitly or by renting the product rather than making an outright sale; or to tie the product to sales of "approved" parts;[13] or to operate a franchise agreement. Similarly, if promotional efforts are best made at downstream levels, and if direct payment for such activities is difficult to calculate, then resale price maintenance or an exclusive franchise arrangement may be used to ensure that the return to such promotional activities accrues to the promoter.

Technical Externalities

If the problem is technical externalities, so the production of the input takes place at declining average cost, use of the market involves two problems. First, the input must be transferred at its marginal cost. Second, continued existence of the firm must be possible under marginal cost pricing. These problems would appear to be solved by integration between the (single) input producer and the users of the input. The new firm will set the internal transfer price of the input equal to its marginal cost, and the input-producing subsidiary can continue to exist despite accounting losses.

Integration, however, simply shifts the problem to a different level if the final output is now produced at falling average costs. For integration to provide a solution requires that enough other inputs are supplied internally at rising average cost so that the average-cost curve for the final product is not falling over the relevant output range. In effect, the accounting loss from production of the declining average-cost input is made up by rents from the increasing average-cost inputs. If inputs are used in fixed proportions, this solution can be shown graphically. Suppose that a final good, X, is produced competitively using two inputs, A and B, in fixed proportions. For simplicity assume that combining one unit of A with one unit of B results in one unit of X. In Figure 2–1, AC_a, AC_b, and AC_x are the average-

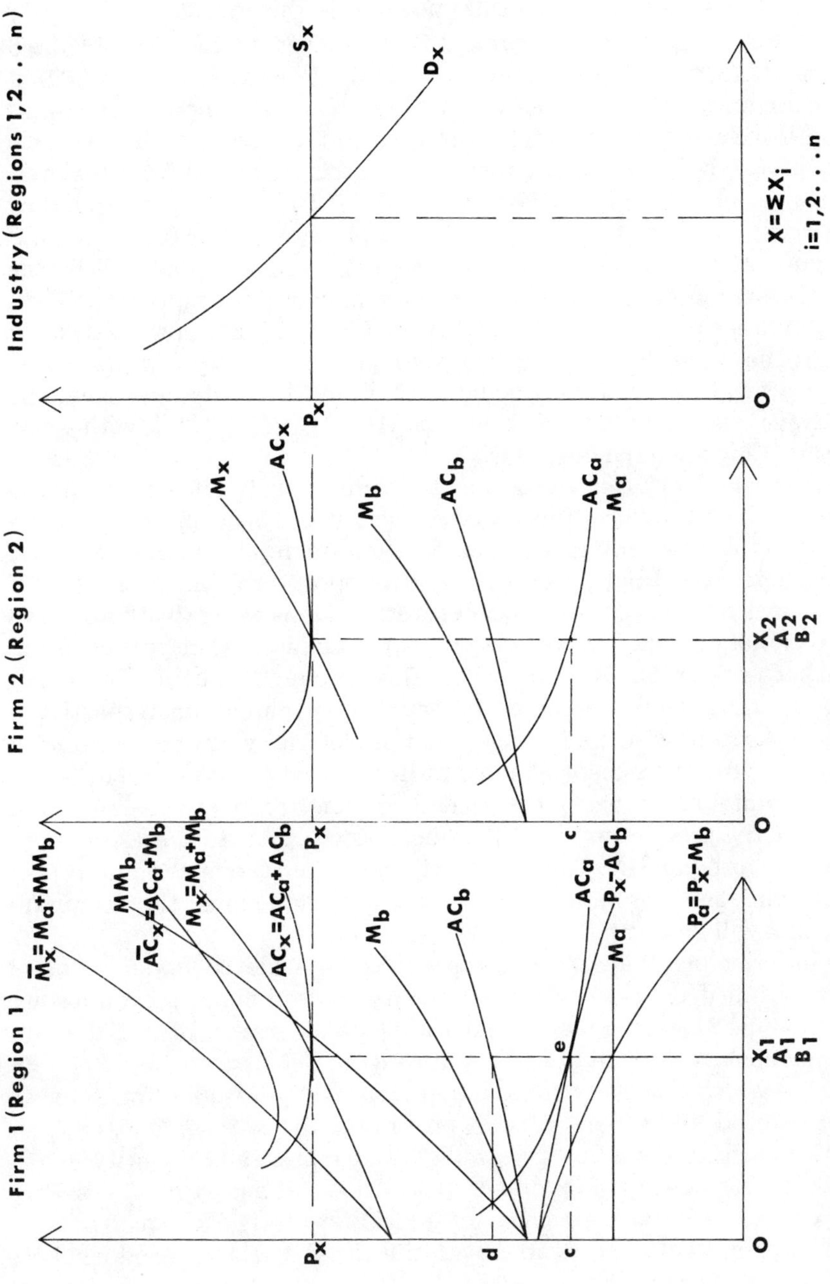

Figure 2–1. Competition With Declining Average-Cost Input

cost schedules for the two inputs and the final product, respectively, while M_a, M_b, and M_x are the corresponding marginal-cost schedules.

If the A firm in Region 1 begins to produce X, purchasing B from competitive independent firms, nothing is gained. Since the supply function for B from independent firms is given by M_b, the integrated firm will act as a monopsonist toward the B industry. Assuming that the integrated firm cannot act as a discriminating monopsonist toward the B industry, the marginal cost of B to the integrated firm is given by MM_b, the curve marginal to M_b. For the integrated firm, the average cost of producing X is $\overline{AC_x} = AC_a + M_b$, with a corresponding marginal cost of $\overline{M}_x = M_a + MM_b$. As is shown later (Chapter 4), if inputs are used in fixed proportions, the level of output will be the same after integration as before, since integration simply transforms an indirect monopsonization of B into a direct monopsonization of B. If the A and B inputs are integrated, however, output will increase. For a single X firm, producing both A and B inputs internally, the average cost of producing X will be $AC_x = AC_a + AC_b$, with a corresponding marginal cost of $M_x = M_a + M_b$.

The problem of ensuring that the firm actually sets price equal to marginal cost for the final product will still remain, however. Since there is a single input supplier, integration results in a single firm producing the final product. The monopoly problem disappears if the final product can be sold in several regions while the inputs have a regional market. This may occur, for example, if transport costs are higher for the inputs than for the final product. Thus in Figure 2.1, A, B, and X could be electricity, bauxite, and aluminum, respectively. Let us assume that neither bauxite nor electricity can be transported between regions except at some prohibitive cost, that transport costs for aluminum are negligible, that increasing returns to scale exist in electricity production, and that decreasing returns to scale exist in bauxite production. The result will be at most one aluminum producer in each region, but—if there are enough regions—the aluminum market will be competitive.

In principle the same results could be achieved under separate ownership if price-quantity agreements or discriminating monopsony is possible. The problem is that the derived-demand curve for an independent A firm in Region 1 of Figure 2-1 is given by $P_a = P_x - M_b$, which lies everywhere under AC_a. Thus no price for A exists that would allow non-negative profits for the A firm. One solution is for both A and B to be supplied under price and quantity agreements that specify A_1 units of A at price Oc, and B_1 units of B at price Od. Such an agreement effectively extracts the rent from the B industry and uses it to cover the fixed costs of producing A.

Alternatively, if a (single) X firm could act as a perfectly discriminating monopsonist toward the B industry, the derived-demand function for A would be given by $P_x - AC_b$. This new demand function is below AC_a at every point except for a tangency at point e. If the A firm now simply sets its optimal price of Oc, the downstream firm will set $AC_b + Oc = P_x$, producing X_1 units of X, and demanding A_1 and B_1 units of the two inputs.

Thus common ownership does not provide a result that *could* not be achieved through a market. But integration may be much less expensive than complex price-quantity or discriminatory arrangements. Once again, the central purpose of integration is to reduce transaction costs.

Public-Good Externalities

Public goods cause market failure because no single price exists that can be efficiently used for both the production and the distribution of a public good. While vertical integration between producer and user may ease the organizational problems created by public goods, it is horizontal integration at the user level that is critical. Thus if defense is a public good, the horizontal integration of all users in the form of a government may be required, but the government does not have to produce its own napalm. Similarly, an industry-financed research program may contract research projects out to universities. The required degree of horizontal integration, however, may cause a new market failure due to monopoly or monopsony power unless public regulation or public ownership is instituted, or the scope of horizontal integration is limited to dealing directly with the public good.[14]

One type of public good directly affected by vertical integration is information on market prices generated by unintegrated firms in a competitive intermediate-good market. Knowledge of "correct" transfer prices, provided at low cost by the market, permits better evaluation of decentralized performance within an integrated firm. In addition, the open-market price presents the option open to integrated buyers between internal and external supply, and the choice to integrated suppliers between internal and external sales. While unintegrated firms must usually provide this information at zero cost, integrated firms are under no compulsion to inform others about their internal prices.

Ideally, integrated firms should be prepared to enter the intermediate market whenever prices in that market diverge from internal marginal costs. Inter-level purchasing instructions may in practice, however, either ignore open-market prices or dictate that external sales or purchases should only be resorted to after certain threshold differences between internal and market prices are reached. The result can be an increasingly thin open market with non-competitive pricing and large short-run price fluctuations. This increases transaction costs for both integrated and unintegrated firms. If the departure of firms from the open market increases the cost of using the market more than the cost of internal transactions, however, the incentive for further integration increases. The result can be a nonoptimal corner solution, where no one firm has the incentive to rely on market transactions, but all firms would be better off if all firms returned to using the market.

A similar argument could be made for futures markets. "[In] real markets, bits of information are dispersed among numerous individuals, the information changes frequently and is costly to acquire and communicate. . . . A formal futures market reduces the cost of transacting because trading is completely centralized. . . . All futures traders acquire this information, and because futures prices are widely publicized, the information incorporated in a futures price can be acquired cheaply by individuals who do not trade in futures markets." (Cox, 1976, pp. 1216-18). Since vertical integration can serve as a substitute for use of the futures as well as spot market, a shift toward integration will increase transaction costs for nonintegrated firms in both markets if the efficiency of these markets is an increasing function of the number of participants.

Thus, public policies requiring large-scale vertical divestiture *may* result in significant improvements in intermediate markets. For estimating the transaction costs imposed on firms by industrywide divestiture, the relevant comparison is between the cost of internal transactions and the cost of using an expanded market, which may be significantly less than the cost of transactions in the narrow, predivestiture market.

RISK AVERSION

Risk aversion exists when, ceteris paribus, individuals prefer a lower variability on the return to their assets. Unless the returns to different assets are perfectly positively correlated, asset diversification can be used to reduce risk. An extensive literature exists in the optimal selection of securities for an individual portfolio.[15] We are interested here in two rather different questions. First, what is the significance of a vertical relationship between firms in determining the degree of correlation between their respective profit streams and hence in determining the desirability of holding the securities of both firms? Second, why would diversification to reduce risk be undertaken by firms rather than by individuals?

Diversification by Firms

If individual shareholders can diversify their own portfolios, why should firms perform this function? In a perfect capital market, individual share prices would reflect not the risk of the share held by itself but rather the risk of the share when held in an optimum combination with other shares in individual portfolios. Under such conditions a merger would reduce the portfolio-combination options open to shareholders and thus lower share prices.

There would appear to be three possible reasons why firms may still undertake diversification to reduce risk. The first is that the costs of diversification through merger may be less than the costs of individual diversification through the market. The second is that the diversifying firm may have superior knowledge of diversification possibilities. The third is that the preferences of shareholders and firm managers concerning risk may not be identical.

On the cost side it is possible that the transaction cost of merger may be less than the total transaction cost of diversification for all shareholders. Suppose that both the shareholders and the firms involved realize that combining the profit streams of firms X and Y would reduce risk, that all shareholders wish to always hold an equal percentage of the shares of X and Y, and that the transaction cost of merging the two firms is less than the sum of the individual shareholders' transaction costs of portfolio diversification. The benefit from firm diversification would then be the same as the benefits from individual diversification, while the costs would be lower. Share prices would thus rise after the merger. In some cases, firm transaction costs may in fact be considerably less than the sum of individual transaction costs. For example, the shares of one firm may not be traded on the relevant stock market because the firm is too small or is a foreign or family firm. Under these circumstances individual diversification may be costly or impossible. In addition, for vertically related firms, less expensive forms of vertical control than integration may reduce risk, and the use of these forms is an option open to firms but not to shareholders.

A second possibility is that firms have better knowledge about diversification possibilities than do shareholders. The firm may have better access to information, and the cost to a single individual of acquiring the necessary information (a public good) may be considerably greater than its value to that individual alone. If managers do have better information than shareholders, however, the optimum policy in terms of the effect on share prices would be for the managers to pass on this information to their shareholders.[16] In addition, both the knowledge and transaction costs of individual portfolio selection may have been significantly reduced by the emergence of the mutual fund. The mutual fund can be seen as a case of horizontal integration in response to the existence of public-good and technical externalities in the capital market. Thus the choice of vehicle for diversification is not really between the individual and the firm, but rather between the mutual fund and the conglomerate, an evolution that should have tipped the scales in favor of the market.

A perhaps more fruitful approach is to examine the third possibility, that a divergence in risk-aversion exists between the shareholders and the firm managers. If ownership is separated from control, managers may be more risk-averse than shareholders, since very little of a large increase in profits may go to managers, while a large reduction in profits may result in dismissal. Excessive risk-aversion can be expected if policies that would maximize share prices also involve a significant chance of bankruptcy, with certain loss of job and, presumably, reputation. This is a management-incentive problem, and the solution would appear to be to equate stockholders and management incentives by rewarding management on the basis of the performance of the firm's stock. Recent work by Masson (1971) seems to show that executive compensation is increasingly determined by stock performance, and that the closer the relationship the better the performance of the stock.

Compensating executives on the basis of stock performance, however, may not completely solve the problem. It may equate the interest of management with the interests of shareholders who own shares only in that firm, but it does not necessarily equate the interests of the management with that of the diversified shareholder. Unless the executive is inordinately wealthy, his "portfolio" will consist almost entirely of the stock of the firm he is managing. The only way for him to diversify his portfolio is through merger. In general, therefore, the executive who is compensated on the basis of stock performance may have an incentive to reduce risk through firm diversification even when such diversification reduces share prices.

Diversification into Vertically Related Industries

If diversification does take place through the firm, under what conditions will such diversification tend to be vertical rather than horizontal or conglomerate? The ideal partners for a diversification merger would be firms whose profit streams could be expected to be highly negatively correlated. For vertically related firms, the direction of this correlation will depend on the particular cause of profit fluctuations. Several such causes can be isolated.

First, the profit fluctuations of two vertically related firms may be due to shifts in demand for the final product and the resulting shifts in derived demand for the input. In this case a high positive correlation can be expected between the profit streams of two vertically related firms. The two firms would therefore be poor candidates for a diversification merger.

A second possibility is negatively correlated shifts in demand between two final-product firms, producing products X and Y, which use a common input, A. If demand for Y increases, for example, the resulting increase in demand for A will raise the price of A (assuming increasing marginal costs in the A industry). Profits will increase in the Y and A industries, but the increased price of A will reduce profits in the X industry. Whenever two final-product firms use a common input that has an upward-sloping supply curve, an increase in demand for the output of one firm will inflict pecuniary external diseconomies on the other firm. The most effective way to reduce risk in this situation would be horizontal integration between an X and a Y firm. Where horizontal integration is expensive or illegal, however, vertical integration can serve as a partial substitute.

A third possible reason for profit fluctuations would be changes in costs at the A level. A fall in intermediate-good costs will tend to increase profits and reduce prices at the A level and hence lower costs and increase profits at the X level. Profits of A and X firms will thus be positively correlated, and vertical diversification is not indicated.

A fourth reason for profit fluctuations would be variations in the price of some other input, B, which is used with A in the production of X. An increase in the price of B will reduce profits in the X industry. Profits in the A industry, however, may rise or fall, depending on whether A and B are complements or substitutes. If B is a substitute for A, an increase in the price of B will increase the demand for A, and profits in the A industry will rise. Profits in the A and X industries will be negatively correlated, and vertical integration between X and A firms will reduce risk. But if B is a complement for A, an increase in the price of B will reduce profits in the A industry.[17] Profits in the A and X industries will then be positively correlated, and vertical integration between X and A firms will not reduce risk.

A fifth reason for profit fluctuations in the A and X industries would be variations in the productivity of the A input. A technological change that increases the productivity of A in X production will reduce its effective cost to users in the X industry and increase profits at the X level. If the demand for A is elastic, X producers will increase their total expenditure on A, and profits in the A industry will increase. If the elasticity of derived demand for A is less than unity, however, an improvement in the productivity of A will shift the demand curve for A to the left and profits in the A industry will fall. Thus if the derived-demand curve for A is inelastic, changes in the productivity of the A input will result in negatively correlated profit fluctuations in the A and X industries, and vertical integration will reduce risk.

The conclusion from this analysis is that in some cases vertically related firms may be good partners for diversification, either through merger at the firm level or through individual portfolio diversification. Prediction of such cases, however, requires information about the expected source of disturbances, and may also require knowledge of specific parameters such as demand and substitution elasticities. In some cases where vertical integration would reduce risk, a more effective method of reducing risk may be horizontal integration at either the final-product or input levels. In addition, alternative forms of vertical control such as requirements contracts or tying arrangements may be used to reduce risk at lower cost than vertical integration.

For example, suppose that demand fluctuations in the Y final-good market are causing negatively correlated profit fluctuations between the X final-good industry and the A input industry (the second case discussed above). Vertical integration between A and X firms will reduce risk, but an easier solution may be for A and X firms to enter into long-term supply contracts for A at a fixed price.

Tying arrangements may also be used in this case (Burstein, 1960b, pp. 69-73). Suppose the A firm is a capital-good supplier to several firms whose profits fluctuate independently. The riskiness of each downstream firm could be reduced if the rental price for A moved with the demand conditions facing each downstream firm. This can be achieved if the A firm reduces the nominal price for A and, in return, the downstream firm agrees to purchase from the A firm all its requirements (at a price higher than the competitive price) of some other input, B, which is used in fixed proportions to its output. The effective price of A facing each downstream firm will then depend on the output of that firm. Some of the profit fluctuations of each downstream firm will thus be shifted to the A level, where they can be pooled. The cost of such an arrangement may be considerably less than the cost of reducing risk by either horizontal integration at the final-product level or by vertical integration.

CONCLUSIONS

We have found only two cases where undesirable vertical control could occur under competitive conditions. First, separation of ownership from control could lead to excessive risk-aversion, leading to vertical control which would not be in the interest of shareholders. Second, moves toward vertical control could reduce the efficiency of market transactions, either by increasing the riskiness of market transactions or by restricting the availability of transfer-price information with public-good characteristics.

The best solution to the first problem, however, is to design a management incentive program that would harmonize the attitudes of managers and shareholders toward risk, a solution which would not require government intervention. The second problem could similarly be solved by negotiation at the industry level. More important, several forms of vertical control can be close substitutes in this case. In practice, it may be impossible to prevent some of these practices, and thus little or nothing may be gained from intervention.

We thus arrive at a somewhat qualified conclusion that government intervention, either to prevent vertical control or alter its form, is undesirable if the industry is competitive and other government policies are neutral toward vertical control. If horizontal market power is clearly present, however, or if the industry is regulated or subject to price controls or certain kinds of taxes, vertical control cannot be simply assumed desirable, and further information is necessary.

We will now turn in Chapter 3 to cases where vertical control is due to government actions, and in Chapter 4 through 6 to cases where vertical control is due to horizontal market power.

NOTES

1. The defense of vertical integration in [the telecommunications] industry is almost unique in its assertion of genuine managerial and technological benefits flowing from it. Not in petroleum, steel, cement, aluminum, motion pictures, or grocery distribution, in all of which integration has been both widely prevalent and strenuously debated, have its protagonists based their arguments so directly on technical grounds. The financial union of crude oil production and refining, iron ore mining and steel-making, the production of ingot steel and the fabrication of steel products, electric power generation and aluminum reduction, the production, distribution, and exhibition of motion pictures, the manufacture of cement and of ready-mixed concrete, the synthesis of nitrogen compounds and the preparation of mixed fertilizers, coffee-roasting and food distribution have all been defended on such grounds as the necessity for assuring a sufficient and regular supply of vital inputs, more effective marketing, the circum-

> vention of monopoly, the saving of selling costs and—it should be conceded—the possibilities it afforded for a closer specification and control of quality, but rarely or never on the ground that the technological interdependencies were so close that each operation had to be done by the same engineers and managers working in close collaboration. . . . One limited exception . . . would be the direct saving in fuel costs made possible by the transfer of pig iron in molten form from the blast furnace directly into the steel converter. [A. E. Kahn, 1971, pp. 300-301]

For a description of these technological economies and a defense of vertical integration in telecommunications, see American Telephone and Telegraph Co. (1969; 1974).

2. For a discussion of the relationship between market structure, size, and technological innovation, see Scherer (1970, pp. 346-78).

3. The underinvestment hypotheses may be invalid for other reasons as well. Demsetz (1969), for example, argues that establishing property rights is not necessarily more difficult for information than for more tangible assets. In addition, Barzel (1968) has shown that competition between potential innovators to obtain property rights from innovations may result in premature applications of discoveries.

4. For a discussion of organization bias toward maintenance or extension of internal operations, see Williamson (1975, pp. 117-31).

5. For a discussion of informal cooperative behavior between firms, see Richardson (1972) and Williamson (1975, pp. 106-109).

6. For an example of the use of requirements contracts, see McKie (1959, pp. 149-50).

7. Crandall (1968b, pp. 91-95), for example, argues that upstream production by automobile assemblers is of assistance in determining contract prices for components purchased from independents. The results of his test for an implied bias toward partial self-supply are inconclusive. This might be expected, however since several other incentives for integration are also present in this case.

8. White (1971, pp. 79, 83) has argued, for example, that repeated strikes against suppliers has been a major motivation for vertical integration in the U.S. automobile industry. It is possible for integration to reduce conflict by increasing both the firm's and the union's desire to settle rapidly, although the range of such cases may be narrow. If a strike at an upstream supplier would cause production disruptions downstream, internalization of these downstream costs through integration should increase the firm's desire to settle rapidly. The external costs of a supplier strike may be quite low, however, if holding an inventory of the intermediate good sufficient to outlast a strike is relatively inexpensive, or if close substitutes are available, or if multiple sources of supply are possible because significant economies of scale at the supplier level are absent, or if penalty clauses in contracts with independent suppliers could be used to shift the cost of downstream production disturbances back onto the supplier. Any of these may be effective substitutes for integration. In addition, there are generally strong pressures for a uniform wage structure within any firm, and thus integration may extend high wage contracts to other levels. Williamson (1975, p. 130), for example, has argued that a principal reason for General Motor's refusal to integrate

into seatbelt production is that, given its contract with the United Auto Workers, labor costs would be higher for GM than they are at present for independent suppliers.

Integration may also increase the union's incentive to settle rapidly. If a strike at one level disrupts production and increases costs at a second level, workers at the second level may also suffer. If firm integration also results in union integration, these costs are internalized. Since labor at different levels will generally be gross complements, union integration can also be expected to lower the union's desired wage. The effect of integration on union incentives should thus reinforce the firm's incentive to integrate.

9. For a discussion of control loss and organizational response, see Williamson (1967, pp. 123-38; 1970, pp. 160-61; 1975, pp. 132-59).

10. "Technical" external economies refer here to nonpecuniary externalities.

11. For the effects of legal liability, see Coase (1960).

12. See *United States* v. *Jerrold Electronics Corp.*, 187 F. Supp. 545, 557, *affirmed per curiam*, 363 U.S. 567 (1961).

13. See *Pick Manufacturing Co.* v. *General Motors Corp.*, 80 F.2d 641 (1935).

14. An example of limited horizontal integration would be an industry research institute, financed by taxes on individual firms, where agreement on the institute budget can be reached without also resulting in agreement on product prices. For a study of industry research cooperatives in the U.K., see Johnson (1973).

15. For a review of this literature, see Hirshleifer (1970, pp. 215-310).

16. For some empirical support of the proposition that the prices of common stocks fully reflect available information on the expected value and dispersion of returns, see Fama and MacBeth (1973).

17. An increase in the price of B has two separable effects on the demand for A. First, it increases the cost of the final product and thus reduces the quantity of the final-product produced, to an extent dependent on the elasticity of demand (η) for the final product. On the other hand, the increase in the price of B induces a substitution of A for B to an extent determined by the elasticity of substitution (σ) between A and B. The net effect is that if η is greater than σ, the output effect will outweigh the substitution effect and an increase in the price of B will reduce the demand for A. The two factors are thus complements. If η is less than σ, the substitution effect will outweigh the output effect, and an increase in the price of B will increase the demand for A. The two factors are then substitutes. For a further discussion, see Hicks (1961).

 *Chapter 3*

Vertical Control Due to Government Actions

Deliberate government policy toward vertical control, as expressed in antitrust actions, has always reflected the belief that the social gains from vertical control cannot be greater than the private gains. Antitrust policy has thus aimed at determining those cases where private and social incentives for vertical control diverge, and then selectively restricting rather than encouraging vertical control in such cases. While we shall postpone an examination of vertical antitrust policy until Chapter 7, we have already seen that vertical and horizontal control can often be close substitutes. Thus an assessment of the net impact of antitrust policy on vertical relationships must consider the possible unintended redirection of internal expansion and merger effort between horizontal, vertical, and conglomerate channels.[1]

While antitrust policy toward vertical control has been restrictive in intent, the unintended and indirect effect of several other types of government intervention has been to encourage vertical control by firms. In particular, taxation, price controls, and regulation can all create very similar incentives for vertical control (see Coase, 1937; Stigler, 1951).

TAXATION

Both vertical integration and tying arrangements have been used to avoid or reduce certain categories of taxation. The clearest example is a turnover tax, which is levied on all sales rather than on value-added or just final sales. If production is not vertically integrated, value-added at the upstream level is taxed at both the intermediate and at the final levels. If production is integrated, upstream value-added is taxed only once, at the final level. This is equivalent to a tax on the use of the intermediate market, since internal transactions are exempt from the tax. While internal transactions could in principle also be taxed, the policing and transaction costs are likely to be excessively high. In particular, since the integrated firm could avoid a simple ad valorem tax on upstream output by setting a zero internal transfer price, effective taxation requires either setting a specific tax or, equivalently, setting both an ad valorem rate and a transfer price for tax purposes.

Imposing taxes on turnover rather than value-added can be undesirable for several reasons. If integration is costless, the additional tax on upstream output can be avoided completely. If integration involves diseconomies, the firm will be willing to incur such diseconomies, at the margin, up to the tax rate. To the extent that transfer is internalized, the tax results in inefficiency without revenue. Even where diseconomies of integration are greater than the tax rate, the relatively higher taxation of upstream value-added distorts the production decision toward excessive use of downstream factors relative to upstream factors. Unless some offsetting distortion exists, or unless factors are used in fixed proportions, the result is an increase in the real unit costs of production. In addition, a turnover tax results in arbitrarily high relative taxation of products that involve multiple stages, especially since each tax payment enters into the costs of successive stages and is itself taxed. Fortunately, turnover taxes have never been important in the United States, and have recently been replaced in Europe by value-added taxes.

While a turnover tax presents an extreme example of distorting the choice between internal and market transactions, any government action that taxes or penalizes external transactions more than internal transactions will provide an incentive for integration. Laidler (1975), for example, has argued that since use of the market requires relatively large holdings of cash balances, inflation (which can be regarded as a tax on cash holdings) can be expected to encourage internal coordination of activities.

Since internal accounting prices also determine the location of accounting profits, integration allows the firm to shift profits to the level with the lowest marginal tax rate on profits. Similarly, a multinational firm can shift its profits to whichever country has the lowest tax rate, if necessary by establishing a completely artificial accounting stage in that country.

The preferential tax treatment given to extractive industries, permitting expensing (rather than depreciation) of exploration costs, and, until recently, a percentage depletion allowance, has probably been the most important example of differential tax treatment between levels that may have encouraged integration.[2] In addition, differences between firms in their ability to take advantage of special investment incentives, and the potential for using leasing to defer profits taxes in capital-goods manufacture, can bias the capital-ownership choice between levels.[3] In general, some or all of any special tax benefits given to one level of an industry can be "sold" to other firms or individuals to whom these benefits are of greater value. If adjusting transfer prices is a relatively efficient method of transferring special tax advantages, vertically related firms become more likely "purchasers" of these benefits, and integration is encouraged. In addition, if the tax benefit is a function of revenue, as with the depletion allowance, and if the internal transfer price can be increased, the integrated firm is uniquely able not only to transfer, but actually to increase the tax benefit.[4] Downstream firms may thus outbid other units for depletable assets, even if these other units face higher marginal tax rates than downstream firms.

Tying arrangements can also be used to avoid or reduce taxes. Purchase of a good that is subject to a high ad valorem tax can be made conditional on the purchase of another good that is taxed at a lower rate. Ideally, all the accounting value of the package would be shifted to the tied good. As a result the tying good would be effectively taxed at the lower rate applied to the tied good.[5]

PRICE CONTROLS

Government attempts at price control can also be circumvented by internalization. In Figure 3-1 a maximum price of *OC* is imposed by the government on a competitive industry producing good *A*. Quantity *OM* is produced and rationed among purchasers.

A competitive market price of *NS* would result in a combined gain to buyers and sellers equal to area *RST*. "In the United States during and immediately after World War II, . . . vertical integration was the simplest way of obtaining this gain. This was the rationale of the integration of radio manufacturers into cabinet manufacture, of steel firms into fabricated products, etc." (Stigler, 1951, p. 119).

The incentive for integration applies to upstream as well as to downstream integration. Since markets do not clear if effective price controls are imposed in a competitive market, at least some downstream users must be rationed. The relevant price for the decision to integrate, therefore, is not the controlled price, but rather the scarcity value at the rationed quantity. Assume, for example, that the demand

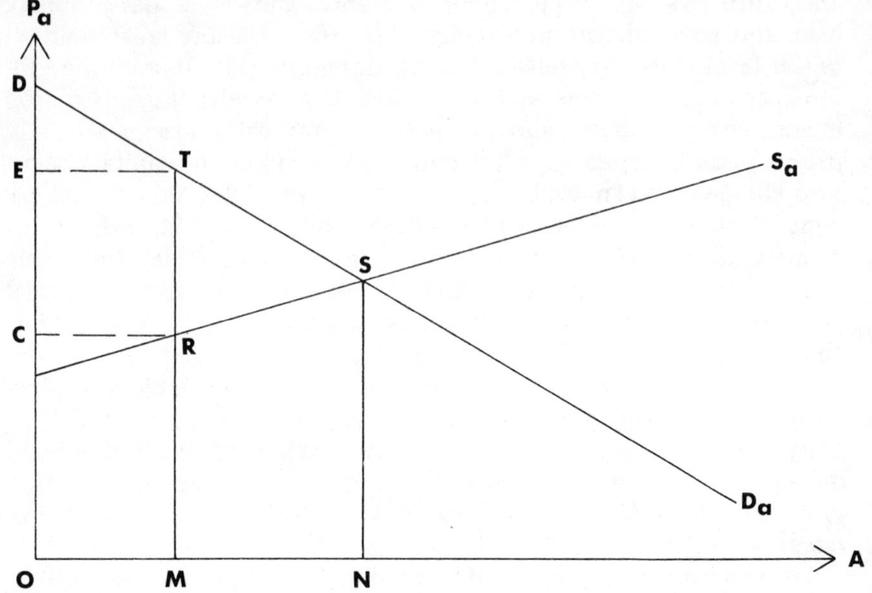

Figure 3-1. Price Control

schedule in Figure 3-1 is that of a single firm, rationed to quantity OM of input A. Since the scarcity value of A is MT, upstream integration will be profitable as long as the internal cost of producing A is less than MT, even if this internal cost is greater than the controlled price. The regulation of interstate prices for natural gas, for example, should be expected to result in an interesting pattern of integration. If there are no technical economies of integration between the exploration and development stage and the distribution stage for natural gas, we should not expect to find rationed gas distributors exploring for natural gas within their own state, since intrastate prices are not controlled. What should be observed is upstream integration by distributors in deficit states into gas production in surplus states.[6]

Tying arrangements can clearly also be used to avoid price controls. The most obvious form of such a tying arrangement would be a requirement by the producer of controlled good A that consumer X also purchase some other good, B, from the A firm at a price greater than the market price for B. More complex or subtle forms are possible, however. One alternative is to make the sale of A conditional upon the supply of B by X to A at a price less than the market price of B. During the 1949-1953 steel shortage, for example, General Motors (X) extended loans (B) to several steel firms (A), presumably at very attractive rates. In return, GM obtained an agreement that the steel firms would supply GM with a certain share of the new output produced by the facilities financed by GM's loans (Crandall, 1968, p. 121). More informally, especially if excess demand situations can be expected to recur, sales of *A* may be restricted to "good" customers who are expected to respond by continuing to purchase from the supplier in later periods when shortages are no longer present, and when alternative sources of *A* may be available on more attractive terms from other suppliers.

One determinent of the choice between a tying arrangement and integration should be the length of time over which excess demand conditions are expected to continue. Using our earlier example, natural gas distributors may have limited access at first to upstream-specific inputs, such as knowledge gained from experience, which are held by upstream firms. We might therefore expect a relatively heavy reliance at first on arrangements such as joint ventures where the distributor's major contribution would be supplying risk capital at favorable rates. In effect, these are tying arrangements which enable payment of a premium to producers in excess demand situations. Over time, however, as distributors gain experience and as expectations of continued shortage persist, distributors might be expected to fully integrate into upstream production.

In practice price controls can result in three kinds of losses: (1) production losses; (2) distribution inefficiencies; and (3) avoidance costs. If the price control cannot be avoided by producers, but a costless secondary black market exists, setting a maximum price for producers of *MR* in Figure 3-1 is equivalent to a unit tax of *RT*, with the tax revenue accruing to whomever had the legal right to purchase the good at the controlled price. The welfare loss will then be given by the area *RST*, and would be due entirely to the reduction in production from *ON* to *OM*.

If a secondary black market is suppressed, however, the value of a marginal unit to users with unlimited access can be as low as *MR*, while the value of a marginal unit to other users may be considerably higher than *MT*. The absence of an efficient secondary market thus results in a further "distribution" welfare loss of some part of area *DTRC*, as well as creating particularly strong incentives for integration by or into the more severly rationed sectors or firms. To take the extreme case, if the marginal and average value to allowed purchasers were precisely *MR* (or if quantity *OM* is exported), the distribution loss would be the whole area *DTRC*, and the total welfare loss would be area *DSRC*.

If vertical integration or tying arrangements are used to avoid price control, the result may be an increase in production and distributional efficiency. Any such gains, however, may be outweighed by the costs incurred to avoid the controls. If the right to purchase the good at the controlled price is not well specified, competition between potential recipients can lead to dissipation of the quasi-rents (area *CRTE*) into avoidance costs. If vertical integration or a tying arrangement is used to reestablish the producer's property right in his output, an increase in output can be expected. Suppose, however, that a distributor of the good acquires it at the controlled price of *MR* from producers, and then raises the effective price to *MT* by making purchase of the commodity conditional upon purchase of some other commodity at an inflated price.[7] While this may reduce any distributional inefficiencies, no gain accrues to the producer, so that production remains at *OM* and the "production" gain of area *RST* is foregone. The avoidance cost of using a tying arrangement rather than a simple price increase will also absorb part of area *CRTE*. In addition, unless the tied and tying goods are sold in fixed proportions, the tying arrangement will result in a distortion of the use ratio against the tied good.

REGULATION

Since vertical integration can be used by a regulated firm to shift income to a level where regulatory restrictions are less stringent or nonexistent, vertical integration has created major regulatory problems, notably in the natural gas and telecommunications industries (and in the electric power industry until the Public Utility Holding Company Act of 1935). The public policy response has been either to require vertical dissolution or to extend regulation, directly or indirectly, to vertically related subsidiaries.

In natural gas, regulation of pipeline rates led inevitably into attempting to determine a value for gas produced by integrated pipeline companies. Less inevitably, and apparently with little enthusiasm, the Federal Power Commission was pushed into regulation of all gas producers—integrated and independent—a mammoth task in an industry with thousands of producers of a product that is both extractive and often jointly produced with oil. This extension of regulation has been severely criticized (see MacAvoy, 1971; Breyer and MacAvoy, 1974). In telecommunications the public policy response has been to involve both state commissions and the Federal Communications Commission in direct or indirect regulation of the equipment manufacture stage, as well as to attempt vertical dissolution.[8] In the non-Bell sector, a civil action filed by International Telephone and Telegraph resulted in a court order declaring the vertical integration into telecommunications equipment manufacture by General Telephone and Electronics to be illegal on foreclosure grounds.[9] (For an analysis of the *ITT* v. *GTE* case, see Braeutigam, 1974.) In addition, in a major suit filed in 1974 the Antitrust Division of the Justice Department is once again attempting to separate Western Electric from AT&T and divide it into several parts (see *U.S.* v. *AT&T*, Civil Suit No. 17, filed Nov. 1974). The issues raised by vertical integration under regulation, particularly upstream integration by a regulated firm into equipment manufacture, are thus of considerable importance.

The analysis of vertical integration in a regulatory context is complicated by what has become known as the Averch-Johnson effect.[10] Briefly, the Averch-Johnson proposition is that if a firm is effectively constrained to some maximum rate of return on its capital that is greater than the cost of capital, then the profit-maximizing capital-labor ratio will be distorted toward excessively capital-intensive production. Furthermore, the factor-ratio distortion will in general be greater, the closer is the allowed rate of return to the true cost of capital. Thus an analysis of vertical integration under regulation raises issues both of avoidance and of efficiency, since if integration reduces the tightness of regulation, an increase in production efficiency can be expected.

The major work rigorously modeling vertical integration in a rate-of-return regulatory context is by Dayan (1972).[11] Dayan begins by showing that limiting rate-of-return regulation to the end-product stage allows the firm to avoid regulation completely. More surprisingly, Dayan shows that extending regulation to include all stages under a single rate-of-return constraint will also be ineffective if the firm can inflate the rate base by raising the transfer price of internally supplied inputs that enter the rate base. Any firm that can arrange such an internal transfer of a capital input can effectively avoid regulation. Thus, "effective regulation of a vertically integrated firm requires that the firm's internal or transfer price, or equivalently that each stage of production, be individually regulated" (Dayan, 1972, p. 200). While integration may complicate and extend the regulator's task, regulation can still be effective. Furthermore, assuming a fixed-proportion technology at the upstream level, Dayan shows that allowing vertical integration and setting the allowed rate of return at the upstream level equal to the cost of capital would be at least as desirable as breaking up the vertically integrated firm, along with regulation of the downstream stage. If a separate upstream industry would be imperfectly competitive, or if real economies from vertical integra-were present, effective regulation of the vertically integrated firm would be preferable to dissolution.

Since the return at each level is within the discretion of the regulatory agency, it appears that the case against vertical integration is weak, and at most a case for more effective regulation of the upstream level. Unfortunately, this conclusion is critically dependent on the use of either of two assumptions—a fixed-proportion technology at the upstream level, or, alternatively, direct regulation of the transfer price rather than rate-of-return regulation. If factor substitution is possible upstream, vertical integration with effective rate-of-return regulation will introduce the Averch-Johnson distortion into the upstream level, and lead to inefficient production at that level.

While the degree of capital-labor substitutability in any particular case is an empirical question, there is no particular basis for expecting a fixed-proportions technology at the upstream stage of regulated, vertically integrated firms. The Averch-Johnson distortion could still be avoided, however, if the regulator's determination of the firm's transfer price is not based on some allowed rate of return on that firm's upstream capital base. If, for example, an independent and competitive upstream industry existed, the regulatory agency could use the resulting market price as the regulated transfer price. Rate-of-return regulation could also be used if a sufficient number of regulated integrated firms existed so that an industrywide average of upstream costs (including the allowed return on capital) could be used for all integrated firms.

Barring collusion among the regulated firms, this would break the link between any one firm's factor-ratio choice and its allowed transfer price. In natural gas, for example, the use of area prices by the FPC should eliminate any incentive toward excessive use of capital at the production level of natural gas. In telecommunications, however, regulators have been unwilling to move away from firm-specific rate-of-return regulation. Troxel (1966) reports:

> The Michigan Commission does not accept Western Electric prices merely because, for some products, they are lower (or not higher) than alternative sources of supply. Indeed the comparative-price test was rejected some years ago in a Supreme Court decision about Illinois Bell. In Michigan, the Commission holds that the rate of return on Western Electric capital should not exceed the rate of return allowed on Michigan Bell capital. And if it does exceed the allowable Michigan Bell return, the expenditure allowance for Western Electric supplies is reduced and the reduction is charged, in effect, against Bell Company earnings. [p. 168]

In order to show in more detail the effects that could be expected from upstream vertical integration into equipment manufacture by a regulated firm, we can construct a simplified model of the effectively regulated firm. Assume a downstream firm producing good A, using two inputs: capital K_a, and labor, L_a. For simplicity, assume the production function is Cobb-Douglas (unitary elasticity of substitution), with constant returns to scale. The production function is thus of the form:

$$A = HK_a^{\beta} L_a^{(1-\beta)} \tag{3.1}$$

All capital is purchased from the equipment level, which produces good E using capital, K_e, and labor, L_e. Again assuming constant returns to scale and a unitary elasticity of substitution, the production function is of the form:

$$E = GK_e^{\alpha} L_e^{(1-\alpha)} \tag{3.2}$$

In a static equilibrium, all demand for equipment is a replacement demand. Assuming the life of capital to be $1/t$ years, the equilibrium production of equipment will be:

$$E = tK_a \tag{3.3}$$

Demand for A is assumed to be a differentiable, decreasing function of the price of A:

$$A = A(P_a); \ \frac{\partial A}{\partial P_a} < 0 \tag{3.4}$$

Effective regulation requires that the regulatory agency impose a maximum rate-of-return constraint on both levels (Dayan, 1972). The allowed rate of return at both levels is assumed to be set at some level higher than the cost of capital, r. The allowed rate of return at the downstream level is $r + \delta_a$, while the allowed rate of return at the equipment level is $r + \delta_e$. There is no regulatory lag, and δ_a and δ_e are assumed greater than zero but small enough so that regulation is effective.

Accounting profits at the A level are total revenues minus the cost of labor at the A level, minus (straight-line) depreciation costs, minus capital costs. The price of labor at each level, P_{la}, and P_{le}, the price of capital at the E level, P_{ke}, and the cost of capital, r, are assumed constant and given:

$$\Pi_a = A(K_a, L_a) \cdot P_a[A(K_a, L_a)] - P_{la}L_a - tP_{ka}K_a - rP_{ka}K_a \tag{3.5}$$

where P_{ka} is the internal transfer price of capital equipment. Accounting profits at the equipment level are revenues from current equipment sales minus current factor costs at the equipment level, plus the return on the accounting value of capital at the downstream level, minus the cost of capital (ignoring any depreciation at the E level) times the real cost of the capital at the downstream level:

$$\Pi_e = P_e E - P_{le} L_e - rP_{ke} K_e + rP_{ka} K_a - rK_a \left(\frac{P_{le} L_e + rP_{ke} K_e}{E}\right) \quad (3.6)$$

Summing Π_a and Π_e gives us total profits for the integrated firm. Note that the internal payment for replacement cancels the current revenue from equipment sales ($tP_{ka}K_a = P_e E$, since $P_{ka} \equiv P_e$ and $E = tK_a$), and the capital cost downstream cancels the return on the accounting value of accumulated sales at the equipment level. Thus:

$$\Pi_{a+e} = P_a A - P_{la} L_a - P_{le} L_e - rP_{ke} K_e - rK_a \left(\frac{P_{le} L_e + rP_{ke} K_e}{E}\right) \quad (3.7)$$

Using Equations (3.1) through (3.3) to eliminate K_a and E:

$$\Pi_{a+e} = R - P_{la} L_a - \left(1 + \frac{r}{t}\right)(P_{le} L_e + rP_{ke} K_e) \quad (3.8)$$

where $R = P_a A$.

If the firm is unconstrained, it sets $\partial \Pi / \partial L_e = \partial \Pi / \partial L_a = \partial \Pi / \partial K_e = 0$. Thus:

$$\frac{\partial R}{\partial L_a} = P_{la} \quad (3.9)$$

$$\frac{\partial R / \partial L_a}{\partial R / \partial L_e} = \frac{P_{la}}{P_{le}(1 + r/t)} \quad (3.10)$$

$$\frac{\partial R / \partial L_e}{\partial R / \partial K_e} = \frac{P_{le}}{rP_{ke}} \quad (3.11)$$

Thus the unconstrained monopoly firm produces E efficiently, using each factor until its price equals its marginal revenue product. We now introduce a regulatory agency, which sets a maximum rate of return at the downstream level, $r + \delta_a$, and a maximum rate of return at the equipment level, $r + \delta_e$. If regulation is effective:

$$R - P_{la}L_a - (r + t + \delta_a)(P_{ka}K_a) = 0 \tag{3.12}$$

$$P_e E - P_{le}L_e - (r + \delta_e)(P_{ke}K_e) = 0 \tag{3.13}$$

Substituting in Equations (3.2) and (3.3), these constraints can be rewritten as:

$$R - P_{la}L_a - \left(\frac{r + t + \delta_a}{t}\right) P_e G K_e^{\alpha} L_e^{(1-\alpha)} = 0 \tag{3.14}$$

$$P_e G K_e^{\alpha} L_e^{(1-\alpha)} - P_{le}L_e - (r + \delta_e)P_{ke}K_e = 0 \tag{3.15}$$

Forming the Lagrangian:

$$\begin{aligned} \Pi_\lambda = {} & R - P_{la}L_a - \left(1 + \frac{r}{t}\right)(P_{le}L_e + rP_{ke}K_e) \\ & - \lambda_a \left[R - P_{la}L_a - \left(\frac{r + t + \delta_a}{t}\right) P_e G K_e^{\alpha} L_e^{(1-\alpha)}\right] \\ & - \lambda_e \left[P_e G K_e^{\alpha} L_e^{(1-\alpha)} - P_{le}L_e - (r + \delta_e)P_{ke}K_e\right] \end{aligned} \tag{3.16}$$

and setting $\partial\Pi_\lambda/\partial L_e = \partial\Pi_\lambda/\partial K_e = \partial\Pi_\lambda/\partial L_e = \partial\Pi_\lambda/\partial P_e = 0$, we can solve for the marginal revenue product of L_a:

$$\frac{\partial R}{\partial L_a} = P_{la} \tag{3.17}$$

the ratio of the marginal revenue product of L_a to the marginal revenue product of L_e:

$$\frac{\partial R/\partial L_a}{\partial R/\partial L_e} = \frac{P_{la}}{P_{le}(1 + r/t - \lambda_a\delta_a/(1 - \lambda_a)t} > \frac{P_{la}}{P_{le}(1 + r/t)} \tag{3.18}$$

the ratio of the marginal revenue product of L_e to the marginal revenue product of K_e:

$$\frac{\partial R/\partial L_e}{\partial R/\partial K_e} = \frac{P_{le}}{rP_{ke}} \left\{\frac{1 + r/t - \lambda_e}{1 + r/t - \lambda_e(1 + \delta_e/r)}\right\} > \frac{P_{le}}{rP_{ke}} \tag{3.19}$$

and the relationship between λ_a and λ_e:

$$\lambda_a = \lambda_e\left(\frac{t}{t + r + \delta_a}\right) \tag{3.20}$$

In addition, we can solve for the effect of the factor-ratio distortion at the equipment level on the marginal (and average) cost of producing E. Denoting $\overline{C}/C$ as the unit cost with distortion to the unit cost without distortion:

$$\frac{\overline{C}}{C} = \frac{1 + r/t - \lambda_e[1 + \delta_e(1-\alpha)/r]}{[1 + r/t - \lambda_e]^{\alpha}[1 + r/t - \lambda_e(1 + \delta_e/r)]^{(1-\alpha)}} > 1 \tag{3.21}$$

Thus if regulation is effective ($\lambda_e > 0$), the integrated firm will produce E at greater than minimum cost, using an excessively capital-intensive process. In addition, excessive capital intensity is also present at the downstream A level. Equations (3.17) through (3.19) show that, of the three ultimate inputs in the model (L_a, L_e, and K_e), L_a is used until its price equals its marginal revenue product, while both L_e and K_e are employed past the level where their prices equal their marginal revenue products. Thus too much K_e is used relative to L_e at the equipment level, and too much of both L_e and K_e are used (as embodied in K_a) relative to L_a at the downstream level. Note that, from Equation (3.20), if regulation is effective, both λ_a and λ_e must be positive, since one constraint cannot be effective unless the other constraint is also effective. Thus the regulatory agency cannot prevent inefficiency at the equipment level unless it completely eliminates effective regulation or sets $\delta_e = 0$.

In addition, Equation (3.21) may be a considerable understatement of the effect of integration on the social marginal cost of E. Clearly, if $\delta_e > 0$, internal production of E would be in the interest of the regulated monopoly even if the elasticity of substitution between K_e and L_e were zero. The Averch-Johnson (A–J) effect is simply one form of the general incentive for a regulated monopoly to increase its capital base. While the A–J effect involves increasing the capital base for any given level of value-added by the regulated monopoly, vertical integration enables an increase in value-added for any given level of final output. Regulation thus results in a strong bias toward internal production over external supply. In general, the price set for E by outside suppliers may have to be considerably lower than the minimum internal cost of production of E. If outside suppliers exist who can produce E at some cost C' which is less than C but greater than the minimum price sufficient to overcome the regulated monopoly's bias toward internal production, then the social inefficiency cost of integration becomes $(\overline{C} - C')$ rather than just $(\overline{C} - C)$.

If vertical integration is to be socially desirable, any inefficiencies from internal production must be more than counteracted by positive economies from integration. If such positive economies exist, the regulatory agency has four alternatives:

1. It can permit vertical integration and accept the resulting inefficiency at the equipment level.
2. It can permit vertical integration but attempt to set $\delta_e = 0$.
3. It can impose vertical divestiture and accept the loss of any economies due to technological interdependencies.
4. It can permit vertical integration and directly regulate the transfer price of equipment, rather than impose regulation in the form of a rate-of-return constraint. If feasible, this would enable any efficiency gains to be achieved without an inefficiency loss due to the A–J effect at the equipment level or the bias toward internal production.

It should be stressed that any case against vertical divestiture is based on the assumption that positive and significant real economies of vertical integration actually exist, after allowing for the administrative costs to both the firm and to the regulatory agency of regulating an additional level. In a purely competitive situation, the firm's decision to integrate could be sufficient support for this assumption, for two reasons. First, no other incentive for integration would apply. Second, if some firms in the industry were unintegrated, and open-market prices existed, considerable information would be available to the firm evaluating integration. Internal costs could be compared with market prices, and overall profitability comparisons between firms could be made.

If the firm is a regulated monopoly, however, alternative incentives for integration exist, and if all firms integrate in order to avoid regulation there is no independent price against which to compare internal production costs. Thus, not only will the regulated firm be *willing* to produce its upstream inputs itself at a higher cost than the cost of purchasing those inputs from independent suppliers, but the firm's *ability* to evaluate its own performance may be reduced, thus encouraging further static inefficiency. The problem is particularly relevant in an industry where most technical change occurs at the equipment manufacturing level, since regulation can be expected to bias the firm's innovational choices. The regulation-induced bias in innovation, however, may or may not reinforce the static misallocation of resources due to regulation. (see Smith, 1974, 1975; Okuguchi, 1975, Magat, 1976)

CONCLUSION

Two alternative strategies are open to governments if vertical control is used to avoid the impact of government policies. The first strategy is to make such cases of vertical control illegal. This would require examination of each instance of vertical control in order to separate legal from illegal cases. The alternative is to redesign government policies so that vertical control could not be used to circumvent these policies. This strategy would require, for example, that turnover taxes be replaced by value-added or final-sales taxes, that profit taxes be set at the same rate for all levels, that import duties be on a specific rather than an ad valorem basis, that the aims of price control be achieved by other methods, and that rate-of-return regulation be replaced by effective transfer-price regulation. The optimal mix of these two alternative strategies depends on the degree to which government aims can be achieved by policies that are neutral toward vertical control, and on the enforcement and inefficiency costs of preventing vertical control.

NOTES

1. "Of the 923 large manufacturing and mining mergers recorded between 1951 and 1966 . . . twenty-seven percent of all horizontal mergers in the group of 923 and seventeen percent of the vertical mergers were challenged, but only three percent of the conglomerates came under attack" (Scherer, 1970, p. 489). While a shift away from horizontal and toward conglomerate mergers may be expected as a result, the effect on vertical mergers is unclear.

2. Until recently, firms producing crude oil, for example, could subtract from their gross income before taxes an amount equal to 27.5 percent of their total revenues from crude production, subject to the condition that the amount of percentage depletion allowance could not exceed 50 percent of the producer's taxable income calculated on a cost-depletion basis. (For a discussion and example of this, see Mancke, 1974, pp. 77-87.) The depletion allowance was reduced to 22 percent by the Tax Reform Act of 1969, and then eliminated, by the Tax Reduction Act of 1975, for all except small unintegrated producers.

Vertical control in the petroleum industry has been a subject of extensive study. See McLean and Haigh (1954); de Chazeau and Kahn (1959); Miller (1963); Erickson, Millsaps, and Spann (1974); Canes (1976); Masson and Allvine (1976); Rusin and Atwood (1976); Teece (1976), and the papers in Mitchell (1976).

3. In the absence of taxation, as Miller and Upton (1976) have noted, "rental rates for capital equipment would adjust until, in equilibrium, the purely

financial advantages of the two arrangements were equal. The choice in any particular case would depend on which method had the lower nonfinancial costs of acquisition, maintenance and disposal. . . ." They continue:

> The presumption of equivalence often breaks down, however, when we allow for the peculiarities of the present U.S. tax laws. What destroys the symmetry is not the way rentals and interest payments are treated for tax purposes, as has sometimes been suggested, but rather the fact that user firms may not always be able to take full advantage of some of the tax subsidies to hardware that Congress bestows. Leasing companies have thus tended to become entities specialized, among other things, to the maximum utilization of these subsidies, which are in turn reflected in equilibrium rental rates. When the leasing company also happens to be owned by the company that manufacturers the equipment, still another twist in favor of leasing is imparted by the deferral of taxes on the manufacturing profit that the manufacturer gains by leasing rather than selling. For nontaxable user firms such as universities, however, and for the special case of consumer durables, there are tax-related financial benefits to ownership that must be considered. [Miller and Upton, 1976, p. 785]

4. The analysis of gains from integration becomes more complex if, for some reason, internal prices cannot diverge from open-market prices. If the integrated firm is not self-sufficient in crude, raising the price it pays for crude will shift profits to independent producers as well as to its own crude production level. One author (Mancke, 1976, pp. 64-67) has calculated that, for a 22 percent depletion allowance, raising the intermediate price would be profitable only for firms producing at least 93 percent of their crude-oil needs, a condition satisfied by only one (Getty Oil) of the seventeen largest integrated refiners. While this argument may be correct, it would be interesting to examine both why internal prices must necessarily correspond to market prices and, if this is the case, why the integrated firms did not respond by moving to complete self-sufficiency, since the tax benefits from doing so would have been quite significant.

5. As a hypothetical example, suppose that an exporter of watches to the United States faced high U.S. ad valorem tariffs. The exporter could try to avoid the tariff by selling the watches at a nominal price to a wholly owned subsidiary in the United States, which would then resell them to U.S. importing firms. The U.S. subsidiary, however, would show large accounting profits, which might result in high U.S. profits taxes. One solution would be to tie the sale of nominally priced watches to the sale, at high prices of some other good (watchbands, for example), which is not subject to tariff duties. By using such a tying arrangement, an exporter could avoid both the tariff and the profits tax. In practice such an extreme and simple arrangement is not likely to successfully deceive the authorities. If designed with sufficient complexity and used in moderation, however, such arrangements can, like internalization through integration, increase policing requirements sufficiently to reduce effective taxation.

6. For example, Lee Liberman, the president of Laclede Gas in St. Louis indicated in a recent conversation with the author that his firm's entry into ex-

ploration in Louisiana is due to shortages resulting from interstate regulation of gas prices.

7. For an early example, see *F.T.C.* v. *Gratz*, 253 U.S. 421 (1920). While such arrangements can easily be discerned by price-control authorities, they do appear with some frequency. My favorite example is the service station operator in St. Louis who, during the recent gasoline shortage, began offering fill-ups conditional on purchase of either a rabbit's foot or a will form, both at remarkable prices but of presumably little value except to his more reckless customers.

8. For a history and analysis of vertical integration in telecommunications, see Irwin (1971, 1977).

9. *International Telephone and Telegraph Corp.* v. *General Telephone and Electronics Corp. and Hawaiian Telephone Co.*, Civil No. 2754, Dist Ct. Hawaii, filed July 14, 1972.

10. A recent and extensive treatment is provided by Bailey (1973).

11. The model presented in this section differs from Dayan's in several respects. First, by introducing a replacement demand for equipment, it permits a positive static equilibrium level of output at the upstream equipment level. Second, it removes the implicit assumption of fixed-proportions technology at the equipment level, thus transforming equipment production cost into a variable. The use of Cobb-Douglas production functions and the assumption that δ_a and δ_e are small enough so that regulation is effective (thus enabling the use of Lagrangian rather than Kuhn-Tucker methods), however, eliminates much of the sophistication and generality of Dayan's formulation.

Chapter 4

Vertical Control Due to Market Power (Fixed Proportions)

Horizontal market power creates four new possible incentives for vertical control: (1) elimination of bilateral monopoly, successive monopoly, or monopsony; (2) achievement of price discrimination; (3) heightening of entry barriers; and (4) maintenance of oligopolistic discipline.

BILATERAL MONOPOLY, SUCCESSIVE MONOPOLY, AND MONOPSONY

Bilateral monopoly exists when a single, monopolist seller (a firm producing good A) faces a single, monopsonist buyer (a firm producing good X); successive monopoly exists when both the A firm and the X firm are monopolists.[1] Successive monopoly can exist without bilateral monopoly. Thus product A may be sold to several firms, producing goods X, Y, and Z, where the X firm has a monopoly in its market but no monopsony power toward the A firm. An example of such a series of successive monopolies without bilaterial monopoly would be a sole seller of copper, selling to a large number of buyers, one of whom is the sole owner of zinc and hence the only producer of brass, who, in turn, sells brass to numerous users, one of whom is the sole producer of a patented brass thermostat, etc. (Machlup and Tauber, 1960, p. 113). Each purchaser treats the price set by his supplier as a parameter, but acts as a monopolist in his own market.

Bilateral monopoly can also exist without successive monopoly. For example, a labor union may face a single employer who, in turn, faces a competitive product market. Monopsony can exist separately or in conjunction with monopoly. An example of a simple monopsonist would be a firm that sells its output in a competitive national market because of low transport costs for its output, but faces an upward-sloping supply curve for a specialized, locally produced input because of high transport costs for this input.

Under conditions of bilateral monopoly, successive monopoly, or monopsony, vertical integration may both increase total profits and lower the price of the final product. The critical requirement for vertical integration to have this effect is that, prior to integration, the parameter set by the supplying monopolist or the purchasing monopsonist/monopolist was the price, rather than the quantity, of the intermediate product. If the vertically related firms can set the quantity as well as the price of the intermediate product, they can choose the joint profit-maximizing quantity and then bargain over the price. Under bilateral monopoly without successive monopoly, the result of either merger or price-quantity contracts is the same as if both levels were competitive. Under successive monopoly, the result of either integration or price-quantity contracts is the same as a single downstream monopoly. If either price-quantity contracts or vertical integration replaces parametric price-setting between the two firms, the result is an increase in joint profits, an increase in output, and—if successive monopoly exists—a decrease in the price of the final product.

If inputs are used in fixed proportions, it is possible to illustrate the above conclusions graphically. In addition, it can be shown that if the downstream firm is a competitor in input and product markets, using inputs in fixed porportions, and if vertical integration does not result in the effects discussed in earlier chapters (that is, informational economies, internalization of externalities, tax avoidance, and so on), then downstream vertical integration by an input monopolist with unrestricted monopoly power will have no effect on either the level of monopoly profits, the prices and quantities of the inputs, or the price and quantity of the final product.

A Taxonomy of Alternative Market Structures

Competition at All Levels. Assume that a final product X is produced using two inputs, A and B, in fixed proportions. The B industry is competitive, with price equal to marginal cost, M_b. B can be a composite of all other inputs, including capital, used at the X stage. If the X industry is also competitive, the demand function for A can be derived by subtracting the cost of the B input, per unit of X, from the demand curve for X:

$$P_x X = P_a A + P_b B$$

or

$$P_a = \left(P_x - \frac{M_b B}{X}\right)\frac{X}{A}$$

If, for simplicity, we assume that one unit of X is produced using one unit of A plus one unit of B, the demand function for A reduces to:

$$P_a = P_x - M_b$$

In Figure 4-1, if competition exists at both input and output levels (A, B, and X), the quantity of the inputs used and the final product produced will be OA, OB, and OX, respectively. At this level of output, $P_x = M_b + M_a$, and $P_a = M_a$.

Single-Stage Monopoly. If we now introduce a monopoly at the A level only, with competition at the X and B stages, the A monopolist will equate his marginal cost, M_a, with his marginal revenue, MR_a, at point b, setting a price for A of P_a'. Sales of A are OA', the final product price is P_x', and final product sale are OX'. Monopoly profits are given by the area *abcd.*

Alternatively, if there is monopoly at the X level only, and competition at the A and B stage, the X monopolist equates his marginal cost, $M_b + M_a$, with his marginal revenue, MR_x, at point l. Production of A, B, and X is OA', OB', and OX', respectively, and profits are the area $klme = abcd = kls = abn$. Thus, under fixed proportions, a single-stage monopoly at the upstream level results in the same production levels for inputs and outputs, and the same level of profits, as does a single-stage monopolist at the downstream level.

Successive Monopoly. Now assume that both the A industry and the X industry are separately monopolized, and that the X monopolist accepts P_a' as a parameter. The X firm's marginal cost of production is now $P_a' + M_b$, equal to P_x'. Equating this marginal cost with marginal revenue in the X market at point f results in a new final price of P_x''. Production of A, B, and X falls to OA'', OB'', and OX'', respectively. Profits at the X stage are now given by *efgh*, but profits at the A stage have fallen to *aijd*. (The A monopolist will still set a price of P_a'. His effective demand curve is now his old marginal-revenue curve, MR_a, and the intersection of his new marginal revenue curve, MMR_a,

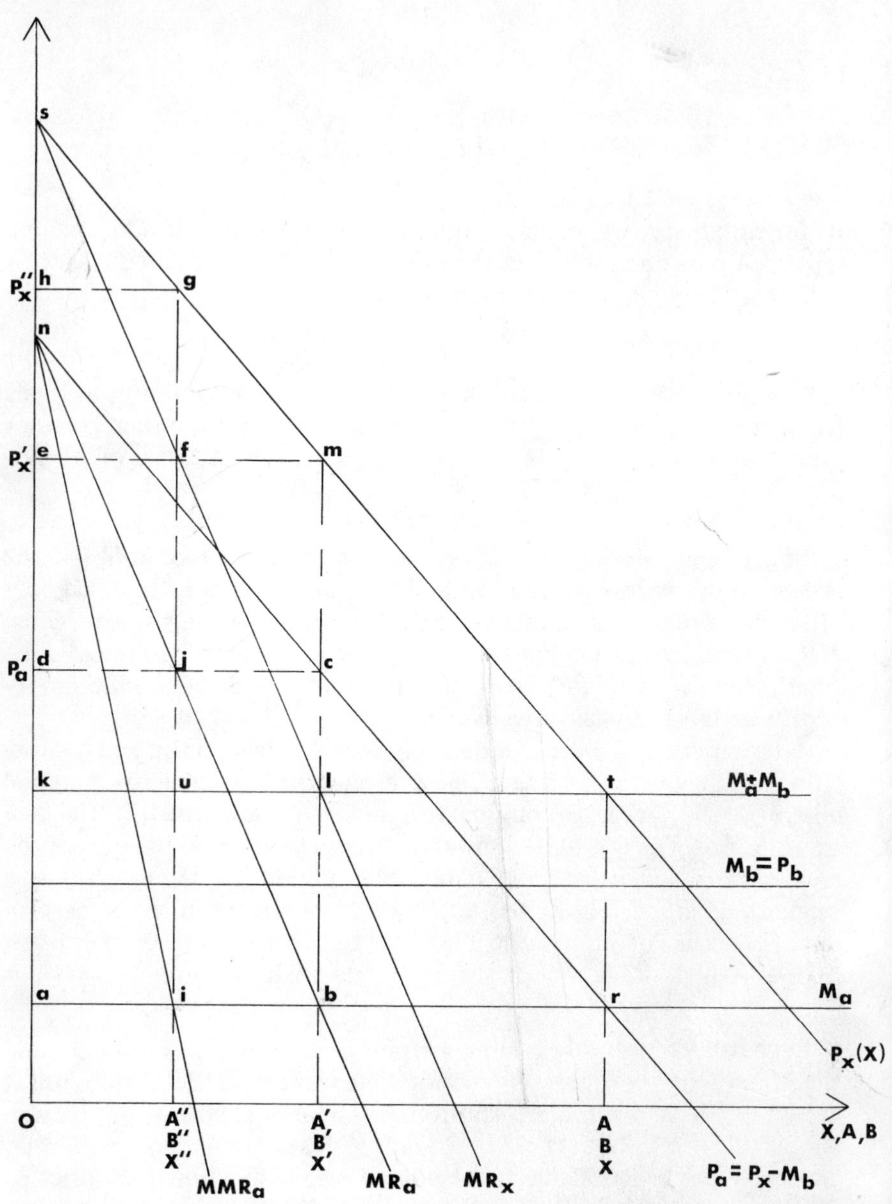

Figure 4-1. Successive Monopoly

with M_a at point i will result in sales of OA'' at price P'_a.)[2] Total joint profits are given by area $aijd + efgh = kugh = kufs = aijn$. Establishing a second monopoly level thus results in a reduction in joint profits by an area $ibcj - efgh = ulf = ibj$, or by one-fourth of original joint profits. The total welfare loss from adding a second monopoly level is given by area *ulmg*, of which area *ulf* represents the loss to producers (reduction in joint profits), while area $lmgf = emgh$ represents the loss to consumers (reduction in consumers' surplus) due to the increase in the price of the final product.[3]

Vertically Integrated Monopoly. If the two monopolies merge into one vertically integrated firm, the new firm will equate MR_x with the internal marginal cost of producing X, $M_b + M_a$, at point l. This results in a final-product price of P'_x and output levels for A, B, and X of OA', OB', and OX', respectively. Profits are given by the area *klme*, identical with the profits from a single-stage downstream monopoly and equal to *abcd*, the profits from a single-stage upstream monopoly.

Alternatively, if the A and X monopolists can agree on the quantity of A, they will set that quantity at OA' and then determine a price for A between M_a and P'_a by bargaining. The price of the final prod- will be P'_x, final output will be OX', and joint profits will be equal to *abcd*.

Two conclusions emerge from this demonstration. First, when the price of the intermediate good is treated parametrically, successive monopoly results in a higher price for the final product and lower joint profits than either a single-stage monopoly or a vertically integrated monopoly. Second, under conditions of fixed proportions, downstream vertical integration by a monopolist supplier into a competitive industry alters neither the level of profits nor the profit-maximizing price for the final product.[4]

Single-Stage Monopoly and Monopsony. These conclusions are unchanged if the supply curve for B is upward-sloping. In Figure 4-2, since M_b, is upward-sloping, a single-stage X monopolist will also act as a monopsonist in the B market, setting $M_a + MM_b$ (where MM_b is the curve marginal to M_b) equal to MR_x at point t. Quantity levels will be OA', OB', and OX', the price of the final product is P'_x, and profits are *klme*.

For a single-stage A monopolist, a rising M_b curve results in a derived-demand curve that is now steeper than the final-demand curve, and hence in a steeper MR_a curve. The single-stage A monop-

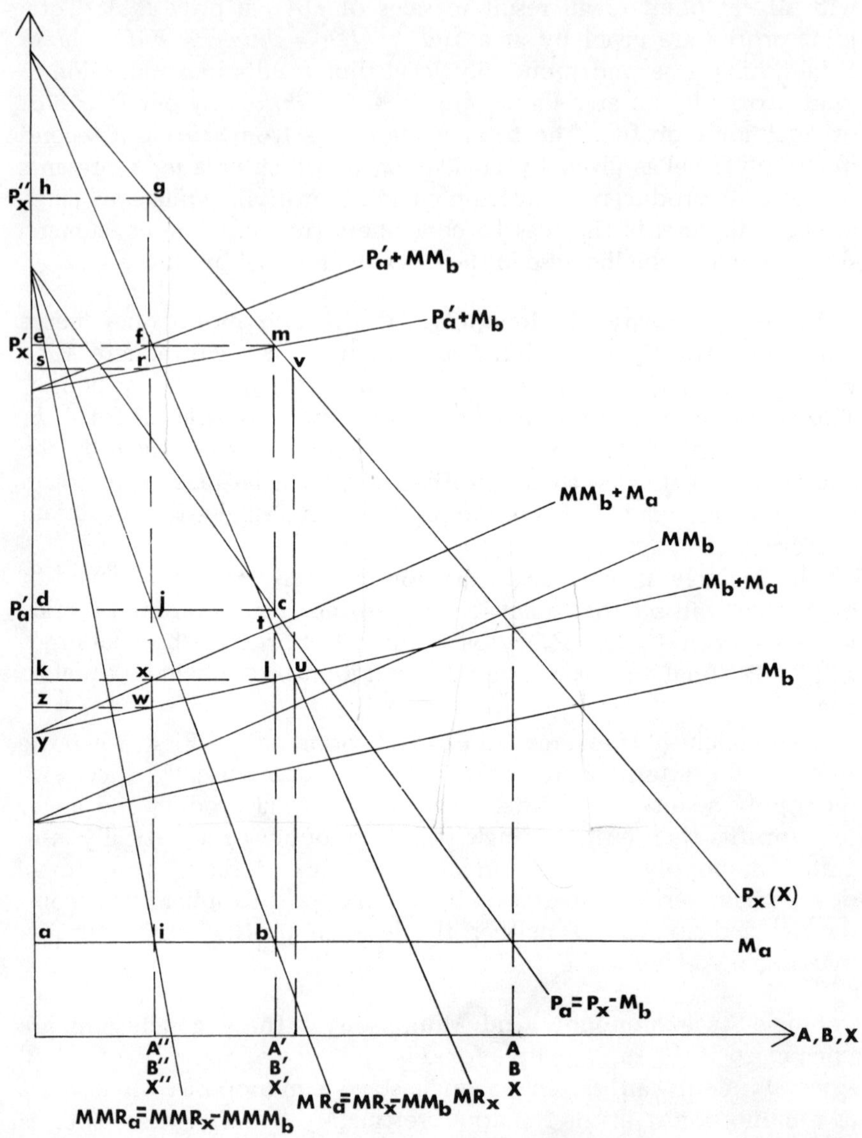

Figure 4–2. Successive Monopoly and Successive Monopsony

olist equates M_a with $MR_a = MR_x - MM_b$ at point b, and sets a price of P'_a, resulting in quantity levels of OA', OB', and OX', a final-product price of P'_x, and profits of $abcd$, equal to $klme$. Note that the decision rule for the single-stage X monopolist/monopsonist (MR_x

$= M_a + MM_b$) is identical to the decision rule for the single-stage A monopolist/indirect monopsonist ($MR_x - MM_b = M_a$).

Thus, with fixed proportions, a single-stage monopolist at either level can act with equal effectiveness as a monopsonist in the B market. Output and input levels, the final-product price, and profits, will all be the same whether the X firm is a monopolist in the X market and a direct monopsonist in the B market, with A and B competitive, or the A firm is a monopolist in the A market and thus an indirect monopsonist in the B market, with X and B competitive.

Successive Monopoly and Monopsony. If both A and X are separate monopolists, the result of a rising supply curve for B will be both successive monopoly and successive monopsony. In Figure 4-2, both A and X will react to the upward-sloping supply curve for B—the X firm directly, since it is the purchaser of B, and the A firm indirectly through a steeper marginal revenue curve. The A firm now sets $M_a = MMR_a = MMR_x - MMM_b$ at point i, resulting in an intermediate product price of P_a', the same price that would be chosen by the A firm if it were a single-stage monopolist and monopsonist. The X firm then sets $P_a' + MM_b = MR_x$ at point f. The result is a price of P_x'' for the final product, quantity levels of OA'', OB'', and OX'', and joint monopoly profits of $aijd + srgh$.

As compared with a single-stage monopoly and monopsony, total welfare is less by area $wlmg$. Joint profits of the X and A firms have fallen by area $klme - aijd - srgh = ibcj - srgh = ibj = xtf$. Producers' surplus in the B industry has fallen by area $srme = zwlk = wltx$, and consumers' surplus is reduced by area $emgh = tmgf$. (Note that $wlmg = xtf + wltx + tmgf$.) Since integration of the A and X levels would return the situation to the single-stage monopoly and monopsony position, integration would now benefit B producers, as well as consumers and the A and X firms.

Bilateral Monopoly. If bilateral monopoly is introduced into a successive monopoly situation, the results will depend on the relative bargaining power of the two firms and on the elasticity of the M_a curve. If the X firm is sufficiently powerful in relation to the A firm, the X firm will face a supply schedule for A that consists of the marginal-cost schedule for A, M_a, as well as a supply schedule for B, M_b. The X firm will then equate $MM_a + MM_b$ with MR_x. The result may be an increase in joint profits and a reduction in the price of the final product as compared to successive monopoly without bilateral monopoly. Monopsony power by the X firm can be used as "countervailing power" against the monopoly position of the A firm.[5] Suppose that the monopsonistic X firm is completely successful in eliminating the monopoly power of the A firm. The X firm unilaterally sets the transfer price and convinces the A firm to accept that price as a parameter. Output levels and joint profits will then be the same as if the A level were competitive. In addition, if M_a is constant ($M_a = MM_a$), the output and joint-profit levels will also be the same as if the A and X levels were integrated.

Integration into the Monopsonized Industry. If the marginal cost schedule for A is upward-sloping, eliminating the monopoly power of the A firm will still result in lower joint profits and output levels than would occur with vertical integration. With increasing M_a, vertical integration would be preferable to parametric price-setting by the X firm because integration would also eliminate X's monopsonization of the A industry. The additional gain from eliminating a monopsony can be examined separately by assuming, as in Figure 4-2, constant M_a and rising M_b, and a monopoly/monopsony at either the A or the X level.

In this case, if the B firms were acquired by either a single-stage X monopolist/monopsonist (vertical integration) or a single-stage A monopolist/monopsonist (horizontal integration), or by an integrated X and A monopolist/monopsonist (vertical and horizontal integration), the result of such integration with the B firms would be production at the point where $MR_x = M_b + M_a$, at the point u. The welfare gain from integration into B will be area $luvm$ (the difference between the cost and the value of the increased output), of which area lut would accrue to producers, and area $tmvu$ to consumers. Not only is it obviously not profitable to monopolize or monopsonize oneself, but such actions would also result in a reduction in the quantity of final output.

Thus, in the absence of transaction costs it is always profitable for a monopsonist to integrate (either horizontally or vertically) into the monopsonized industry and eliminate the inefficiency caused by monopsony. The "absence-of-transaction-costs" assumption, however, is more restrictive than might appear at first glance. If the supply curve of a good (in this case an intermediate good) is upward-sloping, at least one of the factors used in the production of that good must be in less than perfectly elastic supply.[6] It is these factors —factors to which rents accrue as output of the good is increased— that are monopsonized, and it is thus these factors that must be purchased if integration is to be profitable. We thus expect that most observed cases of monopsony (that is, those which have not been eliminated by integration) will involve inelastic factors for which no market exists, or for which the market is imperfect. The classic example of such a factor is, of course, labor (at least since the Thirteenth Amendment). If the supply curve of a competitively produced intermediate good is upward-sloping purely because of an increasing supply price for labor to that industry, integration by a vertically or horizontally related monopsonist into production of the intermediate good will not generally eliminate monopsonization.

The introduction of monopsony into the analysis appears so far only to reinforce our earlier results. Integration will be even more beneficial when successive monopoly and monopsony is present than when only successive monopoly exists. In addition, if integration results in internalizing the ownership of previously monopsonized factors, an integrated monopoly will be preferable to a single-stage monopoly/monopsony (at either the upstream or downstream level) with competition elsewhere.

Thus if horizontal or vertical integration is the only practical alternative to either successive monopoly, successive monopoly and monopsony, or a single-stage monopoly and monopsony, then integration is clearly desirable. Unfortunately, if integration is expensive, the private costs of integration may be greater than the private gain from integration, but still less than the social gain. In Figure 4–1, for example, the private gain (increase in joint monopoly profits) from integrating the A and X levels, and thus eliminating successive monopoly, is area ulf, while the social gain is $ulmg = ulf + lmgf$ (two and one half times the private gain, for the linear case). In Figure 4–2, if the A firm acquired the monopolistic X firm and all competitive B firms at the market price for those firms, the private gain would be given by wuf, while the social gain is $wuvg = wuf + uvgf$.

If integration also results in positive economies due to improved control or information, these private and social benefits are increased. But even if integration results in diseconomies, integration may still be desirable. Suppose that all costs of integration are fixed costs. Examples would include bargaining and legal costs of arranging a merger and defending the merger against antitrust and regulatory agencies. These costs may well exceed the private gain from merger, especially if the acquiring firm undertaking these costs must pay a significant premium over the pre-merger market value of the acquired firm, thus reducing the private (but not social) gain from initiating integration.[7] Under these conditions, the desirable public policy may be to actively encourage integration beyond the level that would be chosen in the absence of government intervention, or at least not to add to the costs of integration.

This argument also holds even if marginal costs rise after integration due to diseconomies of control or information. An increase in marginal costs will reduce the fall in the price of the final product after integration, but the price will still fall and consumers will still gain as long as the increase in marginal cost is less than the original monopoly markup on the intermediate good. For integration to be profitable, however, the increase in marginal costs must be considerably less than the original monopoly markup on the intermediate good. For integration to be socially desirable, therefore, the increase in marginal costs must be less than the original monopoly markup on A, but the maximum increase in marginal costs for integration to be socially desirable will be greater than the maximum increase under which integration would still be profitable.[8] Thus, once again, we should expect integration to stop short of the socially optimal level.

As Perry (1975, 1976) shows, however, the simplicity of this analysis is critically dependent on the assumption of fixed proportions in the production of the monopsonized good. With fixed proportions in production, integration becomes an all-or-nothing proposition. The monopsonist will decide either to produce none of the monopsonized good or to integrate completely and produce all his requirements internally. Thus partial integration is not a relevant alternative. In addition, throughout the analysis we have ruled out (as does Perry) the possibility of a predatory "squeeze" imposed by the monopsonist. For legal or other reasons, we assume that the monopsonist cannot temporarily restrict (or threaten to restrict) his purchases, drive down the price of the monopsonized good, and then purchase, at distress prices, the factors used to produce the good. Combined with the fixed-proportions assumption, this implies that the cost to the monopsonist of purchasing the factors used to produce the monopsonized good will be determined by the level of rents being earned by those factors in the unintegrated but monopsonized situation.

For simplicity, assume that the monopsonist and the monopsonized-factor owner have the same discount rate, and that the factors in noninfinitely elastic supply have a zero value in alternative uses. The rental cost to the monopsonist of acquiring the monopsonized factors will then equal the rents earned by those factors before integration. In Figure 4–2, for example, the rental cost to a single-stage X monopolist/monopsonist of acquiring the monopsonized factors is given the area ylk. If A and X were successive monopolists/monopsonists, however the rental cost of acquiring the monopsonized factors would be only area ywz. Thus if the A firm initiated integration in a successive monopoly/monopsony situation, the preferred strategy would be to integrate simultaneously into X and B. But in either case the monopsonized factors do not lose from integration.

Thus in the fixed-proportions case, integration will be complete, the monopsonized independent factor suppliers will not be harmed, and the only incentive for integration is elimination of the inefficiency loss from monopsony. While we shall defer discussion of Perry's results for the variable-propositions case until Chapter 5, we should simply note here that all of these conclusions may be altered once the element of variable proportions is introduced.

Qualifications of the Defense for Integration

This kind of defense of vertical integration is subject to two critical qualifications. First, successive monopoly, monopsony, and bilateral monopoly can be eliminated by a number of different forms of vertical control, some of which may be socially preferable to vertical integration through merger. Second, the conclusion that downstream vertical integration by a monopolist into a competitive industry will not affect prices or profit levels depends critically on the assumptions of a fixed-proportions production function and unrestricted monopoly power before integration.

Alternative Solutions for Successive Monopoly. The undesirable effects of successive monopoly can be eliminated by a number of different forms of vertical control. In the first place, a price-quantity agreement may be possible that would provide the benefits of vertical integration without also resulting in other, perhaps less desirable, effects of integration. Where bilateral monopoly is also present, the close relationship of the parties is particularly likely to lead to joint profit-maximization, with quantities set at the integrated level, while the price of the intermediate good—and thus the distribution of profits—is determined by bargaining.[9] This solution is probably least likely where "one or both parties have incomplete control over quantity because they are merely agencies for a group of buyers or sellers rather than single firms" (Machlup and Tauber, 1960, p. 112). Several separate price-quantity agreements would be needed, for example, between a labor union and multiple employers, or between bilateral oligopolists. The information, control, and separability requirements of such multiple agreements, however, may make this alternative impractical.

Vertical integration may also be less likely in such situations, however, since the quantity of the intermediate good transferred to each downstream firm may be a small proportion of the output of the intermediate firm or of the total input requirements of the downstream firm. Unless vertical integration is costless, therefore, complete vertical control may not be worthwhile. Where vertical integration is expensive, and price-quantity agreements difficult to administer, other alternatives are possible. Suppose a manufacturer of a patented product sells his product through a number of retail outlets, each of which possesses market power in its own area. The result will be successive monopoly without bilateral monopoly. The manufacturer could, of course, vertically integrate into retail sales. But if the sale of his product is a very small share of the total sales of each retail outlet, the control and other costs of integration may far exceed the gain in profits from elimination of successive monopoly in one item.

One solution would be for the manufacturer to set maximum resale prices. In terms of Figure 4-1 the manufacturer would set a maximum resale price of P'_x, permitting a resale markup of cm (see Hawkins, 1950, pp. 179-91). If resale price-fixing were used only to prevent successive monopoly, the result would be a lower retail price for the final product as well as increased total profits. Another alternative would be for the manufacturer to set a price for A of M_a but require a lump-sum payment from the retailer equal to $klme$. If the exact lump-sum amount is uncertain, or if the retailer also possesses some bargaining power, the A monopolist could set a price of M_a but also receive a percentage of the profits made at the downstream level. The share received by the A firm could, of course, be less than 100 percent and still leave him as well off as he was under successive monopoly. The effects of all these arrangements would be the same as the effects of vertical integration or price-quantity bargaining, but the costs of these alternatives may be lower.

Probably the most important reason for questioning the desirability of vertical integration by merger in a successive monopoly situation is that prohibition of a merger between successive monopolists may well lead to mutual entry. Especially where bilateral monopoly is also present, the vertically related firm has a greater incentive for entry than does a firm in an unrelated industry. A vertically related firm can be expected to have better knowledge of the other industry than would an outside firm, and economies of integration, of the type described in Chapter 2, may also exist. In contrast a merger might strengthen the market power of the remaining single integrated firm by increasing entry barriers (discussed below under that heading). Furthermore, by eliminating the most likely entrant, a merger will reduce potential competition and hence may eliminate an existing entry-price constraint on monopolistic pricing. As Berry (1970) has stated:

> If economies of joint (vertical) operation are present, it is likely that each of the two firms, if merger were denied, would integrate backwards and forwards respectively to gain the benefit of such economies. Each firm is

> presumably a more likely entrant to the market of the other than a firm of equivalent size acting in neither market. Alternatively, if structure at either stage of the vertical process permits noncompetitive behavior at that stage, that too would create an incentive for entry by corporations active at the other stage where the costs of that noncompetitive behavior are borne directly. Merger, under these circumstances, would permit an accommodation between potentially competitive corporations which would preserve the opportunity for that noncompetitive behavior. If such mergers are proscribed, such accommodation is denied. [p. 277]

Thus mutual vertical integration through entry should generally be encouraged as the ideal solution to the successive-monopoly problem. If mutual entry is impossible, then price-quantity contracts or partial forms of vertical control might be encouraged, with vertical integration through merger as a third-best solution.

Equivalence of Single-Stage and Integrated Monopoly. The second conclusion that has been used to defend vertical integration was that vertical integration by a monopolist into a competitive (and not monopsonized) industry would alter neither the level of monopoly profits nor the price of the final product. This implies that the existence of monopoly power at one stage provides neither any incentive for vertical integration into a competitive stage nor any reason for society to oppose such integration. Any such vertical integration must, therefore, be due to cost reductions resulting from improved control, information flows, and the like. Thus integration can only increase welfare.

This conclusion has been used to defend vertical integration without explicit recognition that its validity depends critically on the assumption of fixed proportions:

> Vertically integrated monopolies can take but one monopoly profit. . . . The gaining of a second monopoly vertically related to the first would not alter price, output, or the allocation of productive resources on the second level monopolized. Therefore, dissolving the vertical integration accomplishes precisely nothing. . . . The second monopoly adds no power the first did not confer. [Bork, 1951, pp. 196-98]
>
> Monopoly power is a horizontal, not a vertical phenomenon. It is in the interest of a (horizontal) monopolist to have all the other functions in his industry—the supply of his inputs, the processing, and distribution of his products—performed at minimum cost and charged for at the minimum price. As long as these two conditions prevail, he has no incentive to integrate vertically: he can appropriate the maximum profit available in the industry in the price that he charges for his own service, being assured that that price will be added to and will have added to it the minimum possible

> charge for all other services upstream and downstream from him. If these conditions do not prevail, it then does pay him to integrate; but in that event (if he made no mistake in doing so) the resultant lowering of the cost or price at which the associated function is performed can only be beneficial to consumers, if it affects them at all. [A.E. Kahn, 1971, p. 260]

As will be shown in Chapter 5, however, if variable proportions exist, downstream vertical integration by a monopolist into a competitive industry will both increase monopoly profits and generally increase the price of the final product. Furthermore, these results will occur whether the monopolist integrates by merger or by entry.

Another assumption implicit in the analysis so far is that an unintegrated monopoly firm has unconstrained power in setting the price of its output in each market at any desired level. This requires first, that where a monopolist faces several markets—each with different demand elasticities—price discrimination between these markets is possible. Second, it requires that the short-run profit-maximizing price is less than the price that would result in entry, so that entry is "blockaded." If either of these two conditions is not present, and if vertical control can raise entry barriers, help maintain oligopolistic discipline, or increase the ability to price discriminate, then new motivations for vertical control arise.

PRICE DISCRIMINATION

Third-Degree Price Discrimination

The type of price discrimination assumed above is third-degree price discrimination.[10] This requires that the A firm can divide its customers into groups, each with its own demand function. If these demand functions have different elasticities, it will pay to set a different price for A in each market.

In Figure 4-3, for example, the A monopolist faces two markets where A is used in fixed proportions; the X industry and the Y industry. For simplicity, assume that one unit of A can be combined with one unit of B to produce one unit of X, or with one unit of C to produce one unit of Y. If price discrimination is not possible, the A monopolist will simply set the marginal cost of A, M_a, equal to the total marginal revenue for A, MR_a, where MR_a is the horizontal summation of the marginal-revenue curve for A in the X market, MR_{ax}, and the marginal-revenue curve for A in the Y market, MR_{ay}. At $M_a = MR_a$, the price for A in both markets would be P_a. At that price, however, demand from the X industry is less elastic than demand from the Y industry. If the A firm can separate these two markets, he will set marginal revenue equal to marginal cost in each market,

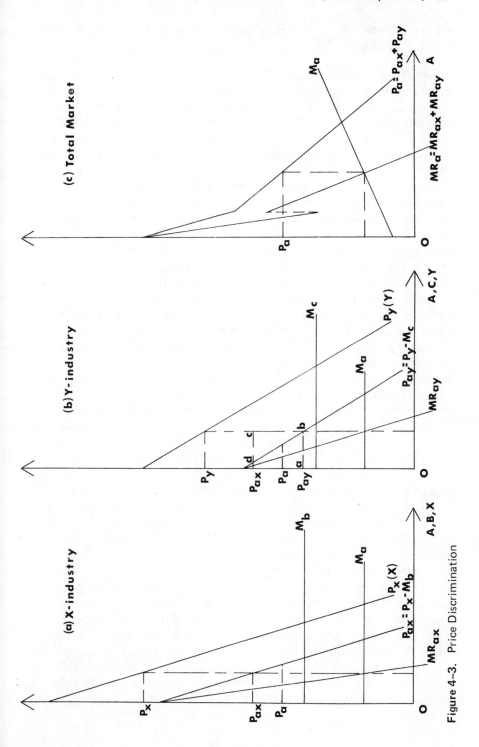

Figure 4–3. Price Discrimination

raising the price for A in the X market to P_{ax}, and lowering the price in the Y market to P_{ay}.

Legality and Separability. The A monopolist faces two potential problems in his attempt to set different prices for A in the two markets. First, such price discrimination may be illegal and difficult to hide. Second, the A firm may not be able to separate effectively the two markets, with the result that customers in the high-price market (industry X) buy A from customers in the low-price market (industry Y).

Vertical control can be used to solve both these problems. If the A firm vertically integrates into the Y industry (the more price-elastic market) it can establish two markets for A—an open market for sales to the X industry and an internal market for sales to its Y-producing subsidiary. By controlling undesirable sales of A from the Y industry to the X industry, integration solves the separation problem. In addition, integration may make price discrimination legal, or at least difficult to establish, since the A firm can set an internal accounting price of P_{ax} for sales to its own Y subsidiary without affecting its total profit levels. The Y-producing subsidiary will, of course, show accounting losses equal to area *abcd* in Figure 4-3b. If integration into the Y industry is tapered, so that some independent Y firms remain in the industry, these independent firms will suffer losses of *bc* per unit output. The independents are being "squeezed," since they are forced to purchase A at price P_{ax} while the producing subsidiary of the A firm sets a maximum price for Y of P_y. Facing such a squeeze, the independents will be forced out, either through exit from the Y industry or through merger with the A firm. Eventually, all of Y will be produced by the A firm. Under fixed proportions, this is not the result of any attempt by the A firm to "monopolize" the Y industry, but is rather the result of the need to internalize the intermediate-good transaction in order to achieve price discrimination. Of course, such a squeeze may have additional short-run benefits for the A monopolist. If some of the factors used by the independent Y firms are fixed, the A firm may be able to buy these fixed factors for less than replacement cost or, equivalently, force the independents to accept less than a "normal" rate of return on their investment.

Inflicting such a squeeze on independent producers may, however, open the A firm to legal attack by the independents. The law on price discrimination has been particularly concerned with harm done to competitors, and the independent Y firms in this case are clearly suffering injury. Thus price discrimination may not be possible if vertical integration is only partial. If the A industry takes over the entire Y industry on terms attractive to independents, damage to competitors will be eliminated. This alternative may be ruled out, however, either by the additional cost of pacifying the Y firms, or by antitrust action initiated by the government. Some interesting phenomena can result in such cases. For example, in an examination of the "two-price system" in the copper industry, McNicol (1975) shows that a partially integrated producer, unable to price discriminate directly and prevented from either integrating fully or squeezing downstream independents, may be able to partially achieve the potential gains from price discrimination by rationing downstream users.

The analysis of price discrimination via selective forward integration has recently been extended by Perry (1977b) to the case of a dominant firm selling its intermediate product to several competitive industries. Perry shows that downstream integration into industries with relatively elastic demands can be profitable for a dominant firm as well as for a monopolist. As a case study he examines downstream integration by Alcoa prior to 1930, and argues that the elasticity of derived demand for aluminum from industries chosen for integration (aluminum cable, cookware, automobile sand castings and pistons) was high relative to the elasticity of derived demand for aluminum from industries where integration was not chosen (aircraft, iron and steel). While such a correspondence does not prove that the only or major incentive for Alcoa's integration was price discrimination, the observed pattern of downstream integration does appear to be consistent with this rationale.

Alternative Forms of Vertical Control to Achieve Third-Degree Price Discrimination. Since vertical integration may create some legal difficulties, and since costs of integration may also exist, the firm wishing to price discriminate between markets may turn to less complete forms of vertical control. In Figure 4-3 the A firm can achieve price discrimination by imposing a tying arrangement on either the firms in the X industry, or on the firms in the Y industry, or on both. Thus A may be sold on the open market at price P_{ay}, but the X firm may be required to purchase its requirements of B from the A firm at a price of $M_b + P_{ax} - P_{ay}$, greater than M_b. Equivalently, the open-market price could be set at P_{ax}, but the Y industry could be offered C at a price of $M_c + P_{ay} - P_{ax}$, less than M_c. Alternatively, if a third input, D, is used with A in different, but fixed, proportions in the manufacture of both X and Y, a single tying arrangement between A and D can be used to set any two different effective prices for A in the two markets.

First-Degree Price Discrimination

The achievement of third-degree price discrimination can generally be regarded as only a first step toward maximization of profits. Ideally the monopolist would also like to achieve first-degree price discrimination, selling each unit at its reservation price. In Figure 4-1, for example, if the X market is a single purchaser or is composed of a number of purchasers whose demand curves are of the same elasticity, area $abcd$ is the maximum profit that can be achieved by third-degree price discrimination. In this situation, however, a consumers' surplus of area $dcn = ems$ and an efficiency loss of $brc = ltm$ still exist, both of which could be added to existing profits if the A firm could practice first-degree price discrimination.

In order to achieve first-degree price discrimination, however, the A monopolist must either face the final consumer himself or face downstream firms that practice first-degree price discrimination. Two alternative strategies are available for the intermediate-product monopolist. He can vertically integrate forward until he faces the final consumer, and then practice first-degree price discrimination himself. Alternatively, he can try to induce the downstream firms to practice first-degree discrimination. For example, the manufacturer of a product sold through competitive dealers could grant the necessary monopoly power for first-degree price discrimination to individual dealers by restricting competition between dealers, while also entering into price-quantity agreements or lump-sum arrangements with the individual dealers, which would transfer the resulting profits back to the manufacturer. Thus where discrimination, either first- or third-degree, can only be practiced at the downstream level, the upstream monopolist may be forced to grant monopoly power to downstream firms with one hand, while appropriating the resulting profits with the other hand.

It should be noted at this point that a tying arrangement between the monopolized product and another input used in fixed proportions with that product clearly cannot be used to achieve first-degree price discrimination. The perfect complementarity of the fixed-proportions input—which makes this input an ideal commodity with which to tie the monopolized product when the purpose is to alter the price of the monopolized product—renders it useless as a vehicle for achieving first-degree price discrimination.[11] While tying arrangements can be used to increase profits above the level possible through third-degree discrimination alone, the tying arrangement must be between two commodities that are used in variable proportions.

Tying arrangements can, however, be particularly useful for achieving (or approximating) first-degree price discrimination in two special cases. If the monopolized input is a capital good, a tying arrangement with a current input can be used to measure different intensities of use by individual users. In addition, if a single seller has market power over several products and if purchasers have different orderings of reservation prices for these products, setting a single price for a package of these products (block booking) can be an effective form of price discrimination.

Measuring Intensity of Use. Whenever the maximum amount that could be extracted for a capital good varies between customers, a monopolistic producer will wish to vary the payment between purchasers. In this situation the familiar problems of price discrimination arise—determining the different maximum lump-sum payments, preventing arbitrage, and avoiding illegality. These problems can be overcome, partially or completely, through several forms of vertical control. Vertical integration could clearly be one solution, although it will usually be a relatively expensive method of achieving the gains from price discrimination. Alternatively, if the reservation price for the machine is a function of intensity of use, the lump-sum payment can be made to vary with the rate of utilization.[12]

Intensity of use can be measured in a number of ways. If the monopolized input is a machine, a meter may be attached. The meter, however, may be tampered with, it may be expensive or result in operating difficulties for the machine, and the expense of reading meters may be significant. If direct metering is inefficient, intensity of use might be measured by the rate of final output, with payment on a royalty basis. Problems may again arise, however, of ensuring correct reporting of final output. In addition there may be difficulties in determining the contribution of the monopolized input to the final product, especially when the input is used in the manufacture of a number of different products.

In many cases intensity of use can best be determined by measuring the rate of use of other inputs used in fixed proportions to final output. A tying arrangement may then provide a method of both measuring and collecting from each user the reservation price for the machine.[13] Use of a tying arrangement to measure intensity of use will be particularly effective if use of the machine results in the same fixed saving per unit output (and hence per unit of a tied good used in fixed proportions per unit of output) for all users, but different users have different output rates. An individual demand curve for the use of the machine will thus look like the *dcf* curve in Figure 4–4. Individual demand curves will differ only in the length of *dc*, which is directly proportional to the quantity of *B* used. A tying arrange-

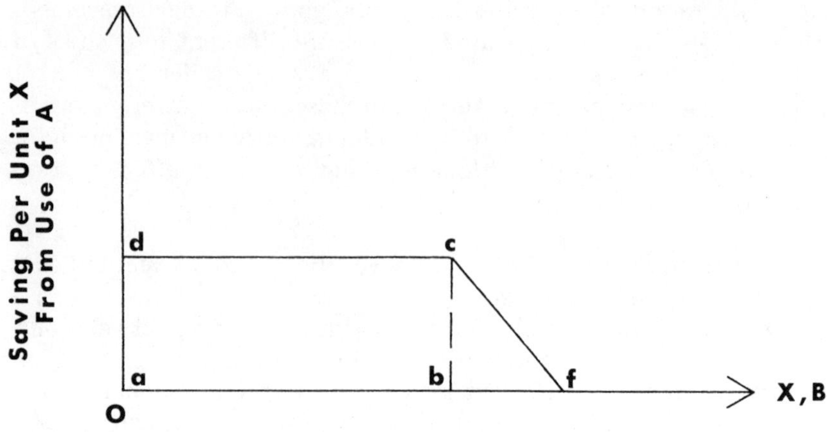

Figure 4-4. Demand, with Fixed Savings per Unit Output

ment where use of the machine is free but the price of B is set at $P_b = M_b + ad$,[14] will result in the maximum payment from each purchaser.[15]

A large number of the tying arrangements that have resulted in antitrust proceedings appear to be examples of the use of tying arrangements as counting devices to achieve price discrimination. Thus toilet paper has been tied to dispensers, buttons to button-fastening machinery, staples to stapling machines, mimeograph supplies to mimeograph machines, punch cards to computers, salt to salt-dispensing machines, steel strapping to applicating machines, rivets to riveting machines, and so on.[16]

Probably the most interesting example has been the use of automobile repair parts as a measure of the intensity of use of automobiles, a case extensively analyzed by Crandall (1968a, 1968b). The cost of determining individual reservation prices for automobiles and the inability to prevent arbitrage make discrimination in vehicle prices impractical. If assemblers vertically integrated downstream, renting rather than selling their product, both these problems could be solved. A uniform per-mile rental would both eliminate arbitrage and automatically generate information on intensity of use. The capital requirements of a rental system would be enormous, but this should not be a significant impediment.[17] We do observe that the major assemblers have integrated into financing retail sales, and companies such as IBM have encouraged leasing despite very large capital requirements. What probably distinguishes automobiles is the tax advantage to consumer ownership of durables and the high cost of controlling their use and maintenance by renters, which makes consumer ownership more attractive than rental except for low-frequency users.[18]

If downstream integration is thus too expensive, assemblers can use the demand for repair parts as a measure of intensity of use (and hence reservation prices). If the assembler can control the supply of repair parts, he can raise prices above marginal costs for parts while lowering the vehicle price, and thus effectively discriminate between high- and low-intensity users. The critical problem for assemblers, however, is to control the supply of repair parts. Control is facilitated by several assembler practices at both upstream and downstream levels. Downstream, assemblers have attempted to force franchised dealers to purchase parts from assemblers. In addition, downstream integration by assemblers into wholesaling can be used to restrict distribution channels open to independent parts manufacturers, if economies of scale in wholesaling are significant.

Upstream, assemblers insist on ownership of special equipment used by independent parts manufacturers to produce original equipment parts sold to assemblers, and can thus prevent the use of such equipment to produce parts for independent sale in the repair parts market. Refusal to standardize repair parts further increases the economies-of-scale barrier to entry. Finally, where economies of volume are important, original-equipment sales may be essential.

Backward integration into parts production by assemblers can thus preempt independent production.[19] The interesting result is that upstream integration provides a substitute for downstream integration to facilitate price discrimination. The far higher rate of return by assemblers in parts production than in vehicle assembly provides strong support for this hypothesis. In addition, Crandall argues, the use of integration to facilitate price discrimination significantly increases barriers to entry into vehicle production (discussed below).

Finally, if metering, royalty arrangements, or tying arrangements are not possible, there is another alternative open to a monopolist of a durable good or machine. He may be able to produce a range of machines, each capable of different rates of output, setting the price of each machine proportionate to its output rate. Even if the production cost of each machine is the same, the resulting price discrimination will increase profits.

Block Booking. Tying arrangements can also be useful as a means to achieve price discrimination where the seller has market power over several products, if purchasers exhibit different orderings of the maximum lump-sum payments they would be willing to offer for each product. The producer may then be able to price discriminate effectively by tying the commodities together and setting a single lump-sum price for the package.[20] Suppose, for example, that a motion-picture producer has two films, one starring John Wayne and the other directed by Ingmar Bergman. He distributes these films to two theaters, one in Houston and the other in Princeton. Suppose further that the maximum amount the theater owners would be willing to pay for each film is:

	Houston	*Princeton*
Wayne	$200	$150
Bergman	150	200
	$350	$350

The maximum revenue that could be achieved if the two films are sold separately at $150 each would be $150 · 4 = $600. If the producer sells the two films as a $350 package to each distributor, however, he could receive revenues of $700.

In general, the greater the difference between purchasers in their preference ordering for the products, and the less the difference between purchasers in the total amounts they are willing to pay for the products as a package, the greater is the profitability of such an averaging technique. To the extent that these conditions do not hold, averaging will be less attractive than other techniques, such as acquisition of some downstream firms. The various forms of vertical control can, of course, be carefully combined. For example, there may be a group of theaters which are large, are in particularly advantageous locations, or are suitable for first-run showings, where block-booking totals would be significantly higher than for the mass of theaters. If setting two block-booking sums is not possible, the answer may be to integrate vertically into one group, while block-booking the other theaters. Similarly, if some theaters face very specialized demands, so that they would pay a very high price for one film, while other films in the package were virtually useless (a theater in Dodge City puts a value of $300 on the Wayne, and $10 on the Bergman for example), supplementing the package offer with a set of single-film prices (the sum of which was considerably higher than the price for the package) could enable additional sales of individual films to theaters that would not have accepted the block. The end result could be an extremely complex pattern of vertical controls involving vertical integration, tying arrangements, unit pricing, royalty arrangements, and so on.

Public Policy toward Vertical Control Used for Price Discrimination

The formulation of public policy toward vertical control used to achieve price discrimination presents two problem. First, it is not clear what should be included in the government's objective function.

While the simplest approach is to maximize total "welfare," public policy may also be concerned with the effect of discrimination on individual competitors, on income distribution, or on the degree of concentration of political and economic power.[21] Second, even if "welfare maximization" is accepted as the goal of public policy, the effect of price discrimination on welfare is *a priori* unknown. One possible proxy for the welfare effect of discrimination is the effect of discrimination on output. Since first- and second-degree price discrimination lead to an increase in output, such discrimination (especially second-degree discrimination used by regulated monopolies with falling average costs) has often been viewed favorably. The effect on total output of third-degree price discrimination, however, depends in a complex manner on the relative characteristics of the demand functions in the separated markets.[22] In addition, for third-degree price discrimination, an increase in total output is generally a necessary but not sufficient condition for an increase in welfare.[23]

Discrimination may also be expensive, and the costs of discrimination can more than offset any increase in welfare due to increased output.[24] For first-degree price discrimination, the increase in profits is due both to the elimination of the welfare loss from monopoly restrictions on output (area *brc* in Figure 4-1for a single *A* monopolist) and the transfer of consumer surplus (are *dcn*) into monopoly profits. If the costs of achieving price discrimination are fixed costs, the monopolist will be willing to incur costs up to area *brc* + *dcn* to achieve discrimination. If the required costs are greater than area *brc* but less than area *brc* + *dcn*, discrimination will reduce aggregate welfare (Williamson, 1975, pp. 11-13; Posner, 1975, p. 822).

In contrast to the case of vertical control used to prevent successive monopoly (see the section "A Taxonomy of Alternative Market Structure," above), the private gains from discrimination are greater than the social gains, and excessive expenditure on achieving discrimination can be expected. This result is reinforced if discrimination increases marginal rather than fixed costs (since output will be correspondingly reduced), if discrimination is third rather than first or second degree, or if discrimination raises entry barriers. On the other hand, if the product would not be produced in the absence of discrimination (that is, the demand function lies everywhere below the average-cost function), discrimination will generally be desirable.

We cannot, therefore, make any general statement about the desirability of price discrimination. In principle the welfare effects of discrimination could be determined in any particular case, although in complex cases this may not be easy. These difficulties are enormously increased when, as would generally be the case, the public-policy choice is not really between discrimination and no discrimination, but rather between alternative methods of achieving discrimination. In antitrust cases, one particular practice is usually examined (for example, a tying arrangement), and the existing situation is compared with the nondiscriminatory result. The relevant comparison, however, is with what would occur if that practice were forbidden (vertical integration, for example). All we can assume is that the particular practice chosen by a firm is the most profitable alternative. As compared to the next-best alternative, however, we do not know if the chosen alternative was more profitable because it enabled greater capture of consumers surplus, or because it involved lower transactions costs. Thus before any comparison can be made, the firm's ranking of alternatives must be known, and a social evaluation of alternative states made. If deemed undesirable, some or all of these alternatives may also be proscribed, but prevention of less desirable alternatives may not be possible.

For example, assume that a manufacturer of a patented machine is using a tying arrangement to measure intensity of use. If this arrangement is proscribed, the manufacturer may vertically integrate downstream. But integration may both increase transaction costs and enable capture of a larger proportion of consumers' surplus, with resulting losses to both the firm and consumers. If we now prevent this alternative, the firm may turn to "skimming" (price discrimination over time)—setting a high price at first and then gradually reducing the price to pick up sales from less urgent customers. Since this cannot be prevented, the relevant choice is between this alternative and a tying arrangement. Quantifying the relative welfare effects of these two alternatives would be a formidable task, and there is no *a priori* reason to choose one over the other. If anything, in the absence of any additional information, the alternative chosen by the firm might be preferred since lower transaction costs are both privately and socially desirable.

Even if the socially desirable alternative can be determined, the costs (legal and other) of imposing that alternative must be considered. Furthermore, since horizontal market power is a prerequisite for discrimination, the legality or illegality of that market power may be relevant, and public policy might be better directed toward eliminating the basic condition of horizontal market power.

Thus polar attitudes are possible with respect to the desirability of public policies aimed at restricting the use of vertical control to achieve price discrimination. For example, "if the horizontal monopoly is legal, there should be no objection to price discrimination, and hence none to vertical integration employed to effect discrimination." (Bork, 1951, p. 198). Alternatively:

> Outlawing vertical control may make it difficult for the monopolist to extract any significant monopoly profits. And where the monopoly power exploited is either publically sanctioned as in the case of patents, or too small to fall within the present interpretation of Section 2, a prohibition against vertical forestalling provides one of the few restraints which may be imposed on the exercise of such power. [*University of Chicago Law Review*, 1952, p. 614]

Although the desirability of vertical control used to achieve price discrimination may be questionable, price discrimination can be clearly established—both in theory and in a number of specific cases—as a motivation for vertical control by firms with market power, even when downstream firms are competitive and no real economies of vertical control exist. The situation is reversed with respect to the second major reason advanced for vertical control in the absence of downstream market power: the raising of entry barriers. Here the difficulty has not been with establishing the undesirability of higher entry barriers. Instead the problems are, first, to show that vertical control can be used to substantially raise entry barriers, and second, to distinguish in practice between cases of vertical control used to achieve real economies and cases of vertical control used to raise entry barriers.

ENTRY BARRIERS

The critical condition for vertical control to raise entry barriers is that the use of some form of vertical control must enable existing firms to impose greater costs on new or potential entrants than on themselves.[25] This requires that vertical control by existing firms can force entrants either to follow suit or suffer losses, and also that vertical control is more expensive for entrants than for existing firms.

Vertical control by existing firms can clearly be used to inflict losses upon entrants. The simplest case is where existing firms are vertically integrated through two or more stages, and a new entrant attempts to operate at only one of these stages. The entrant will thus be forced to deal with one of the existing firms, either as a supplier or as a purchaser. The integrated firms can then set the transfer prices between levels so as to squeeze the entrant to any desired degree.[26] Alternatively, the existing firms could simply refuse to deal with the entrant and thus foreclose him completely from existing markets or supplies. Other forms of vertical control such as exclusive dealing arrangements, requirements contracts, or tying arrangements can also be used to foreclose the entrant.

Although existing patterns of vertical control may deter entry, it is difficult to establish in practice that this is the rationale for the particular pattern of vertical control occurring in any given industry. Vertical restrictions may be necessary in order to achieve price discrimination and thus maximize the returns from a market position already held. Restrictions may also be necessary in order to achieve real economies of vertical control.[27] If vertical control by existing firms both reduces costs for those firms and increases cost to new firms, a policy conflict results between the goals of increasing efficiency and reducing market power.

The second requirement for vertical control to be used as a barrier to entry is that vertical control must be more expensive for new or potential entrants than for existing firms. This could occur either because entrants face higher prices for the factors required for vertical control or because of economies of scale at the vertically related level. If either of these conditions exists, vertical control by existing firms could discourage entry and increase profits even if vertical control also raises costs for existing firms.

Differential Factor Prices

Defensive vertical control may require the raising of relatively large quantities of capital.[28] If the marginal cost of capital is higher for an actual or potential competitor than for the firm that initiates vertical control,[29] a "capital requirements" entry barrier[30] results. Firms that would be willing to enter or remain at one level may be unwilling to operate at both levels,[31] thus permitting higher output prices and profits for the existing firms exerting vertical control.

If vertical control by existing firms can force potential entrants to enter at more than one level simultaneously, unit-factor costs other than capital may also be increased for the entrant. Technically efficient entry may be sequential, since the information and management requirements for large-scale multilevel entry may be overwhelming. The setting up of production requires considerably greater management input than its maintenance. In addition, gradual expansion increases the supply of information and permits experimentation, learning, and goal reformulation (see Penrose, 1959).

The problem of lumpy managerial requirements could perhaps be solved by a firm which was large enough to regard entry into this particular industry as a marginal expansion and which was capable of reabsorbing surplus management after full integrated production is established. The entering firm would then have to be considerably larger than the minimum efficient size of an integrated firm in the industry. And if experience at any single stage were valuable in entering other stages, then simultaneous balanced entry may impose inefficiency costs on even a very large firm.

The entrant must thus weigh the costs of rapid expansion against the pecuniary losses that can be imposed by existing firms until integration is completed. The minimum amount of such cost increases and pecuniary losses may be a substantial fixed cost of entry, a cost that was not incurred by existing firms. Thus the integration of existing firms may enable them to maintain a profit rate substantially above that which would be acceptable to new entrants. In addition, these entrants may have to come from a small class of large firms, with higher than "normal" acceptable profit rates.

Economies of Scale

Even if all firms faced the same unit prices for factors used in vertical control, vertical control by existing firms could force higher costs on entrants if the minimum efficient scale for separate operations at the vertically related level is greater than the minimum efficient scale at the original level. If all firms at the vertically related level have ownership ties or other exclusive relationships with existing firms, the new entrant may be forced either to establish his own firm at the vertically related level or to persuade an existing firm at that level to abandon its present ties. A firm desiring to enter at minimum efficient scale can thus be required to enter at every level at a scale that will satisfy minimum efficient size requirements at the level exhibiting the largest scale economies. If average-cost curves are U- rather than L-shaped, efficient balanced integration may even require several plants at the level exhibiting the largest scale economies.

While such a requirement may result in large economies-of-scale entry barriers even in the manufacture of an undifferentiated product,[32] the problem seems most acute in product-differentiated industries where exclusive-dealership arrangements are general practice.[33] Sufficient volume for an efficient separate dealership system may require the entrant to produce a range of differentiated products. Due to entrenched consumer preferences, it may be very difficult to achieve a sufficiently large market share in all product lines in a short time without prohibitive market-penetration costs. Meanwhile, existing dealers will be unwilling to abandon their present lines, although they might be willing to add the entrant's product to their present lines if they were not prevented from doing so. In addition, there may be a limited supply of effective dealers in particular areas.

In some areas where demand is relatively dense, separate dealership arrangements may be efficient for the entrant. Exclusion from other markets, however, may reduce the attractiveness of his product elsewhere, especially if servicing is important. And total sales in areas where separate dealerships are efficient may not be sufficient to exhaust scale economies at the production level.

Exclusive arrangements by existing firms can thus be used to impose large artificial scale economies on entrants.[34] The effect has been noted in industries as diverse as automobiles[35] and dress patterns,[36] and it has even been argued that such arrangements in one industry can create entry barriers in another industry.[37] If the existing firms are large enough so that they can provide all the requirements, or demand, for vertically related firms of minimum efficient size, exclusive agreements will not prevent their realization of scale economies at the vertically related level. Vertical control can then be forced on the entrant at no cost to existing producers.[38]

A closely related situation can occur where vertical control facilitates price discrimination. Although the usefulness of price discrimination as a method of achieving market power appears questionable,[39] price discrimination has been effective in protecting an existing market position in a number of industries.[40] If only some downstream firms are large enough so that monopolistic pricing toward these firms would result in their integrating backward, a firm with market power may seek to discourage the most likely entrants. They could do this by setting low prices to large customers while setting higher prices to smaller firms which are effectively deterred from backward integration by the presence of scale economies at the upstream level. The effect can be to deter entry at both levels, since smaller downstream firms suffer a competitive disadvantage as compared with their larger rivals who are receiving discriminatory price concessions.[41]

In some cases price discrimination may encourage entry. Discrimination will increase industry profits, and if entrants can discriminate as effectively as existing firms, the expected profitability of an entrant is increased. Depending on the particular case, however, discrimination by existing firms may result in either a comparative advantage or disadvantage to entrants, and thus in either reinforcing or reducing the effect of a higher overall industry rate of return on the expected profitability of entry. On the one hand, new firms may be able to selectively enter less elastic markets where profit margins are high, a process usually referred to as creamskimming. If entry does not force existing firms immediately to end discrimination,[42] entry is in effect subsidized. On the other hand, discrimination may be easier for existing firms, and may even result in rates of return to entrants that are lower than what the industry average would be in the absence of discrimination. In effect, entry may—at least temporarily—only be possible into the more elastic market where profit margins are lower than the industry average. The automobile industry may be one example. Entry into vehicle assembly is a precondition for entry into the production of parts that are specific to the assembler. If parts are complements to vehicles but the demand for parts is less elastic than for vehicles, and if integration improves control over parts supply, then the preferred price for vehicles will be a decreasing function of the degree of integration, and the most integrated firm will be the price leader:

> Since [entrants] cannot hope to enter the industry as fully integrated as any of the Big Three, they must depend upon independent suppliers and Big Three firms for parts requirements. As a result, these firms are able to successfully tap the repair-parts market demand for parts from the entrant, reducing his ability to capture rents from these markets. But at the same time the entrant must compete for buyers of new vehicles at the prices established by the larger firms which are depressed . . . in order to stimulate a large market for repair parts. If the entrant cannot gain a large share of the parts demand generated by his vehicles, profit margins in vehicle supply may be so low as to forbid his continued production, especially given the natural cost disadvantages of low-scale production faced by the nascent producer. In short, the pricing mechanism developed by the large assemblers may serve to impede entry at the assembly stage. [Crandall, 1968b, p. 230]

MAINTAINING OLIGOPOLISTIC DISCIPLINE

In addition to influencing the height of barriers to new entry, the extent and character of vertical control may also be a factor in determining the strength of oligopolistic discipline among any given number of firms. In several industries, differences between existing firms in their degree of vertical integration appear to have led to difficulties in agreement on the desirable vertical price structure or on changes in that structure in response to the threat of entry.[43] In addition, even changes in the degree of vertical integration that are uniform across firms may influence the conditions for oligopolistic coordination. Changes in the extent of vertical integration may alter the ratio of fixed to variable costs for existing firms,[44] or may permit the bypassing of a level which, for some reason, is not conducive to oligopolistic control.[45] Integration, franchising, or resale-price maintenance may be used to prevent retail price-shading that might induce retaliatory wholesale price cuts by rival manufacturers. Tying contracts may be expressly motivated by the desire to prevent the disruption of an oligopolistic pricing structure in a second industry.[46] Tying arrangements may also reduce the sensitivity of the market to price changes[47] and reduce price instability.[48] On the other hand, if they facilitate hidden price reductions, vertical integration or tying arrangements can increase the information costs of policing an oligopolistic pricing arrangement.[49] Similarly, by increasing the lumpiness and infrequency of transactions, the use of a requirements contract can increase the temptation for individual firms to break industry pricing rules.

CONCLUSIONS

Based on the analysis so far, it would appear that vertical control by unregulated firms with market power could be assumed beneficial unless it could be shown that such control significantly increased the height of entry barriers or the strength of oligopolistic discipline, or resulted in price discrimination. The first two of these conditions are difficult to prove, and the welfare effect of price discrimination is *a priori* indeterminate. In industries where entry barriers are already so high as to eliminate the possibility of entry even without vertical control, any further rise in entry barriers due to vertical control would become irrelevant. If the industry were composed of a single firm, the question of oligopolistic discipline would also not be applicable. The result would be a wide range of cases where the extent and form of vertical control chosen by firms with horizontal market power could be assumed to correspond with the public interest Horizontal diverstiture, regulation, or appeals to social conscience would then be the only possible policy approaches.

Put in other terms, no basis has been supplied so far for an "extension-of-monopoly" effect from vertical control. A firm that is secure in its monopoly and free to discriminate in price cannot increase the level of its monopoly profits by foreclosing competitive firms from a vertically related level and establishing a "second monopoly" at that level. The only remaining incentive and effect of vertical control is increased efficiency.

The assumption of fixed proportions, however, turns out to be critical for such a conclusion. The existence of variable proportions provides an incentive for vertical control that is independent of all the other motives discussed so far, and the effect of vertical control due to variable proportions can be shown to have a predictable effect on both profits and prices. In other words, the achievement through vertical control of a meaningful "second monopoly" is now possible.

NOTES

1. The extensive early literature on bilateral monopoly and successive monopoly is excellently reviewed and analyzed in Machlup and Tauber (1960).

Citing no less than 58 references, they date the discussion back to Cournot in 1838.

2. This result—that the monopoly price of the intermediate good is not affected by monopolization downstream—does not hold in general. As Rees (1962) poins out, for the special case discussed in the text (constant costs, linear demand curves), the elasticity of derived demand, E, will not change if the downstream industry becomes a monopoly. In terms of Figure 4-1, the linearity of the derived-demand curve for A implies that, at any intermediate price (such as P_a'), the elasticity of the marginal-revenue curve (at point j) will be the same as the elasticity of the demand curve (at point c). This isoelastic relationship holds for a broader class of derived-demand functions than just linear. Foran (1976) notes that it also holds for constant-elasticity demand functions, and Greenhut and Ohta (1976a) extend this class to demand functions of the form $p = a - bq^{\alpha}$ (for appropriate parameters), which includes the linear ($\alpha = 1$; a, $b > 0$) and constant-elasticity ($a = 0, b < 0, -1 < \alpha < 0$) cases. Since the decision rule for the A monopolist is $P_a = M_a E/(E - 1)$, if M_a is constant, the A monopolist will not alter his price when the downstream level is monopolized. *If* M_a is an increasing function of A, however, P_a will fall after successive monopolization; while if M_a is a decreasing function of A, then P_a will rise after integration. (Note that introducing a nonconstant but linear M_b schedule, as in Figure 4-2, will not alter P_a since the linearity of M_a is preserved.)

Clearly, a large number of cases could be developed, involving alternative specifications for the final demand function and for the input cost functions. As Perry points out, however, the effect of successive monopoly on the intermediate price is of limited interest in a fixed-proportions context "since input price changes cannot affect productive efficiency . . . [and] thus, the welfare analysis for this model requires no information about the input price" (Perry, 1977a, p. 6.) When the fixed-proportions assumption is removed (see Maurice and Ferguson, 1973; and Foran, 1976), the effect of a downstream monopoly on the elasticity of derived demand will depend on the type of production function assumed and the values for the parameters of the function, as well as on the final-demand and input cost functions. Thus, "the conclusion must be that the manner in which [downstream] market structure affects the elasticity of derived demand [and thus the price chosen by an upstream monopolist] must be viewed as an empirical question" (Foran, 1976, p. 87).

3. It should be noted that the use of consumers' surplus as a measure of welfare requires particular assumptions; for example, homotheticity of preferences (see Rader, 1972, pp. 234-43). For possible ambiguities in the use of producers' surplus later in this chapter, see Mishan (1968).

4. These are extremely well-known results. Since Machup and Tauber's (1960) review, they have been restated and discussed by, among others, Bork (1951; 1969), Burstein (1960b), Singer (1968), Scherer (1970, p. 243), Hay (1973), McGee and Bassett (1976), and (incredibly referring to these results as somehow mislaid!) Greenhut and Ohta (1976b).

5. See Galbraith (1956) and the discussion in Scherer (1970, pp. 241-52).

6. Almost tautologically, all cases of production functions showing decreasing return to scale are really misspecified, since some input (such as managerial

skills, the ability to form new firms, and so on) is omitted from the production function.

7. For a discussion of the costs of acquisition and the effects of public policy on those costs, see Manne (1965).

8. For the linear case illustrated by Figure 4-1, the maximum increase in marginal cost for integration to be socially desirable is approximately 47 percent of the monopoly markup on A, while the maximum increase in marginal costs for integration to be profitable is only approximately 27 percent. Denote the monopoly markup (distance $ad = ke = uf$) as y; the original level of output ($OA'' = ku = ul$) as x; the increase in marginal costs as a proportion of the monopoly markup as α; and the increase in monopoly profits after integration as $\Delta\pi$. Then:

$$\Delta\pi = \frac{(1-\alpha)\,x\;(1-\alpha)y}{2} - \alpha xy$$

and $\Delta\pi = 0$ when $\alpha = 2 - \sqrt{3} \cong 0.27$
The increase in total welfare, ΔW, is given by:

$$\Delta W = (1-\alpha)x(1-\alpha)y + (1-\alpha)\frac{x\alpha y}{2} + \frac{(1-\alpha)x}{2} \cdot \frac{(1-\alpha)y}{2}$$

and $\Delta W = 0$ when $\alpha = 2 - \sqrt{21}/3 \cong 0.47$

9. See Bowley (1928), Morgan (1949), Fellner (1947), Machlup and Tauber (1960), and the discussion in Scherer (1970, pp. 239-52).

10. First-degree, or perfect, price discrimination involves selling each unit at its reservation price, so that no consumer surplus remains. Under second-degree price discrimination, blocks of units are sold at the reservation price for each block. Third-degree price discrimination involves dividing customers into two or more groups and charging different prices to each group. The terminology is due to Pigou (1920, pp. 240-46). For an alternative classification (personal, group, and product), see Machlup (1955, pp. 400-23). For a general discussion of the types and effects of price discrimination, see Scherer (1970, pp. 253-72).

11. This applies whether the tied good is another input or the final product, as long as there are fixed proportions between the tying and the tied goods. Thus if the proportion of A to B is technologically fixed, tying A to B is equivalent to a change in the price of A. If the proportion of A to X is fixed, a tie with the final product, through a royalty arrangement, for example, is similarly equivalent to a change in the price of A.

12. The fixed-proportions assumption here is that the output from the machine, per unit time operated, is technologically fixed. This requires, for example, that the machine is used with a fixed number of operators, that the life of the machine cannot be altered by increasing labor, maintenance, and so on, and that, if the output of the machine is itself an intermediate good, that this output is combined in fixed proportions with other inputs to produce the final product.

13. The earliest published analysis of the use of tying arrangements as counting devices to achieve price discrimination is Director and Levi (1956, pp. 291-92).

The argument has been presented in greater detail in numerous other articles, notably Burstein (1960b, pp. 64-65); Bowman (1957, pp. 23-24); and Hilton (1958, pp. 268-76).

14. Assuming that the proportion of B to X is fixed at unity. If not, then $P_b = M_b + (ad)(X/B)$.

15. With this arrangement, revenue from some low-volume users may be less than the marginal cost to the monopolist of providing the machine. In order to prevent this occurance, the monopolist may insist on a minimum quantity of B sales. Alternatively, he could rent or sell the machine at its marginal cost, in addition to insisting on a tying arrangement with B. If dc is horizontal, this will reduce the effectiveness of the tying arrangement. If dc is downward-sloping, however, setting a lump-sum rental in addition to the tie will increase profits.

16. *Morgan Envelope Co.* v. *Albany Perforated Paper Co.*, 152 U.S. 425 (1894); *Heaton-Peninsular Button-Fastener Co.* v. *Eureka Speciality Co.*, 77 F. 288 (6th Cir. 1896); *Rupp & Witgenfeld Co.* v. *Elliot*, 131 F. 730 (6th Cir. 1904); *Henry* v. *A.B. Dick Co.*, 224 U.S. 1 (1912); *International Business Machines Corp.* v. *United States*, 298 U.S. 131 (1936); *Morton Salt* v. *F.T.C.*, 132 F.2d 48 (4th Cir. 1942); *Judson L. Thompson Mfg. Co.* v. *F.T.C.*, 150 F.2d 952 (1st Cir. 1945).

17. We do not wish to enter into detailed consideration of the cost of capital in relation to the choice between renting (leasing) and buying, a subject that has been extensively explored in the finance literature. In a competitive situation without differential transaction costs or taxes, financing will be provided by intermediaries with the lowest cost of borrowing, and there is no *a priori* reason why producers of a capital good should have a comparative advantage over specialized financial institutions in financing purchases of their output. (See Miller and Upton, 1976.) Differential taxation may affect the decision (see Chapter 3, above), as well as differential transaction (information, control, and the like) costs. Market power by other financial intermediaries would encourage even competitive producers to provide credit, since a reduction in financing charges would increase demand for the consumer durable. As Crandall points out, however, this does not explain why assemblers tied financing to the dealer franchise. One possible—though unlikely—explanation is to prevent side-payments to dealers from monopolistic financial institutions. A more likely—though untested—explanation first offered by Burstein (1960b, p. 92), is that producers with market power may find that credit customers have a lower price-elasticity of demand than cash buyers. Assemblers can then price discriminate by requiring dealers to use high-cost financing provided by the assembler. In addition, if such price discrimination requires larger amounts of capital, it may also serve to increase entry barriers at the assembler level (see discussion in the section "Public Policy Toward Vertical Control . . . ," below).

18. In general, rental becomes more attractive relative to ownership to the extent that: (1) user negligence is unimportant; (2) providing maintenance service is less expensive for a rental firm than for users (although separate maintenance contracts are also possible). (3) changes in users are frequent and transactions in the second-hand purchase market are more expensive than in the rental market (due mainly to the higher legal and bargaining costs of transferring

ownership than transferring a lease); and (4) rental firms have better information on product quality, but this information cannot be easily transmitted to users.

19. Strictly speaking, integration is not necessary. Assemblers can use the threat of entry, and the resulting loss of original equipment sales, to extract the large profits in repair parts sales. Independents can be allowed to set high prices for sales to the independent repair market but forced to supply original equipment parts to assemblers at prices far below cost. There is considerable evidence of such a differential pricing system which is difficult to explain otherwise. (See Crandall, 1968b, pp. 250-72). Price discrimination can thus be carried out by assemblers, using independent parts manufacturers who earn overall only a normal rate of return. If this differential pricing system is attacked by antitrust authorities on a Robinson-Patman or other basis, assemblers should be expected to turn to integration as an alternative. (For a review of antitrust action in this area, see Nelson, 1970.)

20. The earliest explanation of block-booking as a method of price discrimination is given in Director and Levi (1956, p. 292). More detailed presentations are given by Telser (1965, p. 493), and Markovits (1967, pp. 1454-58). Two antitrust cases which appear to illustrate this practice have concerned the tying together of advertising space in different newspapers under the same ownership (*Times-Picayune Publishing Co.* v. *United States*, 345 U.S. 594 (1953), and block-booking in the motion picture industry (*United States* v. *Loew's, Inc.*, 371 U.S. 38 (1962)). For a discussion of vertical control in the motion-picture industry, see Whitney (1955, pp. 491-98); and Stigler (1963).

21. For a discussion of the political purposes of antitrust, see Blake and Jones 1965a.

22.

> It is possible to establish the fact that total output under [third-degree] price discrimination will be greater or less than under simple monopoly according as the more elastic of the demand curves in the separate markets is more or less concave than the less elastic demand curve. . .
>
> On the whole it is more likely that the introduction of price discrimination will increase output than that it will reduce it. [Robinson, 1933, pp. 190, 201]

See also Samuelson, 1947, pp. 42-45. Edwards (1950) introduces an alternative criterion based on "slope ratios," and examines the relationship between the two criteria. Greenhut and Ohta (1976a) provide a counter-example to the adjusted concavity test.

23. "From one point of view, price discrimination must be held to be superior to simple monopoly in all those cases in which it leads to an increase in output. . . . But against this advantage must be set the fact that price discrimination leads to a maldistribution of resources as between different uses" (Robinson, 1933, p. 206).

Suppose that third-degree price discrimination did not alter total output (as, for example, when all demand curves are linear), and there are no offsetting distortions (such as positive externalities from use of the good in the more elastic market, or successive monopoly only in the more elastic market). As output is shifted from the less elastic market to the more elastic market, each unit is shifted from a higher price (value) use to a lower price (value) use. Aggregate value (welfare) must therefore fall.

24. These costs are usually described as the costs of determining reservation prices (or price elasticities for group discrimination) and preventing arbitrage. They may not be obvious, however. A good example is the cost of refusal to standardize repair parts in the automobile industry (Crandall, 1968b).

25. See Director and Levi (1956, p. 293), or Bork and Bowman (1965, pp. 366-68). These writers express doubts that this requirement can be satisfied: "It is difficult to imagine that such a mechanism exists, but it is perhaps conceivable" (Bork and Bowman, 1965, p. 367).

26. The existence of such power raises the question as to why an integrated monopolist would oppose entry at a single level. The entrant can be restrained from earning more than "normal" profits, and can be regarded as providing an input into the final product for a price less than, or equal to, the cost the integrated firm would incur if it carried out this function internally. Under fixed proportions, it would not matter whether the entrant operated at the upstream or downstream level since, by shifting its internal vertical price structure, the integrated firm can take its monopoly profit at any level. One reason why the integrated firm might oppose such entry under fixed proportions is that, once entered at one level, the new firm might subsequently expand its operations to other levels (or other firms might enter at these levels), thus escaping the control of the integrated firm and seriously threatening the integrated firm's market power.

27. For example:

> For packers' cans there is voluminous and convincing evidence that requirements contracts are necessary and beneficial to the buyer, and that any possible damage to competition from using them is of negligible importance if certain ancillary restraints are prohibited. . . . The basis of this need . . . is the unpredictability of can requirements and the necessity of having them immediately and in the proper quantities when the food is ready to be packed. . . . Spot brokerage . . . would be greatly inferior to the requirements contract as a means of allocating can supplies. . . . But the can manufacturer will not provide standby capacity nor try to meet emergencies unless he contracts to do it in return for advance assurance of all the canner's business, or unless the price rises sharply. [McKie, 1959, pp. 149-50]

28. The capital requirement for vertical control may be very large. For example, "the control of ore by the present major steel producers is particularly limiting for new entrants. . . . Most of the new [ore development] projects have been on a scale that only very large firms could handle. . . . Each has required an initial investment of more than $100 million. Some have come as high as $300 million" (Weiss, 1967, pp. 145-47).

It should be noted that vertical integration is not the only form of vertical control that would involve increased capital requirements. Under tying arrangements the tying good may itself be the provision of capital. For example, in *Fortner Enterprises Inc.* v. *United States Steel Corp.*, 394 U.S. 495 (1969), U.S. Steel was accused of foreclosing the market for prefabricated houses by tying the provision of a large loan at low cost to the purchase of its houses. (Capital has also been the tied good, as in *General Motors Corp.* v. *United States*, 121 F.2d 376, where GM was accused of excluding competitors from the auto-financing business by requiring its dealers to finance installment sales of automobiles through the General Motors Acceptance Corporation.) The practice of rental rather than outright sale may be regarded as a form of tying contract, and may impose large capital requirements on entrants. The best example is probably the computer industry (see Scherer, 1970, p. 102).

If existing tying contracts force the effective entrant to undertake the production of several inputs, capital requirements are increased in the same way as under vertical integration. For the tying of cans to can machinery, see Mckie (1959, pp. 185-97); and for full-line forcing in shoe machinery, see Kaysen (1956).

29.

> Large firms . . . tend to pay lower interest rates on short- and long-term debt than smaller enterprises, and they can float equity issues at lower costs per dollar of usable funds received, other things being equal. . . . In a statistical analysis of 238 common stock issues floated by firms of widely varying sizes between 1960 and 1962, Archer and Farber (1966) found that flotation costs ranged from 5 to 44 percent of the total value of shares sold, and flotation costs as a percentage of total share value was inversely correlated with both size of firm and size of the issue. . . . [In addition], investors are evidently willing to buy the securities of large firms at lower interest and profit yields than similar securities of small firms, partly because the large firms are better known and have longer earning histories, and partly because investments in large firms are demonstrably less risky, in the sense that earnings tend to be more stable and defaults rarer. [Scherer, 1970, p. 100]

In addition, the short-run supply curve for capital may be upward-sloping, leading to high marginal costs for capital for rapid expansion. Such an upward-sloping capital supply curve (for a model, see Hirshleifer, 1970, pp. 200-202) may result from lenders' information and control costs (Williamson, 1971, p. 119), or a "principle of increasing risk" (Scherer, 1970, p. 102). Alternatively, there may be some maximum or optimal degree of leverage (see Baumol and Malkiel, 1967, pp. 547-78). Once this degree of leverage is reached, maintenance of this degree of leverage requires that retained profits plus revenue from sale of new stock provide a share of total new capital requirements equal to the existing equity to equity-plus-debt ratio. Where expansion must be rapid, and internal financing is difficult (since profits are held low due to the disadvantages of not yet being integrated), this may force the firm either to float new stock issues (generally a high-cost source of capital) or to accept increased debt-financing rates as leverage is increased.

Thus small entrants can face higher unit capital costs than do large entrants or existing firms, and their unit capital costs may be an increasing function of the absolute capital requirements for initial entry and the rate of subsequent expansion to achieve vertical control. These differential capital costs are not based on irrational behavior by capital suppliers, in constrast to Bork's assertion that "it must be explained why the irrationality of the capital suppliers would take the particular form of denying funds to would-be entrants in vertically integrated industries . . . [a] suggestion that capital suppliers are hare-brained" (Bork, 1965, p. 407).

30. The concept of absolute capital requirements as a barrier to entry was first presented in Bain (1956, pp. 144-66). One attempt (Hall and Weiss, 1967) to measure the height of the capital-requirements barrier to entry estimated that firms in industries with capital requirements of about $500 million could increase profits as a percentage of equity from 8.8 percent to 10.4 percent and could increase profits as a percentage of assets from 5.7 percent to 6.8 percent, without attracting entry from those capable of breaking into industries with capital requirements in the neighborhood of $50 million. They concluded that "there is a significant though probably not enormous capital requirements barrier . . . and this barrier very likely has a greater effect on profit rates than concentration." (Hall and Weiss, 1967, p. 329). But see Shepherd (1972) for evidence that profit rates are a decreasing function of firm size, ceteris paribus.

31. There is, of course, the possibility of simultaneous entry by different firms at each level. "If the industry is attractive—if it is not, there will be no entry anyway—the prospective entrant in manufacturing should have no difficulty in finding someone else to enter distribution" (Bork, 1965, p. 410).

Finding an entrant for a vertically related level may not be easy, however. For example, in the GMAC case, it is difficult to imagine an independent financing company persuading another firm to enter the automobile industry. In addition there may be difficulties in coordinating simultaneous entry by independent firms. And even if multiple-firm entry is achieved, problems of bilateral and successive monopoly may arise unless the firms subsequently merge. (See Blake and Jones (1965b, pp. 445-48, 463.)

32. For example, in aluminum, "the size of the barriers to entry attributable to economies of scale depend upon whether new entrants must be as vertically integrated as the existing three primary producers. If such vertical integration is required, then the aluminum industry ranks near the top quarter in Bain's sample on the economies of scale barrier. Without vertical integration, aluminum ranks in the lower half" (Peck, 1961, p. 169).

33. "Strategic underlying considerations in strong product differentiation seem frequently to include . . . integration of retail dealer-service organizations by manufacturers, either through ownership or exclusive-dealing arrangements" (Bain, 1956, p. 142). See also Comanor (1968, pp. 1419-38).

34. In addition to the barrier created by requiring a large market share for effective entry, this obviously also increases the absolute factor requirements for entry.

35. See Pashigian (1961). Another author concludes that "if all formal and informal pressures toward exclusive dealing in autos could be eliminated and if a sufficient number of dealers were willing to take on additional makes, the

growth of competition from smaller and foreign automobile producers would be greatly stimulated" (Scherer, 1970, p. 510). The elimination of exclusive dealing may, however, be of little effectiveness in inducing entry by domestic firms. "Since the barriers to entry for domestic automobile manufacturing are very high on other grounds, the benefits to domestic manufacture would be small. But a foreign manufacturer considering entry into retailing in the American market might find entry somewhat easier under these conditions" (White, 1971, p. 238).

36. See *Standard Fashion Co.* v. *Magrane-Houstaon Co.*, 258 U.S. 346 (1922).

37. Major oil companies have put pressure on their service stations to sell only products produced or sponsored by that oil company. In return for their sponsorship of a particular tire manufacturer's product, for example, the oil companies receive a commission on tire sales. The commission both keeps the major oil companies from entering the tire industry and excludes small tire manufacturers from a substantial share of the market:

> The sales commission payments . . . can be interpreted as the payment by the tire companies for the erection of a barrier to the entry of new manufacturers and the expansion of existing firms in the industry. Without these barriers other tire producers . . . would be able to nibble at the fringes of the service station market, injecting price competition for the patronage of the individual station dealers. [Miller 1963, p. 234]

38. The larger the number of existing firms, however, the less likely that oligopolistic discipline will be strong enough to prevent existing firms from making mutually profitable arrangements with an entrant. The foregone benefits of such a transaction represent in effect an "investment in entry barriers," but the return to this investment accrues to the oligopoly as a whole, rather than to the refusing firm. The temptation to deal with entrants will be particularly strong if the existing firms are themselves not perfectly balanced and the marginal costs of additional production are low. (For examples from the petroleum industry, see de Chazeau and Kahn, 1959, pp. 560-62.) In addition, if there are differences between existing firms in degrees of vertical integration, joint agreement on a vertical price structure (and on changes in that structure in response to entry) may be difficult to achieve (see Scherer, 1970, pp. 191-92).

39. See McGee (1958) and Elizinga (1970). For an opposing view, see Scherer (1970, pp. 273-76).

40. See McKie (1959, pp. 58-64, 160-82); Kaysen (1956, pp. 126-34); and *Federal Trade Commission* v. *Morton Salt Co.*, 334 U.S. 37, 43, 49 (1948).

41. Interestingly enough, however, the use of tying arrangements as metering devices results in discrimination against more intensive users who are usually also the larger firms. The effect of these tying arrangements should thus be to reduce entry barriers downstream.

42. The parallel here is with the declining-dominant firm model.

43. Examples include copper (see McCarthy, 1964, p. 93), steel (see Adams and Dirlam, 1964), petroleum (see de Chazeau and Kahn, 1959, p. 564), and aluminum (see Scherer, 1970, p. 172).

44. See Scherer (1970, pp. 13-14), and de Chazeau and Kahn (1959, p. 564).

45. See Comanor (1967). But see also the discussion by McGee that follows Comanor's article.

46. Suppose a firm has a monopoly in the production of one input, A, which is used in fixed proportions with input B, but B is produced by a number of oligopolistic firms, so that P_b is greater than M_b. Normally, the A firm will have an incentive to force competition on the B industry by producing B itself and setting $P_b = M_b$, while setting a price for A such that $MR_a = M_a$. But if B is combined with A in only one market, and if the A monopolist is already selling B in other markets, the A monopolist may not wish to disturb the oligopolistic pricing situation for B in these other markets. The solution is to tie A to B, leaving the price of B at P_b, but reducing the price of A to $P_a - (P_b - M_b)(A/B)$. See Burstein (1960b, pp. 65-68).

47.

> Because the can-makers must make separate charges for machinery and service, the price of cans is now unmixed with other inducements. Competitive tension in the market has increased throughout the complex market structure as a result. [McKie, 1959, p. 278]

48.

> The shortened term of the present contract gives all buyers more frequent opportunities to switch suppliers or add new sources. . . . While only a small number may switch in any year, the mere opportunity is enough to increase the competitive pressure markedly. [McKie, 1959, p. 277]

49. Suppose that a firm in an oligopolistic industry wishes to lower its price without provoking retaliation. A tie with another good (with the tied good supplied at a price below its prevailing market price) may be less noticeable or more difficult to retaliate against than a direct reduction in the price of the tying good. This form of price reduction would be particularly difficult to police if the tied good is a quality of the tying good such as the provision of transport or servicing.

Chapter 5

Vertical Control with Variable Proportions

If a monopolized factor or intermediate good can be used in variable proportions with other inputs by downstream producers, pricing of the monopolized input above its marginal cost will distort the input ratio chosen by downstream users. Vertical control by the input monopolist can prevent this distortion and thus increase monopoly profits. This proposition has been established several times in the literature, notably by Burstein (1960a, 1960b), and a graphic formulation has been presented by Vernon and Graham (1971). Other recent work in this area has been done by Schmalansee (1973), Bowman (1973), Warren-Boulton (1974b), Hay (1973), Perry (1975), and McGee and Bassett (1976).

Vernon and Graham's graphic proof of the profitability of vertical integration with variable proportions is reproduced in Figure 5-1, where X' is the level of final-product output before vertical control. The ratio of the monopoly price of A to the price of B is given by the slope of PP', while the ratio of the (assumed constant) marginal cost of A to the price of B is given by the slope of MM'. Measured in units of B, the monopolist's premerger profit before any fixed costs is PM. After merging and shifting production from point E to point F, the integrated firm could increase its profit by at least MN. If the profit-maximizing postmerger output differs from X', the increment to profit will be even larger than MN.

For public policy, however, the critical problem is to determine the effects of vertical control on the prices of the inputs and the final product and hence the effect on welfare.[1] This chapter examines these effects, assuming a constant elasticity of substitution

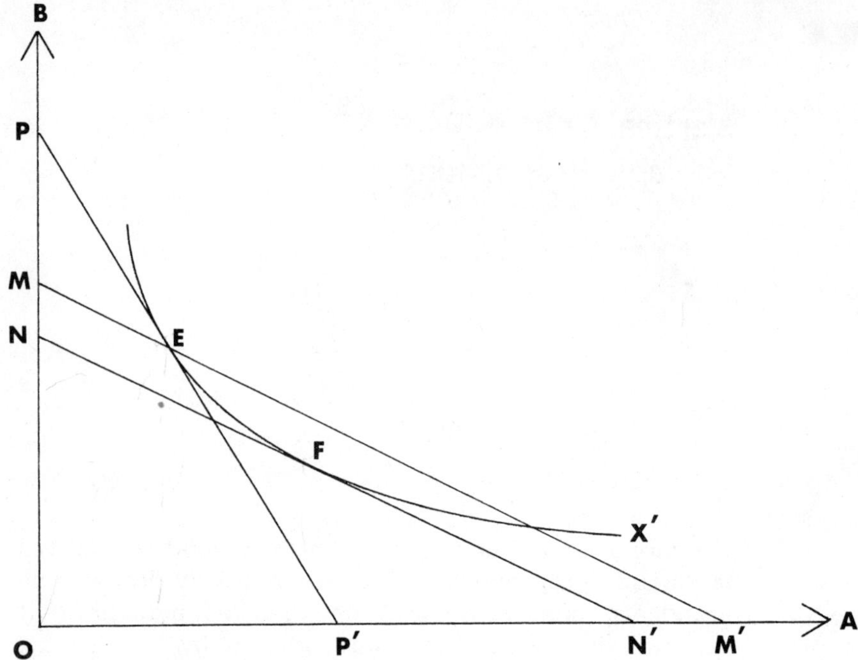

Figure 5-1. Profitability of vertical control

(CES) downstream production function and a constant elasticity of demand for the final product. A combination of analytic results and simulation experiments is used to show that, except under particular cost conditions in the input industries, vertical control results in higher prices for the consumers of the final product and reduced demand for nonmonopolized inputs. The direction of the "combined" welfare effect on consumers, producers of nonmonopolized inputs, and monopoly profit receivers, however, depends on the specific parameter values in the demand and production functions.

The chapter is divided into three sections. The first assumes constant marginal costs in the input industries; the second extends the results to cases of nonconstant input marginal costs; and the third examines the effect of relaxing other assumptions and attempts to draw some conclusions for public policy.

VERTICAL CONTROL WITH CONSTANT INPUT COSTS

Assume that a final product X is produced by competitive firms using two inputs. The first input, A, is monopolized; the other input, B, is supplied competitively. The production function for the final product is of constant elasticity of substitution, σ, and constant returns to scale:

$$X = Y\left[\delta A^{(\sigma-1)/\sigma} + (1-\delta)B^{(\sigma-1)/\sigma}\right]^{\sigma/(\sigma-1)}$$

$$Y > 0,\ 0 < \delta < 1,\ 0 \leqslant \sigma \leqslant \infty \qquad (5.1)$$

Assume also a constant-elasticity demand function for the final product of the form:

$$X = Z/P_x{}^{\eta} \qquad Z > 0,\ \eta > 1 \qquad (5.2)$$

Throughout this section it will also be assumed that the marginal cost of producing the monopolized input, M_a, is constant over the relevant range, and that B is available in infinitely elastic supply at price P_b.

The first step in determining the effect of vertical control on the price of the final product is to derive the profit-maximizing price for A before vertical control. Since the supply of A is monopolized:

$$P_a = \frac{M_a}{1 - 1/E} \qquad (5.3)$$

where E, the elasticity of derived demand for A, is given by:[2]

$$E = \frac{\sigma(\eta + e) + k_a e(\eta - \sigma)}{\eta + e - k_a(\eta - \sigma)} \qquad (5.4)$$

where e is the elasticity of supply of B, and k_a is the share of the cost of A in the total cost of producing X. Since B is assumed to be available in infinitely elastic supply, $e = \infty$, and Equation (5.4) reduces to:

$$\underset{e=\infty}{E} = k_a\eta + (1 - k_a)\sigma. \qquad (5.5)$$

From the first-order conditions for cost minimization:[3]

$$K_a = \frac{1}{1 + ((1-\delta)/\delta)^{\sigma}(P_a/P_b)^{\sigma-1}} \qquad (5.6)$$

Substituting Equations (5.5) and (5.6) into Equation (5.3):

$$(\eta - 1)P_a + \left[\left(\frac{1-\delta}{\delta}\right)^{\sigma}\left(\frac{\sigma - 1}{P_b{}^{\sigma-1}}\right)\right] P_a{}^{\sigma}$$

$$-\left[\left(\frac{1-\delta}{\delta}\right)^{\sigma}\left(\frac{\sigma}{P_b{}^{\sigma-1}}\right)\right] P_a{}^{\sigma-1}$$

$$-\eta M_a = 0 \tag{5.7}$$

Equation (5.7) cannot readily be solved explicitly for P_a. We do not, therefore, have an expression for P_a that can be used in further derivations. P_a can, however, be computed over the range of the various parameters, notably η, δ, and σ. Since the downstream X industry is assumed competitive, the price of X is equal to its marginal cost. Thus, once P_a is determined, we can solve for P_x:[4]

$$P_x = \frac{1}{Y}\left[P_b{}^{(1-\sigma)}(1-\delta)^{\sigma} + P_a{}^{(1-\sigma)}\delta^{\sigma}\right]^{1/(1-\sigma)} \tag{5.8}$$

After vertical control, an unconstrained integrated monopolist will set marginal revenue equal to marginal cost in the X market. The resulting price for X will be:

$$\overline{P}_x = \frac{\overline{M}_x}{1 - 1/\eta} = \frac{\left[P_b{}^{(1-\sigma)}(1-\delta)^{\sigma} + M_a{}^{(1-\sigma)}\delta^{\sigma}\right]^{1/(1-\sigma)}}{Y(1 - 1/\eta)} \tag{5.9}$$

The A monopolist may not, however, be able to set a price of $\overline{P}_x$ for the final product after integration. The integrated firm cannot set a price for X that is higher than the independent downstream firms' cost of producing X. The cost of producing X for an independent producer—a function of the price of A set by the A monopolist—is thus the "entry price of X," $\hat{P}_x$. If the A monopolist is prepared to raise the price of A after vertical control to any arbitrarily high level, $\hat{P}_x$ becomes the cost of manufacturing X using only B (or, equivalently, the value of P_x in Equation (5.8) as $P_a \to \infty$). If $0 \leqslant \sigma \leqslant 1$, $\hat{P}_x$ is infinite, since X cannot be produced without using A. But for $\sigma > 1$, $\hat{P}_x$ is less than infinity,[5] and may even be less than $\overline{P}_x$. Thus the ratio of the price of the final product after vertical control to the price of the final product before vertical control is:

$$R = \min\left(\frac{\overline{P}_x}{P_x}, \frac{\hat{P}_x}{P_x}\right) \tag{5.10}$$

R can easily be shown to be equal to unity if the elasticity of substitution is zero or infinity since, for either of these two extreme values for σ, factor proportions cannot be affected by vertical control.[6] In addition, for the special case of $\sigma = 1$, it is possible (see Appendix A) to derive an explicit expression for R which, with constant costs in both input industries, reduces to:

$$\underset{\substack{\sigma=1 \\ e=g=\infty}}{R} = \frac{(1 - 1/E)^{\delta}}{(1 - 1/\eta)} > 1, \tag{5.11}$$

where

$$\underset{\substack{\sigma=1 \\ e=\infty}}{E} = 1 + \delta(\eta - 1)$$

and g = elasticity of the marginal-cost schedule in the A industry (assumed infinite, in this section). For this special case, R is always greater than unity and approaches unity as η approaches infinity or as δ approaches 1.[7] Thus the price of the final product must go up after integration if the elasticity of substitution is unity and there are constant costs in both input industries. The price of the final product will go up by a larger proportion after vertical control, the smaller are δ and η. Thus the smaller the share of the cost of the final product that is due to the monopolized input, and the less elastic the demand for the final product, the greater the percentage increase in the price of the final product after integration. In addition, for this special case we can show that the welfare effect of integration is always negative (see note 12, below).

The direction of the price effect can also be determined for two other special cases. For the $\sigma = 2$ case, Hay (1973) has shown that integration results in an increase in the price of the final product. Finally, we can also show that $R > 1$ when $\sigma > \eta$. If $\sigma \geqslant \eta$, then $E \geqslant \eta$.[8] The monopoly markup on A before vertical control, P_a/M_a, is thus less than or equal to the markup on X after vertical control, $\overline{P}_x/\overline{M}_x$. Furthermore, an increase in the price of one input by any proportion must result in a rise in the price of the final product by a lesser proportion if the prices of other inputs are held constant. Thus P_a/M_a must be greater than the ratio of P_x to the price of

X that would exist if there were competition in both input and final-product industries. With constant input costs, this competitive price for X, P'_x, is also the integrated monopolist's marginal cost of producing X, $\overline{M}_x$. Thus, if $\sigma \geqslant \eta$:

$$\frac{P_x}{P'_x} < \frac{P_a}{M_a} = \frac{1}{1 - 1/E} \leqslant \frac{1}{1 - 1/\eta} = \frac{\overline{P}_x}{\overline{M}_x}$$

and since $\overline{M}_x = P'_x$, it follows that $P_x < \overline{P}_x$.

The conclusion that vertical control results in a rise in the price of the final product for three special cases, $\sigma = 1$, $\sigma = 2$, and $\sigma \geqslant \eta$,[9] leads one to expect this result for the general case of $0 < \sigma < \infty$. The inability to derive an explicit expression for P_a from equation (5.7) prevents the derivation of an analytic proof. The effects of vertical control for the general case of $0 < \sigma < \infty$ can be examined, however, through the use of computer simulations, using a range of values for each important parameter. In particular, the effect of vertical control on the price of the final product and on the levels of consumers' surplus[10] and monopoly profits was computed for all combinations of:

$$\begin{aligned} \sigma &= 0.00, 0.25, 0.50, \ldots, 4.00 \\ \eta &= 1.1, 1.5, 2, 3, 4, 5 \\ \delta &= 0.05, 0.10, 0.25, 0.38, 0.50, 0.63, 0.75, 0.95 \end{aligned}$$

Other parameter values were:

$$\begin{aligned} Y &= 1.00 \\ M_a &= 1.00 \\ P_b &= 1.00 \\ Z &= 1000 \end{aligned}$$

The conclusions from these simulations follow.

Effect of Vertical Control on the Price of the Final Product

With constant costs in both input industries, the price of the final product always increases for elasticities of substitution between zero and infinity:

$$R > 1$$
$$0<\sigma<\infty$$
$$g=e=\infty$$

As the elasticity of substitution is increased from zero, R rises above unity, reaches a maximum, and then declines, approaching unity again as the elasticity of substitution approaches infinity.

The lower the elasticity of final demand, the greater is $\overline{P}_x/P_x$, although $\overline{P}_x$ and P_x are both decreasing functions of η. Thus if the entry contraint is not effective, a lower elasticity of final demand will increase R.

The entry price, $\hat{P}_x$, is not a function of η. A lower η will, however, increase P_x. Thus $\hat{P}_x/P_x$ is an increasing function of η; and, if the entry constraint is effective, a lower elasticity of final demand will decrease R.

The effect of varying η is illustrated in Figures 5–2a and 5–2b, which plot R as a function of σ for $\eta = 2$ and $\eta = 4$. Figure 5–2a assumes $\delta = 1/4$, so that, after some value for σ, the $\hat{P}_x$ constraint is effective. Thus, for example, if $\sigma = 1$, an increase in η reduces R, while if $\sigma = 2$, an increase in η increases R. In Figure 5–2b, $\delta = 3/4$, and the $\hat{P}_x$ constraint is never effective. Thus an increase in η will lower R for all values of σ.

The effect of varying δ parallels that of varying η. A higher value for δ shifts $\overline{P}_x/P_x$ down, but shifts $\hat{P}_x/P_x$ upward. Figure 5–2c shows R for $\eta = 2$ and $\delta = 1/4, 1/2, 3/4$.

These results for η and δ are consistent with the analytic results from the $\sigma = 1$ case (since for $\sigma = 1$, the $\hat{P}_x$ constraint is never effective), and are intuitively plausible. Ceteris paribus, the less elastic the final demand, and the less "important" the monopolized input (the lower is δ), the greater the difference that can be expected between an unconstrained monopoly over one input and an unconstrained monopoly over a final product. On the other hand, if δ is large there is less likelihood of the input monopolist being confronted after vertical integration with effective competition from other firms in the final-product industry (a low $\hat{P}_x$). Similarly, the more elastic the final demand, the less likely that the desired monopoly price for the final product will be high enough to exceed $\hat{P}_x$.

Thus the effect of η and δ on R cannot be determined in general without information as to the effectiveness of the entry constraint. For $0 \leqslant \sigma \leqslant 1$, if the A monopolist is willing and able to raise the open-market price of A to any height (ultimately, but simply refusing to sell A at any price), then the P_x constraint is not effective and

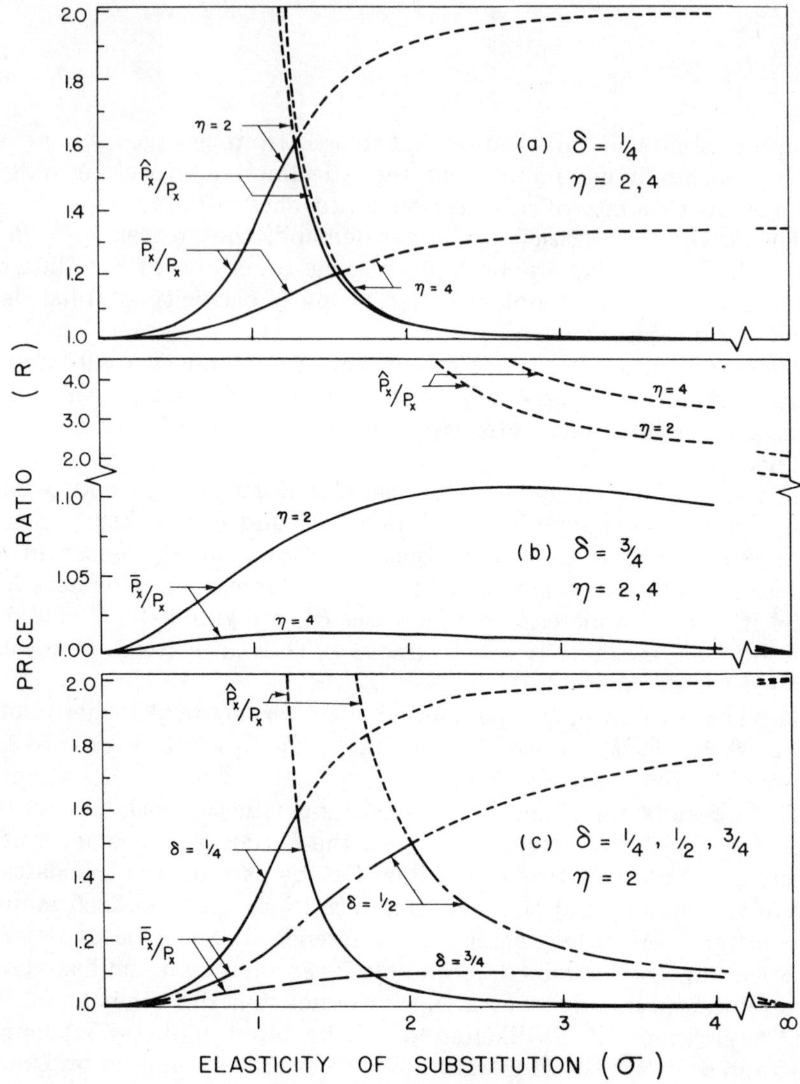

Figure 5-2. Effect of vertical control on the prices of the final product

R is a decreasing function of η and δ. Even over this range of σ, however, if the A monopolist does not raise the price of A sufficiently after vertical control, he may be confronted with a maximum price for the final product that is less than the desired monopoly price for the final product.

Effect of Vertical Control On Monopoly Profits and the Incentive for Vertical Control

Monopoly profits must increase after vertical control for $0 < \sigma < \infty$. This increase reaches a maximum at some $\sigma > 1$. The lower are δ and η, the greater the magnitude of the increase in profits, and the lower the value for σ where the increase in profits is at a maximum.

While the absolute magnitude of the increase in monopoly profits is relevant for calculating the total welfare effect, a better proxy for predicting the likelihood of vertical control might be the proportion by which monopoly profits could be increased by vertical control, or the increase in profits as a proportion of either the cost of manufacturing A or the total costs of manufacturing X. These three alternative indicators of the likelihood of vertical control are also higher, the lower are δ or η, except that—where the $\hat{P}_x$ constraint is effective—a higher value for δ increases the gain in monopoly profits as a proportion of the costs of A or X.

Since an increase in the price of the final product after vertical control may be impossible or undesirable in some cases (due to regulation, threat of antitrust proceedings, possible entry at the A level, or loss of sales of A in other markets if P_a is increased), it is useful to separate the total increase in monopoly profits into two components: the increase in profits that would be possible without changing the price of the final product after vertical control ($EFCY$), and the further increase in profits due to the change in the price of the final product ($\Delta\pi\Delta P_x$). If there are constant costs in the B industry, the first component can be regarded as a pure "efficiency" effect. It reflects the increase in efficiency of production of the final product (the reduction in the cost, pricing inputs at their social marginal cost, of producing any given amount of the final product) due to the elimination of the input-ratio distortion.[11]

Graphically, vertical control results in both a downward shift in the cost curve for X and an increase in the price of X (Figure 5-3). Note that, due to the previous existence of monopoly power in the input industry, the welfare loss due to the price increase, $\Delta W\Delta P_x$, is not just the "welfare triangle" (kfg in Figure 5-3), but the area $ibfg$.

Since the welfare effect of the efficiency component is unambiguously positive, and since it may be the only effect of vertical control, the efficiency component is worth separate examination. As a function of σ, δ, and η, the efficiency component shows the same pattern as the total increase in profits. As a proportion of the total increase in profits, however, the efficiency gain is higher, the lower

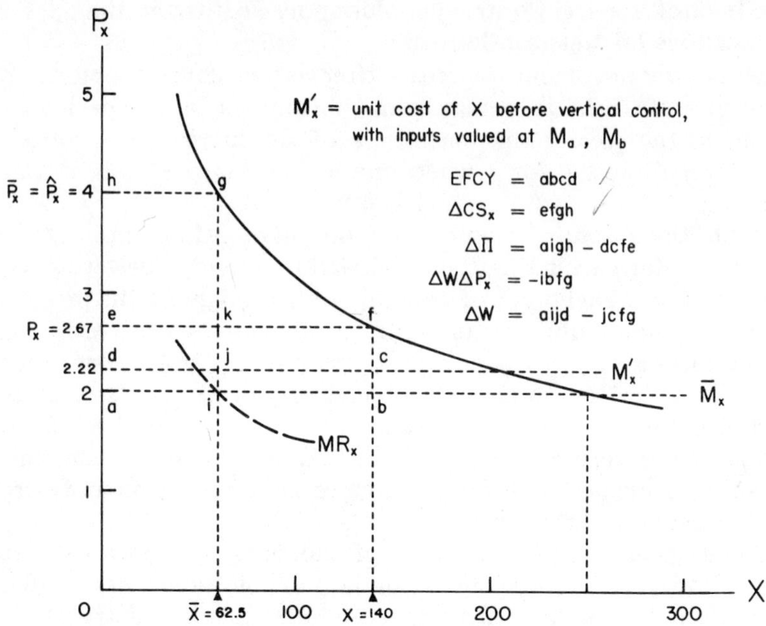

Figure 5-3. Effect of vertical control on final-product industry (numerical results assume $\sigma = \eta = 2$, $\delta = ½$)

is σ and the higher are δ and η. As σ rises, and as δ and η fall, the incentive for vertical control increasingly becomes the achievement of market power rather than the elimination of inefficiency.

If the price of the final product is prevented from increasing, the likelihood of vertical control occurring (as measured by the ratio of the efficiency gain either to monopoly profits before vertical control, or to the costs of *A*) is higher, the lower are δ and η. The maximum percentage gain is reached at lower σ for lower δ and η. As a proportion of the total costs of *X*, the efficiency gain is greater for lower values for η; but, over high values for σ, the proportion is higher for larger values for δ.

Whether or not the price of the final product is permitted to rise, therefore, the maximum incentive for vertical control will exist under a combination of very small values for δ and η, and an elasticity of substitution only slightly greater than unity. As δ and η increase, so does the "optimal" elasticity of substitution.

Effect of Vertical Control on Welfare

With constant costs in the *B* industry, the effect on welfare is the combination of the change in monopoly profits and the change in consumer surplus. For $0 < \sigma < \infty$, the change in consumer surplus is always negative, while the change in profits is always positive. If income-distribution effects are ignored, the change in consumers' surplus, ΔCS_x, and the change in profits, $\Delta\pi$, can be lumped together to arrive at a "total" welfare effect from vertical control:

$$\Delta W = \Delta CS_x + \Delta\pi$$

Alternatively, the total change in welfare, ΔW, can be viewed as occurring in two steps (see Figure 5-3 for an illustration). First, holding the quantity of the final good constant, vertical control reduces the real cost of producing that quantity of the final product. This efficiency effect, $EFCY$, is one component of the increase in profits resulting from vertical control. In the second step the integrating monopolist raises the price of the final product, causing a further increase in monopoly profits, $\Delta\pi\Delta P_x$, and a reduction in consumers' surplus, ΔCS_x. The combined welfare effect of this price increase, $\Delta W \Delta P_x$, is necessarily negative. Thus:

$$\begin{aligned} \Delta\pi &= EFCY + \Delta\pi\Delta P_x > 0 \\ \Delta W\Delta P_x &= \Delta CS_x + \Delta\pi\Delta P_x < 0 \\ \Delta W &= EFCY + \Delta W\Delta P_x \end{aligned}$$

The following conclusions can be drawn from simulations of the welfare effects of vertical control.

As a function of the elasticity of substitution, the effect of vertical control on total welfare, ΔW, rises from zero as σ increases from zero, reaches a positive maximum, declines to a negative minimum, and then rises again. For parameter values under which the $\hat{P}_x$ constraint is never effective (as in Figure 5-4a), ΔW approaches zero again from below as $\sigma \to \infty$. If the $\hat{P}_x$ constraint eventually becomes effective at some value for σ (Figure 5-4b), ΔW reaches a second positive maximum before declining again to zero from above as $\sigma \to \infty$.

If the $\hat{P}_x$ constraint is not effective, lowering η or δ increases the absolute value of the net welfare effect. In addition to this scale effect, the value for σ at which the net welfare effect first becomes negative,

$$\sigma_{\substack{\Delta W = 0 \\ \partial(\Delta W)/\partial\sigma < 0}},$$

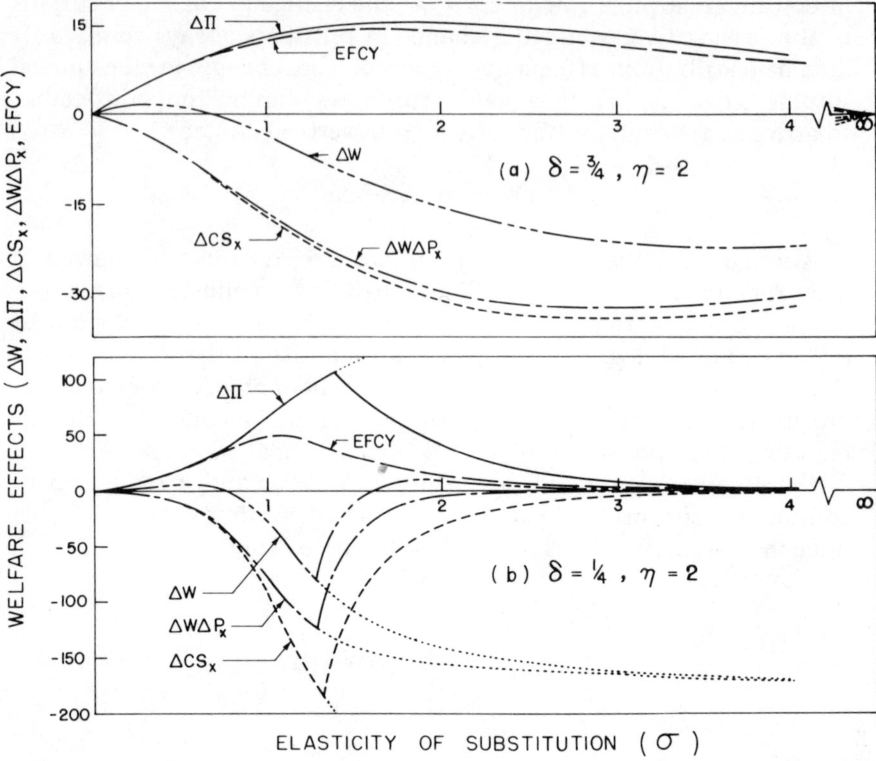

Figure 5-4. Effect of vertical control on profits, consumer surplus, and welfare

is higher, the lower are δ or η. As $\delta \rightarrow 1$, or as $\eta \rightarrow \infty$,

$$\sigma_{\substack{\Delta W = 0 \\ \partial(\Delta W)/\partial \sigma < 0}} \rightarrow 0.$$

As $\delta \rightarrow 0$, or as $\eta \rightarrow 1$,

$$\sigma_{\substack{\Delta W = 0 \\ \partial(\Delta W)/\partial \sigma < 0}} \rightarrow 1.$$

Thus if the $\hat{P}_x$ constraint is not effective, the net welfare effect will be negative over a minimum range for σ of $\sigma \geqslant 1$. Over this range for

σ, the absolute value of the welfare effect will be greater, the lower are δ and η. For the $0 < \sigma < 1$ range, a lower δ or η will increase the range for σ over which ΔW is positive, and increase the magnitude of ΔW.

If the $\hat{P}_x$ constraint is effective, however, the net welfare effect will become positive again at some σ, and the value for σ where ΔW again becomes positive will be lower, the lower are δ or η. As $\Delta \to 0$ or as $\eta \to 1$,

$$\sigma_{\substack{\Delta W = 0 \\ \partial(\Delta W)/\partial\sigma > 0}} \to 1.$$

Thus the effect of lower values for δ and η, if the $\hat{P}_x$ constraint is effective for some σ, is to narrow the range around $\sigma = 1$ where $\Delta W < 0$ and increase the scale of the welfare effect.[12] Figure 5-5a graphs ΔW as a function of σ for $\delta = 1/4$; $\eta = 3, 4$. Figure 5-5b shows $\Delta W(\sigma)$ for $\delta = 3/4$; $\eta = 3, 4$. Figure 5-5c shows $\Delta W(\sigma)$ for $\eta = 2$; $\delta = 1/4, 1/2, 3/4$.

It is thus difficult to draw any general conclusions for the direction of the welfare effect. If the particular case is such that it is clear that the input monopolist exerting vertical control would have the power to set any desired price for the final product after vertical control, then the net welfare effect could be assumed negative if $\sigma \geqslant 1$. If, however, the input monopolist were constrained from raising the price of the final product after vertical control to the full monopoly price, then the net welfare effect cannot be assumed negative unless the elasticity of substitution is close to unity. If σ is significantly less than unity, and if the values for δ and η are relatively low, then the welfare effect might be presumed positive.

The result that the net welfare effect can be positive or negative is to be expected. The welfare effect of an acquisition of a "second monopoly" is *a priori* indeterminate, given the presence of an existing monopoly distortion. Vertical control by an input monopolist can be viewed as the achievement of a "constrained second monopoly" over the other input industries. Assuming constant costs in the input industries, a joint monopoly over all input industries is equivalent to a monopoly over the final product. If the $\hat{P}_x$ constraint is not effective, then the same level of monopoly profits and the same price for the final product also result from vertical control by a single input monopolist, either in the form of vertical integration

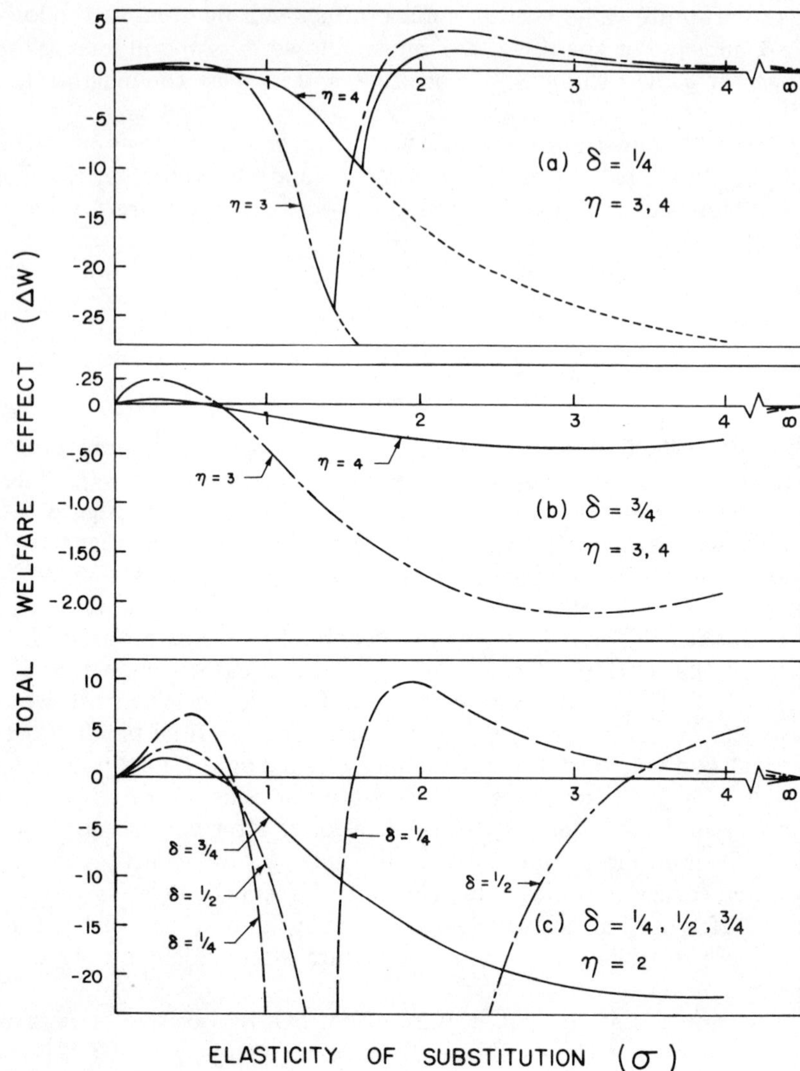

Figure 5-5. Total welfare effect of vertical control

or by the imposition of a tying arrangement (the requirement that purchasers of *A* also purchase their requirements of *B* from the *A* monopolist). If the $\hat{P}_x$ constraint is effective, however, profits and the final-product price will be lower, and total welfare higher, under vertical control than under a joint monopoly of all inputs. Under vertical control the *A* monopolist sets the input prices P_a^* and

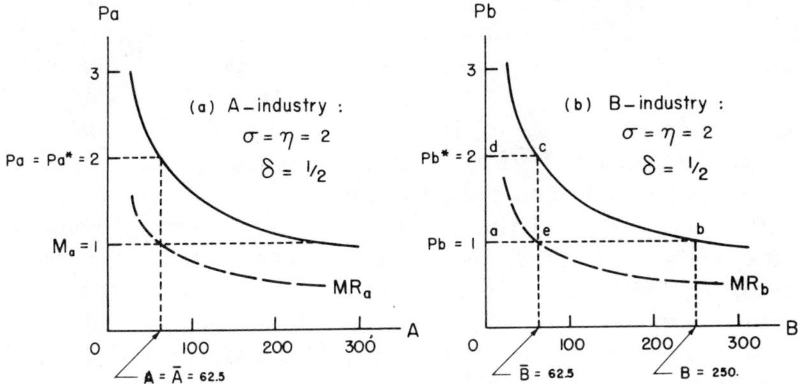

Figure 5-6. Effect of vertical control on input industries for $\sigma = \eta$

P_b^* (either directly in a tying arrangement or implicitly through internal pricing under vertical integration) such that:

$$\frac{P_a^*}{\overline{M}_a} = \frac{P_b^*}{\overline{P}_b} = \min\left(\frac{\overline{P}_x}{\overline{M}_x}, \frac{\hat{P}_x}{\overline{M}_x}\right) \tag{5.12}$$

This "second monopoly" over the other input industries can be illustrated graphically if $\sigma = \eta$, since in this case the cross elasticity of demand between the inputs is zero and the input derived-demand curves do not shift in response to changes in the prices of other inputs. If $\sigma = \eta$ (see Figure 5-6), the effect of vertical control is simply to increase the price of the cooperant input while leaving the price of the monopolized input unchanged. In Figure 5-6b, $\Delta CS_x = -abcd$, $\Delta \Pi = aecd$, and $\Delta W = -ebc$. If $\sigma > \eta$, then $E > \eta$ and $P_a^* > P_a$. Since $P_b^* > P_b$, the total welfare effect must therefore be negative if $\sigma \geqslant \eta$ and the $\hat{P}_x$ constraint is not effective. If $\sigma < \eta$, $P_a^* < P_a$, and ΔW can be positive or negative. Since $\eta > 1$, however, this conclusion is weaker than the simulation result that, if the P_x constraint is not effective, $\Delta W < 0$ if $\sigma \geqslant 1$.

VERTICAL CONTROL WITH NONCONSTANT INPUT COSTS

If we relax the assumption that all input costs are constant, a fall in the price of the final product, after vertical control, becomes possible. In addition, the effect of vertical control on producers' surplus in the competitive-input industry must be considered.

The effect on R of a rising or falling marginal-cost schedule for A can be determined from the effect of vertical control on the quantity of A used. For example, if the quantity of A used increases after vertical control ($\Delta A > 0$), a rising M_a schedule will reduce ΔA and hence increase R. However, while the magnitude of ΔA will be affected by the form of the M_a schedule, the sign of ΔA will be the same whether M_a is rising, falling, or constant. With constant M_a, the simulation results show that if the $\hat{P}_x$ constraint is not effective, the quantity of A used always falls after vertical control if $\sigma > \eta$; remains constant if $\sigma = \eta$; and increases if $\sigma < \eta$. If the $\hat{P}_x$ constraint is effective, however, the quantity of A used may increase even if $\sigma > \eta$. Thus, if $\sigma < \eta$, then $\Delta A > 0$, and rising marginal costs in the monopolized input industry will increase R, while falling M_a will reduce R.

Since the quantity of B used always falls after vertical control, the only way the price of the final product can decline after vertical control is if the quantity of A used increases sufficiently to offset the reduction in B. The most favorable conditions for a large increase in A would be a combination of $\sigma < \eta$ and a rapidly declining M_a.[13] If the elasticity of the marginal-cost schedule for A, g, is less than zero and small in absolute value, then $R < 1$ becomes possible. For example, in the $\sigma = 1$ case, with constant costs in the B industry only ($e = \infty, g \neq \infty$), R reduces to:

$$R = \left[\frac{(1 - 1/E)^{\delta g}}{(1 - 1/\eta)^{(g+1-\delta)}}\right]^{1/g+E} \tag{5.13}$$

where:

$$\underset{\substack{e=\infty \\ \sigma=1}}{E} = 1 + \delta(\eta - 1)$$

As expected, since $\sigma < \eta$:

$$\frac{\partial R}{\partial g} = \frac{\delta R}{(g + E)^2} \quad [E\, ln(1 - 1/E) - \eta\, ln(1 - 1/\eta)] < 0$$

(since $\sigma < \eta \rightarrow E < \eta$).

While the second-order conditions (if $g < 0$, then $g < -\eta$) restrict the range over which Equation (5.13) can be less than unity, they do not exclude the possibility entirely. The simulation results show a rather narrow range for g where the price of the final product will fall after vertical control. Thus if $\sigma < \eta$, a declining marginal-cost schedule clearly improves the welfare effect of vertical control (since the monopoly profits from vertical control are also increased), and may even result in a situation where vertical control improves the welfare of both consumers and profit receivers.

A finite elasticity of supply of the competitive input ($e \neq \infty$) introduces a monopsony element. In the absence of vertical control, the elasticity of supply of B enters indirectly through the elasticity of derived demand for A (the lower is e, the lower is E in Equation (5.4)). Vertical control, however, in addition to establishing the A monopolist as a "second monopolist" in the sale of B, now also enables the A monopolist to act directly as a monopsonist toward the B industry. It is thus easy to understand why other input producers would object strenuously to vertical control by a firm with market power over an input with which their product can be used in variable proportions.

From the viewpoint of consumers of the final product, however, a rising supply curve for B improves the effects of vertical control. Since the quantity of B always falls after vertical control, a rising supply curve for B acts to reduce the fall in B after vertical control and hence reduce R. If the supply of B is sufficiently inelastic, and if $\sigma < \eta$ so that $\Delta A > 0$, the price of the final product can fall after vertical control even if there are constant costs in the A industry. For example,[14] if $\sigma = 1$ and $e = 0$:

$$\underset{\substack{e=0\\ \sigma=1}}{R} = \delta^{\delta g/[\delta g+\eta[1+g(1-\delta)]]} < 1 \tag{5.14}$$

Any such gain to consumers of the final product must, however, be balanced against the loss of producers surplus in the B industry. The total welfare effect of vertical control on consumers, monopoly-profit receivers, and competitive-input producers can, of course, be positive or negative depending on the particular parameter values. For any given quantity of the final product, however, nonconstant costs in the B industry clearly reduce the potential efficiency gain from vertical control. Before vertical control, the ratio of A to B is lower than the efficient ratio; but after vertical control, the input ratio is higher than the efficient ratio if $e \neq \infty$:

$$\frac{\overline{A}}{\overline{B}} = \left[\frac{\delta \overline{P}_b(1 + 1/e)}{(1-\delta)\overline{M}_a}\right]^{\sigma} > \left[\frac{\delta \overline{P}_b}{(1-\delta)\overline{M}_a}\right]^{\sigma}$$

Integration into the Monopsonized Industry

We have already examined the incentive for a monopsonist to integrate upstream in a fixed-proportions context (see Chapter 4, *supra*). With fixed-proportions production functions at both levels, the analysis was relatively simple. Three conclusions emerged from that discussion. First, the private incentive for integration is due entirely to the potential gain from eliminating the inefficiency loss from monopsony. Second, integration is an all-or-nothing choice. In the absence of transaction costs, complete integration is always preferred. Third, if the monopsonist is also a monopolist in the final-product market, the social gain from integration will be greater than the private gain. If transaction costs are present, integration may be unprofitable but still socially beneficial. Thus in contrast to downstream integration used to facilitate price discrimination, a case can be made for encouraging monopsony-induced integration beyond the privately chosen level.

Introducing variable proportions at the downstream X-stage complicates the analysis but does not affect these conclusions. As Perry (1975 and 1976) shows, however, variable proportions at the monopsonized upstream B-stage does significantly alter the analysis. Perry's approach is to assume that the monopsonized input is produced using two inputs: a specialized factor, N, in fixed supply, and a variable factor, L, in infinitely elastic supply. Upstream integration can then be defined as the fraction of N which is owned by the monopsonist firm. The crucial observation is that the monopsonist will utilize N more intensively than will the independent monopsonized suppliers of B. The optimal L/N and B/N ratios are thus higher for the integrated producer than for the independents, and total production of B increases as the monopsonist integrates backwards. In the open market, the reduction in the monopsonist's demand for independently-produced B is thus greater than the reduction in the independent supply of B. An excess supply of B develops, the market price of B falls, and rents to independent B-firms are reduced.

Variable proportions at the upstream level thus alters the effects of monopsony-induced integration in several respects. First, rents of the remaining independent producers are effectively transferred to the monopsonist as integration proceeds, via the fall in the open-market price of B. This provides an additional incentive for integration by the monopsonist, independent of the efficiency gains. The welfare effect of integration is therefore no longer unambiguously positive. Second, partial integration is now a possible outcome. In particular, suppose that all purchases of N must be made at a price which reflects pre-integration rents. Since the open-market price of B falls steadily as integration proceeds, it may eventually be less expensive for the monopsonist to purchase a marginal unit of B at this reduced price than to produce an additional unit of B internally by acquiring additional N at its preintegration price.

SUMMARY, EXTENSIONS, AND CONCLUSIONS

Summary

This chapter has examined the welfare effects of vertical control by a monopolist of an input that can be used in variable proportions with other inputs. For the specific case of a CES production function and a constant-elasticity demand function for the final product, the following conclusions can be drawn.

1. If the marginal costs of producing all inputs are constant, vertical control will always result in an increase in the price of the final product. If vertical control enables an unconstrained monopoly over the final product, the percentage increase in the price of the final product will be greater, the less elastic the demand for the final product, η, and the less "important" the monopolized input (more specifically, the lower is the distribution parameter, δ, in the production function for the final product). However, if the final-product monopoly achieved through vertical control is effectively constrained by potential competition from firms that can produce the final product without using the monopolized input, the price increase will be less, the less elastic the final demand and the less important the monopolized input.

2. If input costs are not constant, a fall in the price of the final product after vertical control is possible if: (a) the elasticity of substitution between the inputs is less than the elasticity of demand for the final product; *and either* (b) the marginal-cost schedule for the monopolized input is downward-sloping; *or* (c) the supply curve of the competitive input is upward-sloping.

3. The combined welfare effect of vertical control on monopoly profit receivers, consumers of the final product, and producers of the competitive input may be positive or negative, depending on the particular parameter values. This result is to be expected, since the welfare effect of a "second" monopoly (in this case, a monopoly over the other input industries) is *a priori* indeterminate, given the presence of an existing monopoly distortion. With constant input costs, the combined welfare effect is always positive over a range for σ immediately above zero, but becomes negative at some $\sigma < 1$. If the final-product monopoly achieved by vertical control is effectively

constrained, the combined welfare effect becomes positive again at some $\sigma > 1$. In general the less elastic the demand for the final product and the less important the monopolized input, the greater the magnitude of the welfare effect and the wider the range for σ over which the combined welfare effect is positive.

Extensions

Further extension of these results would involve relaxing the assumptions made about parameter values and the institutional context.

1. The critical parameter assumption has been that the elasticity of substitution is constant over the relevant range for vertical control. The price effects of vertical control for production functions which are less 'well-behaved' than CES have not been extensively examined. Bowman (1973), however, has discovered a numerical example where downstream integration by an input monopolist into a competitive industry results in a fall in the price of the final product. Bowman's example assumes constant returns to scale and a discontinuous linear marginal physical product schedule for the competitively-supplied input. Since discontinuity is not crucial, we can translate Bowman's numerical table (Bowman, p. 79) of output as a function of the quantity of the competitively-supplied B-input (for $A=1$) into a continuous function:

$$X = .50 + .55B - .05B^2 \tag{5.15}$$

Since constant returns to scale are assumed, the implied production function is:

$$X = .50A + .55B - .05B^2/A \tag{5.16}$$

which gives us a linear marginal physical product function for B:

$$\partial X/\partial B = .55 - .10B/A \tag{5.17}$$

and a convex marginal physical product function for the monopolized input, A:

$$\partial X/\partial A = .50 + .05B^2/A^2 \tag{5.18}$$

Before integration, the competitive, independent X-firms set the marginal rate of input substitution equal to the input price ratio. Thus the downstream factor proportions ratio before integration is:

$$\alpha = B/A \tag{5.19}$$
$$= - P_a/P_b + [(P_a/P_b)^2 - 10 + 11\, P_a/P_b]^{1/2}$$

Substituting (5.19) into (5.16), the average product of A before integration is:

$$\beta = X/A \tag{5.20}$$
$$= .50 + .55\alpha - .05\alpha^2$$

Given any demand function for the final product and a supply function for the competitively-supplied input, we can now solve for the derived-demand function for the monopolized input. Bowman assumes a linear demand function which, in continuous form, is given by:

$$P_x = 10 - .02X \tag{5.21}$$

With competition and constant returns to scale at the X and B levels, Equations (5.20) and (5.21) can be used to solve for the demand for A as a function of P_a and P_b:

$$A = (500\beta - 50P_a - 50\alpha P_b)/\beta^2 \tag{5.22}$$

We could use Equation (5.22) to solve for the profit-maximizing price for A, but the resulting expression is rather complex. Instead, we use a gradient method to solve for the optimal price. Bowman assumes a constant, unitary marginal cost for each input. Thus $M_a = 1$ and $M_b = P_b = 1$. The resulting profit-maximizing price for A is $P_a = 7.67$, resulting in $\alpha = 3.87$, $\beta = 1.88$, $A = 102.69$, $B = 397.51$, $\pi = 684.90$, $P_x = 6.139$, $X = 194.9$, and a 'real cost' per unit of X of $M'_x = 2.59$.

If the A monopolist now integrates downstream, the integrated firm will set the marginal rate of input substitution equal to the ratio of input marginal costs. Replacing P_a with M_a in Equation (5.19) results in a post-integration factor-proportions ratio of $\overline{\alpha} = .414$, and thus in $\overline{\beta} = .719$ and a marginal (equal to average) cost of X of $\overline{M}_x = 1.966$. The profit-maximizing monopoly output is $\overline{X} = 200.84$ at $\overline{P}_x = 5.983$, resulting in $\overline{A} = 279.33$, $\overline{B} = 115.64$ and $\overline{\pi} = 806.76$. Integration in this example would thus result in a fall in the price of the final product by 2.54 percent as well as an increase in monopoly profits. The welfare effect is unambiguously positive.

These price effects from integration appear to be caused by the asymmetric marginal physical product functions for the two inputs. The monopolized A-input is the only essential input. Since $\partial X/\partial A$ in Equation (5.18) approaches .5 as α approaches zero, X can be produced using only A at a cost per unit of $2P_a$. From Equation (5.17), production is technically efficient only for $\alpha < 5.5$. The result is a relatively inelastic derived demand for A and a relatively elastic derived demand for B. Equivalently, we can observe that the elasticity of substitution for this production function is given by

$$\sigma = \frac{110 - 20\alpha + 11\alpha^2 - 2\alpha^3}{20\alpha(10 + 11\alpha - \alpha^2)}$$

where $\sigma > 0$ for $\alpha < 5.5$, and $\partial\sigma/\partial\alpha < 0$.

Since the B/A ratio must fall after integration ($\bar{\alpha} < \alpha$), production before integration occurs in a region where factor substitution is relatively difficult. The effect (see Equation (5.3)) is a relatively low elasticity of derived demand and a correspondingly high monopoly price for the monopolized input before integration. Since σ increases rapidly with integration, however, a significant increase in efficiency is still possible. In Bowman's example, the elasticity of substitution rises from $\sigma = .03$ to $\bar{\sigma} = .73$, the B/A ratio falls from $\alpha = 3.87$ to $\bar{\alpha} = .414$, and the real unit cost of X falls from $M_x' = 2.59$ to $\overline{M}_x = 1.97$.

Clearly, it would be desirable to know the general conditions for a price reduction to occur after integration. Unfortunately, knowledge of the production function alone appears insufficient to sign the price effect. In particular, some experiments using the production function of Equation (5.16) indicate that both the direction and the strength of the price change are quite sensitive to both the elasticity of final demand and the ratio of input marginal costs.[15] These results imply that the information required to definitely sign the price effect may be beyond that available in most policy situations. In the absence of such information, some restraint is indicated in using the Bowman example as a defense of integration. As noted above, while the $\partial\sigma/\partial\alpha < 0$ characteristic of the production function results in a relatively inelastic derived demand for A, it also results in a relatively elastic derived demand for B. If A is competitively supplied while B is monopolized, the profit-maximizing monopoly price for B would be $P_b = 1.057$, resulting in $\alpha = .1949$, $\beta = .6053$, $A = 661.4358$, $B = 128.9404$, $\Pi = 7.3490$, $X = 400.3782$, and $P_x = 1.9924$. Integration by the B monopolist will thus result in an increase in the price of the final product. The integrated *B*-monopolist cannot impose the full monopoly price for *X* of 5.983, however, since *X* can be produced using only *A* at a cost of 2.00. The increase in P_x after integration is thus constrained to a maximum of 0.38 percent. The general conclusion, therefore, is that if the sign of $\partial \sigma / \partial \alpha$ is not known, the price effect from integration may be either better or worse than would be predicted if a CES production function (i.e. $\partial \sigma / \partial \alpha = 0$) is assumed.

2. The welfare effect would also clearly be improved if the *A* monopolist were unable to raise P_a significantly after vertical control. This inability to raise the price of *A* to independent *X* producers could be due to regulation, threat of antitrust proceedings, or potential entry at the *A* level. In addition, if markets for *A* other than the *X* industry are present, an increase in P_a in these markets might be unavoidable if P_a is to be increased for independent *X* producers. If raising P_a in these other markets would reduce monopoly profits, the *A* monopolist may be unwilling to raise P_a to independent *X* firms after vertical control.

3. Some interesting problems arise when the *A* industry is a regulated monopoly. In general, if economies of scale are present at the *A* level, the price of *A* will be greater than its marginal cost, even if regulation is effective in setting price equal to average cost.[16] The downstream factor ratio chosen by independent *X* firms will thus be distorted toward underutilization of *A*, and downstream vertical integration by the regulated firm will remove this distortion.

Integration, however, creates two problems, as noted in the third section of Chapter 3, above. First, if the vertically related subsidiary of a regulated firm is unregulated, the firm can avoid effective regulation by adjusting accounting prices between the regulated and unregulated levels. Unless the regulatory agency moves to control—directly or indirectly—the accounting price between levels, any restraint on monopoly conduct becomes voluntary. Second, the regulatory process itself may induce production inefficiencies, notably the Averch-Johnson effect. If, in order to maintain effective regulation after vertical integration, the regulatory agency sets a maximum rate of return on capital at the downstream *X* level, the Averch-Johnson distortion will be introduced at that level. Integration will thus remove one distortion at the *X* level (between *A* and other inputs), while adding another distortion (between capital and other inputs). The final effect can be to raise or lower the real social costs of production at the *X* level, depending on the specific parameter values.

4. The goal of the *A* monopolist may not be profit-maximization,

or other goals may also exist in addition to profit-maximization. For example, if the goal is sales maximization, subject to an absolute profit constraint, then the achievement of the efficiency gain will permit a reduction in the price of the final product after vertical control, and the welfare effect will be greater than the efficiency effect alone. If a higher level of monopoly profits reduces the pressure for efficient management, however, the potential increase in profits from vertical control may be absorbed by increased organizational slack and other "*X*-inefficiencies," so that a reduction in consumer surplus can become the only effect of vertical control.

5. If the *A* industry is an oligopoly rather than a monopoly, it becomes difficult to determine the price effect of vertical control. There will clearly be some pressure toward raising the prices of *A* and *X* after all members of the oligopoly have vertically integrated. However, since the price of *A* on the open market must rise by a relatively large proportion for any given rise in the price of *X*, the profit margin on sales of *A* to independents will be high compared to the profit margin on internal sales of *A*, and the temptation facing any one firm to make such sales of *A* to independent *X* producers will be correspondingly strong. The efficiency effect could also be expected to be less significant, since the oligopoly markup on *A* before vertical control can be expected to be less than the full monopoly markup. In general, therefore, the magnitude of the welfare effect from vertical control, and particularly the incentive for vertical control, could be expected to be significantly less if the *A* industry were an oligopoly than if it were a monopoly. The effect of vertical control on entry into the *A* industry appears indeterminate, since while vertical control may raise entry barriers (by increasing capital requirements for entry, for example), the increased profitability of the integrated firms and the potential profits from sales of *A* to independents will make the industry more attractive to potential entrants. In addition, unless vertical control is through merger with the independent *X* producers, the *X* producers will have a particularly strong incentive to integrate backwards.

6. The income redistribution effects of vertical control are relatively clear. Monopoly profits are increased, consumers' surplus generally falls, and producers' surplus in competing input industries always falls. Independent *X* firms are necessarily eliminated, although if the removal is accomplished by an advantageous merger with the input monopolist, they may share in the increase in profits resulting from vertical control. In general the effect of vertical control will be to increase income inequalities, and the increase in monopoly profits may thus be given a lower social-welfare weighting than the fall in

consumers' and producers' surplus outside of the *A* industry. Under certain conditions, of course, this weighting could be reversed. One example might be that of vertical control by a union in a low-wage industry producing a luxury good. Another example might involve exports or foreign investment. From a national point of view, if the eventual consumers are foreigners and the firm is owned by nationals, the welfare gain could be regarded as the entire increase in monopoly profits due to vertical control

7. The sensitivity of the welfare effects of vertical control to the particular parameter values implies that accurate estimation of these parameters is necessary. Most of the empirical work on the elasticity of substitution has concentrated on estimating σ between capital and labor in a value-added production function. The estimated values fall mainly in the $0.5 < \sigma < 1.5$ range (see Nerlove, 1967), where significant effects from vertical control on final-product prices and monopoly profits could be expected (see Figures 5-2 and 5-4). Estimated values for the elasticity of substitution between intermediate inputs and value-added, on the other hand, have usually been low (see Theil and Tilanus, 1964, p. 268; Balassa, Guisinger and Schydlowsky, 1970, pp. 1157-61). Humphrey and Moroney (1975), however, have recently estimated partial elasticities of substitution between capital, labor, and natural resource products. Their results suggest that "labor and, to a lesser degree, capital are substitutable for natural resource products among most of the resource-using product groups of American manufacturing" (p. 78). For several two-digit product groups, substitution appears easier between natural resource products and a primary factor (capital or labor) than between primary factors.[17]

In addition, the elasticity of substitution between one particular monopolized capital good (or one category of labor) and all other capital and labor inputs can be expected to be higher than between capital and labor aggregates. Similarly, even if the elasticity of substitution between intermediate inputs and value-added is negligible, substitution possibilities between different intermediate inputs may be significant. Thus we cannot rule out the intermediate inputs case, nor can we ignore the results for high levels of σ.

Nevertheless, vertical control by labor unions or capital-goods producers should be of particular interest. An additional consideration is that the original basis of market power for unions and patented capital-good producers may be legally unassailable, while policies can still be formulated toward extensions of that market power through vertical control. Since an analysis of vertical control by labor unions requires reformulation of the model presented in this chapter, in terms of both the objective function and the institutional constraints, we will now turn in Chapter 6 to the special case of vertical control by labor unions.

NOTES

1. While Vernon and Graham (1971) assume that the price of the final product is unchanged after integration, Burstein's (1960b) opinion appears to be that the price of the final product will rise after integration or an equivalent tying arrangement, since "the very existence of substitution possibilities will in general prevent the monopolist from facing the competitive producers of the final product with production costs high enough to *force* them to charge a price (for the final product) equal to the monopoly price" (p. 81). Schmalensee (1973) has examined the effects of vertical integration with variable proportions under assumptions of a linear homogeneous production function for the final product and constant costs for all inputs. The implication of Schmalensee's results is that the price effect of vertical control cannot be signed without additional information on the cost and demand conditions.

2. See Hicks, 1964, p. 244.

3.

$$(1) \quad k_a = \frac{P_a A}{P_x X}$$

or

$$(2) \quad k_a = \frac{1}{1 + (P_b B)/P_a A)}$$

Efficient factor use by the competitive firm implies:

$$(3) \quad \frac{A}{B} = \left[\frac{\delta P_b}{(1-\delta)P_a}\right]^{\sigma}$$

Substituting (3) above into (2) above results in Equation (5.6).

4. For a derivation, see Nerlove, 1967, p. 111.

5. For the CES production function with $\sigma > 1$, the average product of B approaches a positive lower limit as the A/B ratio approaches zero (see Arrow, Chenery, Minhas and Solow, 1961, pp. 230-31). Hence production is possible with B alone, and the unit cost of producing X using only the B input, P_x, is a finite upper limit to the integrated monopoly's price.

It should be noted that if $\sigma > 1$, this finite upper limit for the integrated monopoly's price holds even if $\eta \leqslant 1$. In addition, if σ is sufficiently greater than unity, the elasticity of derived demand for A may also be greater than unity even if $\eta \leqslant 1$ (see Equations (5.4) and (5.5)), so that the price of the final product before integration will also be finite. For such cases, the restriction that $\eta > 1$ (see equation (5.2)) can be removed.

6. See Burstein (1960b) or Vernon and Graham (1971).

7. That R approaches unity as η approaches infinity or as δ approaches unity is obvious by substitution. By using the series expansion of $ln(1 - 1/\eta)$ and $ln(1 - 1/E)$, it can be shown that $\partial R/\partial \eta$ and $\partial R/\partial \delta$ are negative. Thus R in equation (5.11) is always greater than unity. Thus result for the $\sigma = 1$, $e = g = \infty$ case is also derived by Schmalensee (1973, pp. 447-48) and by Hay (1974, pp. 191-93).

8. From Equation (5.4), if $\sigma = \eta$, then $E = \sigma = \eta$. If $\sigma > \eta$, then $E > \eta$, and if $\sigma < \eta$, then $E < \eta$.

9. For an alternative proof for the $\sigma > \eta$ case, see Hay (1973, pp. 193-94).

10. It should be noted that the use of consumers' surplus as a measure of welfare requires particular assumptions: for example, homotheticity of preferences (see Rader, 1972, pp. 234-243). For possible ambiguities in the use of producers' surplus later in this chapter, see Mishan (1968).

11. It is this "efficiency" effect that is shown graphically by Vernon and Graham (1971).

12. The net welfare effect is always negative at $\sigma = 1$ if there are constant input costs. With $\sigma = 1, e = g = \infty$:

$$\Delta \underset{e=\infty}{W} = \Delta CS_x + \Delta \Pi$$

$$\Delta \underset{\substack{\sigma=1 \\ e=g=\infty}}{W} = \frac{Z}{(\eta - 1)} \left[\frac{(2\eta - 1)}{\eta \bar{P}_x{}^{(\eta-1)}} - \frac{(2E - 1)}{EP_x{}^{(\eta-1)}} \right]$$

$$= \frac{Z}{(\eta - 1)} \left[\frac{Y\delta^{\delta}(1 - \delta)^{(1-\delta)}}{M_a{}^{\delta} P_b{}^{(1-\delta)}} \right]^{(\eta-1)} \left[\frac{(2\eta - 1)(\eta - 1)^{(\eta-1)}}{\eta^{\eta}} \right.$$

$$\left. - \frac{(2E - 1)(E - 1)^{(E-1)}}{E^E} \right] = Q\,[\,f(\eta) - f(E)\,]$$

By using the series expansion of $ln(1 - 1/\eta)$, it can be shown that $\partial f(\eta)/\partial \eta < 0$. Thus, since $Q > 0$ and $\underset{\sigma=1}{E} < \eta$, $\Delta \underset{\substack{\sigma=1 \\ e=g=\infty}}{W} < 0$.

13. If the $\hat{P}_x$ constraint is effective, R must be greater than unity. Thus any increase in A if $\sigma \geqslant \eta$ cannot result in a fall in the price of the final product after vertical control.

14. $\underset{\substack{e=0 \\ \sigma=1}}{R} > 1$ would require that:

$$\frac{\delta g}{\delta g + \eta[1 + g(1 - \delta)]} < 0$$

and thus:

$$0 > g > \frac{-\eta}{\delta + \eta(1-\delta)}$$

or: $0 > g > -E$, since:

$$\underset{\substack{e=0\\ \sigma=1}}{E} = \frac{\eta}{\delta + \eta(1-\delta)},$$

which is excluded by the second-order conditions.

15. For example, if the linear demand function of equation (21) is replaced by a constant-elasticity demand function, the $\bar{P}_x/P_x$ ratio is 0.78 for $\eta = 4/3$, 0.95 for $\eta = 2$, and 1.02 for $\eta = 4$. Alternatively, if the marginal cost of B is increased to $M_b = 2$, $\bar{P}_x/P_x$ is 1.65 for the linear demand function, 2.21 for $\eta = 4/3$, 1.11 for $\eta = 2$, and 1.003 for $\eta = 4$.

16. In principle, a second-degree price-discriminating rate structure could result in each user facing a price for the marginal unit equal to the marginal cost of production. In practice, however, such a rate structure is unlikely.

17. For the "primary metals" two-digit product group, for example, the estimate from a translog cost function for 1963 of the partial elasticity of substitution between capital and labor is 0.726, while the partial elasticity of substitution between labor and natural resources is estimated at 5.918 (Humphrey and Moroney, 1975, p. 76).

 *Chapter 6*

Vertical Control by Labor Unions

The literature on labor unions provides voluminous evidence of the complexity of the collective bargaining process. To some extent this complexity is due to the multidimensional nature of both the service offered (requiring specification of job classifications, production standards, hours, safety rules, and so on) and the form of payment (requiring specification of wage-rate structure and differentials, allowances, bonuses, vacations, sick leave, health and insurance plans, pension, and the like). In addition, administration of the transaction requires agreement on such issues as union security and grievance procedures.[1] Complex labor contracts would not even be necessarily inconsistent with a competitive labor market (see Macdonald, 1967; Rice, 1966).

Much of this complexity can be conceptually reduced to the choice by a union of some point along a given derived-demand curve for labor, with employers free to determine the level of employment. Many union actions often labeled "restrictive practices" or "featherbedding" do not, however, easily fit into this framework.[2] Instead they appear to result in a wage-employment combination that lies entirely off the derived-demand curve for labor. They involve either fixing the total amount of employment or fixing the labor-capital (or labor-output) ratio, in addition to setting the wage rate. Examples are legion. The American Federation of Musicians has required that a minimum number of men be hired per theater orchestra, and that when nonunion musicians are hired, union musicians must also be hired on standby or the equivalent salaries paid into the local's unemployment fund (Countryman, 1948; 1949). Railroad unions have attempted to set a minimum size for train crews and have guaranteed absolute employment levels for nonoperating crafts (Rehmus, 1971). In Pacific Cost longshoring, at least up to the 1960 Mechanization and Modernization Agreement, the union enforced work rules that required firms to employ a fixed quantity of labor inputs, or required that labor be used in fixed proportions to other inputs or outputs (Goldberg, 1971, pp. 316–40; Hartman, 1969). On the East Coast the longshoring unions have gradually shifted from setting a minimum gang size to establishing an annual income guarantee for the registered work force (Goldberg, 1971, pp. 341–72). Seafaring unions have imposed minimum crew sizes (Goldberg, 1971, pp. 373–402). In the building trades, restrictions have occasionally been placed on the use of particular techniques such as the use of spray guns or preglazed sash (Chamberlain and Cullen, 1965, p. 242 ; Rees, 1962, p. 137; Haber and Levinson, 1956, pp. 103–203).[3] Numerous other early examples of restrictive practices are cited by Ulman (1966, pp. 536–66).

Unions have also used more subtle measures—essentially taxes on output or capital—that operate through a pricing mechanism but can have a similar effect to direct controls. Perhaps the best known example is the United Mine Workers (UMW), which finances its Welfare and Retirement Fund through a royalty on each ton of coal produced in union mines (Christenson, 1962 , pp. 209–15, 248–49; Myers, 1967; Lewis, 1970). Similarly, the Mechanization and Modernization Fund in West Coast longshoring is financed on a tonnage basis (Goldberg, 1971, p. 330), while the unemployment fund on the East Coast is financed by a royalty on containers, which is proportional to the degree of anticipated labor displacement (Goldberg, 1971, p. 346). Airline pilots are paid according to a complex formula that closely resembles a tax on either output or capital. Base pay, which increases with length of service, accounts for only about one-sixth of pilot earnings. The remainder is accounted for by hourly pay (which varies with aircraft speed), mileage pay, and gross-weight pay (M.L. Kahn, 1971, pp. 526–66; and for other case studies of the Air Line Pilots Association, see Baitsell, 1966; Hopkins, 1971). In trucking, the Teamsters Union has negotiated mileage-rate differentials based on truck size and cargo capacity (Levinson, 1971, p. 55), and has also imposed a royalty payment on the transportation of highway trailers on railroad flatcars (Levinson, 1971, pp. 43–51, 58–71). In addition, profit-sharing plans in general can be regarded as a direct tax on capital (unless the debt-equity ratio is fixed, however, "profits" should ideally include interest payments on debt).[4]

There are several possible reasons why unions might wish to impose absolute employment levels, labor-output or labor-capital ratios, output taxes, or taxes on other inputs. Some of these reasons do not involve operating off the derived-demand curve for labor. For example, the wage structure imposed by the Air Line Pilots Association has resulted in particularly large benefits to seniority (since senior pilots have priority in flying the faster, heavier airplanes), and has also been very effective as a bargaining tool in an industry where productivity has increased rapidly. Tying wages to particular equipment may also have enabled effective price discrimination by the union.[5] In addition, certain practices have the effect of regularizing employment[6] or spreading the same amount of work over a larger number of employees.[7]

Nevertheless, all these practices can be used by a union to achieve a wage-employment combination that lies off to the right of the derived-demand schedule for labor. Analytically these actions bear a close resemblence to vertical control by firms with market power over an input who face a variable-proportions technology in the downstream production process. For example, suppose a powerful union in a competitive-product industry wishes to increase the earnings per hour of its members, but is unwilling to force up the wage rate because of the effect on employment. Increasing the wage rate would reduce employment for two reasons. First, the increase in wage rates would increase production costs and product prices, lower output levels, and thus decrease employment for any given labor-output ratio. Second, the increase in the wage rate relative to the cost of capital would lead to substitution of capital for labor, lower the labor-output ratio, and thus decrease employment for any given level of output. Vertical control by the union, however, can be used to reverse the substitution effect.

Since formal vertical integration by unions is rare, let us assume that the union decides to impose a tax or royalty on the final product (the UMW case is the clearest example in practice). If the union wishes to increase earnings per worker with no change in employment, it can raise the royalty rate while simultaneously reducing the wage rate. The fall in the quantity of labor demanded due to the effect of the higher royalty rate on output can thus be balanced by the increase in labor demanded due to the effect of a lower wage-rental ratio on the labor-output ratio. As we shall see, this balancing act can continue until some finite (assuming that the elasticity of demand for the product eventually becomes greater than unity) maximum level of earnings per worker (from wages and royalties) is reached. The crucial requirement for the process to work, of course, is that the elasticity of substitution between labor and other inputs be greater than zero, since in the absence of a substitution effect there is no difference between the effects of a tax on labor and a tax on output.

This incentive for vertical control by unions has not gone unnoticed in the literature. The earliest, and still clearest, exposition is by Lewis (1951) and is worth quoting at length:

> The law and social canons against extortion . . . in effect require labor monopolies to depend chiefly upon wage taxes for their monopoly gains. But employers can avoid wage taxes to some extent by substituting untaxed services for the taxed labor services.
>
> Unions remedy or partially remedy this defect of a wage levy in two ways. First, they supplement wage taxes with other levies, output royalties, for example, which do not have this defect. Second, they place hurdles in the way of the substitutions in order to make wage taxes approximate excise taxes in their revenue effects. These hurdles include standby rules, work demarcation regulations, and other "make-work" and "featherbedding" rules. [1951, p. 284]

This argument has been essentially restated by Hilton (1959), Nutter (1959), and Rees (1962). Leontief (1946) has interpreted the guaranteed annual wage in a graphic pure-exchange model as a price-quantity agreement equivalent to first-degree (perfect) price discrimination. In addition, several writers have attempted to determine the effect of featherbedding using a graphic analysis (Weinstein, 1960; Simler, 1962), but such attempts inevitably founder due to the inability to determine the output effect in an isoquant diagram. In this sense the problem is very similar to the limitations of Vernon and Graham's (1971) analysis of vertical control by firms. What is needed is an explicit model of vertical control by unions, based on some reasonable union objective function, which can specify optimal union policy toward vertical control, analyze the determinants of such a policy, and establish the theoretical relationships between vertical control by unions and vertical control by firms. Before presenting such a model, however, we must first justify the choice of an objective function for labor unions and ask if any special constraints are applicable to the labor union case.

The Objectives of Labor Unions

An extensive literature exists on the objectives of labor unions. At one extreme is the position that unions do not maximize anything,[8] or are essentially political institutions (Ross, 1948). At the other extreme are models that assume unions are purely economic units, very similar to firms but with profit-maximization replaced by some other single goal such as maximizing net revenue (Berkowitz, 1954) or the wage bill (Dunlop, 1950). Both political and economic goals have been incorporated into a single framework, notably by Atherton (1973). In addition, Martin (1972; 1976) has taken a property-rights approach to the analysis of union behavior.

We shall assume that the objective function for a union is representable by a utility function, $U = U(W,L)$ whose only components are earnings per worker and employment. Graphically (see Figure 6-1), the union selects the wage that results in the wage-employment combination where the derived-demand schedule for union labor is tangent to the union's highest indifference curve. As Cartter (1959, pp. 80–90) points out, this general preference-function approach allows several often-suggested models of trade union behavior as sub-cases, including: maximization of profits or economic rent to union

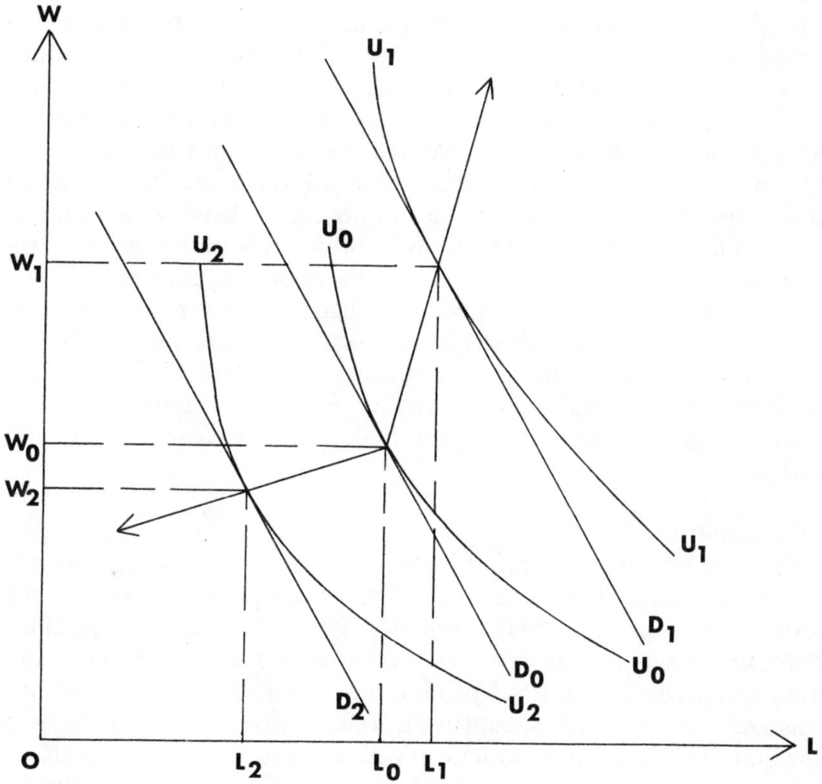

Figure 6.1 Wage-Preference Path

members or union officials (maximizing union dues); maximization of the gross wage bill; and maximization of the wage rate only, or of union membership only.[9] In general one would expect the union's indifference mapping to be nonsymmetrical in response to demand shifts. "Unions will prefer to use an increase in demand primarily for a wage increase, only accepting large increments of employment if the increase in demand is quite substantial. Similarly, with a decrease in demand, a wage cut will be resisted unless the decline is quite substantial" (Cartter, 1959, p. 92). The resulting wage preference path is illustrated in Figure 6-1, where an outward shift of the demand curve for labor for D_0 to D_1 results in a large increase, from W_0 to W_1, in the wage chosen by the union, and a small increase, from L_0 to L_1, in the employment level chosen by the union. A decrease in demand to D_2 results in a small decrease, from W_0 to W_2, in the union preferred wage, and a large decrease, from L_0 to L_2, in employment. In general, the kink could be expected to occur at the point of full employment for existing union members.

In the context of a labor monopoly, vertical control can best be viewed as a method of shifting outward the demand curve for union labor. Assuming that neither earnings per worker nor employment are inferior goods to the union, the effect of vertical control on earning per worker and on employment will lie between one of two extremes. First, the union could take all the gains from vertical control in the form of increased employment, leaving earnings per worker unchanged (a horizontal wage-preference path). At a second extreme, the union could leave employment unchanged and take all gains in the form of increased earnings per worker (vertical wage-preference path). In most cases a relatively horizontal wage-preference path could be expected until existing union members are fully employed. Once full employment is reached, a union could be expected to use vertical control mainly to increase earnings per worker.

Constraints

What factors could limit the use of vertical control by a union? The union cannot force the price of the final product above what it would cost to produce that product without the use of union labor. If the union has complete control over labor supply, this maximum price would be the cost of production when no labor is used. If a constant elasticity of substitution (CES) production function is assumed, the cost of production without the use of one factor is finite only if the elasticity of substitution is greater than unity. In many cases, however, the power of a union to increase production costs may also be constrained by the existence of nonunion labor. If the union forces the cost of production up too far, new firms using nonunion labor may enter the industry or existing firms may switch to nonunion labor. The cost of production using nonunion labor will then set an upper limit for the price of the final product after vertical control.[10]

Even if the union has effective control over labor supply, however, the imposition of vertical control could involve enforcement costs. If a strike is necessary, the union will incur, over the contract period, a cost in foregone earnings. These costs can be expected to be greater the greater the loss to employers in reduced profits. Recognition of these costs results in an additional constraint on the extent of attempted vertical control.[11]

Having specified the objective function and constraints, we proceed first to set out the simplest form of the union model, assuming a Cobb-Douglas production function with constant returns to scale.[12] The model is then generalized to a CES production function, nonunion labor and enforcement costs are introduced, and the model is applied to union vertical control in coal mining.

UNION VERTICAL CONTROL WITH A COBB-DOUGLAS PRODUCTION FUNCTION

Assume a Cobb-Douglas production function with constant returns to scale:

$$X = YL^{\delta}K^{(1-\delta)} \tag{6.1}$$

where X = final good, L = unionized labor, K = capital (or other inputs), Y = efficiency parameter, and $0 < \delta < 1$.

Assume also a constant-elasticity demand function for the final product of the form:

$$X = Z/P_x^{\eta} \tag{6.2}$$

where $Z > 0$, $\eta > 1$.

The X industry is assumed competitive, setting price equal to marginal cost:

$$P_x = M_x = \frac{P_l^{\delta}P_k{}^{(1-\delta)}}{Y\delta^{\delta}(1-\delta)^{(1-\delta)}} \tag{6.3}$$

where M_x = marginal cost of X, P_l = wage rate, and P_k = rental price of capital.

Assume also a constant-elasticity supply function for K of the form:

$$K = H P_k^e \tag{6.4}$$

where $H > 0$, and e = elasticity of supply of K. Using Equations (6.1) through (6.4), we can solve for the derived-demand curve for labor before vertical control:

$$L = C/P_l^E \tag{6.5}$$

where E, the elasticity of dervied demand for labor, is given by:

$$E = \frac{\eta + e + \delta e(\eta - 1)}{\eta + e - \delta(\eta - 1)}$$

and, for convenience:

$$C = Z^{(E-1)/\delta(\eta-1)}\, Y^{(E-1)/\delta}$$

$$\delta^E (1 - \delta)^{(E-1)e(1-\delta)/\delta(1+e)}\, H^{(E-1)(1-\delta)/\delta(1+e)}$$

Facing (6.5), the union chooses the wage-employment combination (P_l, L) where the demand curve for labor is tangent to the union's highest indifference curve. If the union decides to exert vertical control, it can choose any one of the forms mentioned earlier. The analysis of vertical control in two such forms, a royalty or a tax on output (as in the United Mine Workers case), and a tax on capital (or profit-sharing agreement) will be presented here. The union's choice between alternative forms of vertical control would appear to depend mainly on transactions, enforcement, and information costs. In the absence of such costs, all forms of vertical control can produce identical results. Uncertainty, technical change, lack of precise technical information, and problems of specification and control lead one to expect that vertical control through a price mechanism, such as output taxes, would be considerably more efficient than direct-control measures such as wage-employment agreements or setting labor-capital ratios. Over time, direct controls can lead to a degree of inefficiency that approximates simple work-sharing. This appears to have happened in West Coast longshoring, and helps to explain the union's willingness to replace the existing work rules with more efficient forms of work-sharing, such as leisure, combined with output royalties. On the other hand, all labor earnings are in the form of wage payments if direct-control measures are used. As we shall see, the use of output royalties (and, to a lesser extent, taxes on capital or an equivalent profit-sharing agreement) reduces direct wage payments and may require the channeling of a significant share of earnings through a union or outside organization.

Tax on Output

Assume that the union imposed an ad valorem royalty or tax, t_x, on the final product. Earnings per worker will then be the new wage rate, $\overline{P}_l$, plus each worker's share of the tax receipts, $t_x\overline{P}_x\overline{X}/\overline{L}$:

$$W = \overline{P}_l + \frac{t_x\overline{P}_x\overline{X}}{\overline{L}} \tag{6.6}$$

With $\sigma = 1$, competition in the X industry, and constant returns to scale, wage earnings are a constant share of the after-tax value of sales of X:

$$\overline{P}_l\overline{L} = \delta(1 - t_x)\overline{P}_x\overline{X} \tag{6.7}$$

Substituting (6.7) into (6.6):

$$W = \overline{P}_l\left(1 + \frac{t_x}{\delta(1 - t_x)}\right) \tag{6.8}$$

After the tax is imposed, firms set the marginal cost of producing X equal to their net price, after tax, of X. Thus we must replace Equation (6.3) with:

$$\overline{M}_x = \frac{\overline{P}_l^{\delta}\overline{P}_k^{(1-\delta)}}{Y\delta^{\delta}(1 - \delta)^{(1-\delta)}} = (1 - t_x)\overline{P}_x \tag{6.9}$$

Using Equations (6.1), (6.2), (6.4) and (6.9), we can solve for the demand for labor after vertical control:

$$\overline{L} = \frac{(1 - t_x)^{(E-1)\eta/(\eta-1)\delta}C}{\overline{P}_l^{E}} \tag{6.10}$$

To characterize the optimal tax rate for the union, we calculate the critical points of the Lagrangian W_λ of (6.8) subject to (6.10):

$$W_\lambda = \overline{P}_l\left(1 + \frac{t_x}{\delta(1 - t_x)}\right) + \lambda\,(\overline{L} - (1 - t_x)^{(E-1)\eta/(\eta-1)\delta}\, C\overline{P}_l^{\,-E}) \tag{6.11}$$

We then solve for the optimal tax rate:

$$t_x = \frac{\eta + e}{\eta(1 + e)} \tag{6.12}$$

Substituting (6.12) into (6.8):

$$W = \frac{\overline{P}_l(1 + 1/e)}{(1 - 1/E)} \tag{6.13}$$

Substituting (6.13) into (6.10), we thus arrive at the new demand for labor as a function of earnings per worker:

$$\overline{L} = \frac{C(1 - 1/\eta)^{\eta(1+e)/[\eta+e-\delta(\eta-1)]}}{W^E(1 - 1/E)^E(1 + 1/e)^{(\eta-1)e(1-\delta)/[\eta+e-\delta(\eta-1)]}} \tag{6.14}$$

Tax on Capital

Before proceeding further, we would like to show that an expression identical to Equation (6.14) can also be derived if we assume that the union places a tax on capital, t_k. Equation (6.8) is now:

$$W = \overline{P}_l + \frac{t_k\overline{P}_k\overline{K}}{\overline{L}} \tag{6.15}$$

or:

$$W = \frac{\overline{P}_l(\delta + t_k)}{\delta(1 + t_k)} \tag{6.16}$$

Equation (6.10) becomes:

$$\overline{L} = \frac{C}{\overline{P}_l^E(1 + t_k)^{(E-1)e(1-\delta)/\delta(1+e)}} \tag{6.17}$$

Using the Lagrangian of (6.16) subject to (6.17), we solve for the optimal tax on capital:

$$t_k = \frac{\eta + e}{e(\eta - 1)} \tag{6.18}$$

Substituting (6.18) into (6.16):

$$W = \frac{\overline{P}_l(1 - 1/\eta)}{(1 - 1/E)} \tag{6.19}$$

Substituting (6.19) into (6.17) then gives us equation (6.14) once again. Thus if vertical control is in the form of an optimal tax on capital (essentially a tying arrangement), the resulting demand curve will be the same as when vertical control is in the form of an optimal tax on output. The same demand curve could also have been arrived at by a union setting the labor-capital or labor-output ratio as well as fixing the wage rate, or by a union setting both the wage level and the absolute level of employment. In this model the only difference between these forms of vertical control is in the share of workers' earnings received in direct wage payments. If the union sets the wage rate and the labor-capital (or labor-output) ratio, all of labor's earnings are in the form of direct wage payments. From comparison of Equations (6.13) and (6.19) it is clear the union members receive a larger share of their earnings in direct wage payments if the tax is on capital then if the tax is on output:

$$\frac{(\overline{P}_l/W)_k}{(\overline{P}_l/W)_x} = \frac{(1 + 1/e)}{(1 - 1/\eta)} > 1 \tag{6.20}$$

The optimal tax rate on capital, however, will be greater than the optimal tax rate on output. From Equations (6.12) and (6.18):

$$\frac{t_k}{t_x} = \frac{\eta e + \eta}{\eta e - e} > 1 \tag{6.21}$$

Thus one form of vertical control may be preferred to another form if union members or leaders are not indifferent as to the relative components of union member earnings. Since tax payments can be expected to be channeled through the union organization, a union with a powerful leadership (such as the United Mine Workers Union[13] or the Teamsters Union), or a leadership particularly trusted by members, would be more likely to choose an output tax, while a union with a more democratic structure might choose to exert vertical control in the form of profit-sharing or the setting of work rules. In addition, tax revenue—by tradition or law—might be assignable only to particular uses,[14] such as a Welfare and Retirement Fund in the UMW case. Such a restriction on the use of tax receipts may result in a union choosing a higher wage rate and a lower tax rate than will maximize W, and thus choosing a (W,L) combination on a demand curve to the left of the maximum demand curve.

Effect of Vertical Control on Earnings and Employment

We can now solve for the proportion by which the demand curve has shifted. Suppose that the union decides to take all its gains from vertical control in increased earnings per worker, leaving employment constant (vertical wage-preference path). Using Equations (6.5) and (6.14), and setting $L = \bar{L}$, we can solve for the ratio of earnings per worker after vertical control, to earnings per worker before vertical control:

$$R_{W:L=\bar{L}} = \left(\frac{W}{P_l}\right)_{L=\bar{L}}$$

$$= \frac{(1 - 1/\eta^{\eta(1+e)/[\eta+e+\delta e(\eta-1)]}}{(1 - 1/E)(1 + 1/e)^{(\eta-1)e(1-\delta)/[\eta+e+\delta e(\eta-1)]}} > 1 \tag{6.22}$$

where:

$$\frac{\partial R_{W:L=\bar{L}}}{\partial \delta} < 0$$

$$\frac{\partial R_{W:L=\bar{L}}}{\partial e} < 0$$

$$\frac{\partial R_{W:L=\bar{L}}}{\partial \eta} < 0$$

Thus the less elastic the supply of other inputs, the less elastic the demand for the final product, or the lower the share of labor costs in total costs, the greater is the proportion by which earnings per worker can be increased. Solving for the values of $R_{W:L=\bar{L}}$ as η, δ, and e reach their limit values:

$$\lim_{\delta \to 1} R_{W:L=\bar{L}} = 1$$

$$\lim_{\delta \to 0} R_{W:L=\bar{L}} = \infty$$

$$\lim_{e \to \infty} R_{W:L=\bar{L}} = \frac{(1 - 1/\eta)^{\eta/E}}{(1 - 1/E)} > 1$$

which approaches unity as a lower limit as $\eta \to \infty$ or as $\delta \to 1$, and approaches $1/\delta$ as $\eta \to 1$.

$$\lim_{e \to 0} R_{W:L=\bar{L}} = \frac{1}{\delta}$$

$$\lim_{\eta \to 1} R_{W:L=\bar{L}} = \frac{1}{\delta}$$

$$\lim_{\eta \to \infty} R_{W:L=\bar{L}} = \frac{1 + \delta e}{\delta (1 + e)(1 + 1/e)^{e(1-\delta)/(1+\delta e)}} > 1$$

which approach unity as $e \to \infty$, and approaches $1/\delta$ as $e \to 0$. Thus vertical control will always enable the union to increase earnings per worker, at the previous level of employment, unless *both* the elasticity of final demand *and* the elasticity of supply of other inputs are infinite. The maximum proportion by which earnings can be increased, $1/\delta$, results as *either* the elasticity of final demand becomes unity (its assumed lower limit) *or* the elasticity of supply of other inputs approaches zero. Because vertical control enables the union to act both as a monopolist in the final-product market and as a monopsonist toward other input suppliers, vertical control can be effective even when the price of the final product cannot be raised.

Similarly, if the union chooses to take all gains in increased employment, we can again use Equations (6.5) and (6.14) to solve for the maximum increase in employment with $W = P_l$:

$$R_{L:W=P_l} = \left(\frac{\bar{L}}{L}\right)_{W=P_l}$$

$$= \frac{(1 - 1/\eta)^{\eta(1+e)/[\eta+e-\delta(\eta-1)]}}{(1 - 1/E)^{E}(1 + 1/e)^{(\eta-1)e(1-\delta)/[\eta+e-\delta(\eta-1)]}}$$

$$= (R_{W:L=\bar{L}})^{E} > 1 \qquad (6.23)$$

Using these results we can now begin to show the relationship between vertical control by a utility-maximizing union and vertical control by a profit-maximizing firm. Assume that a profit-maximizing firm produces good L with a constant-elasticity marginal-cost function, and faces the downstream production, demand, and cooperant input supply conditions given by Equations (6.1) through (6.4). We can then solve (see Equation A.17 in Appendix A) for the ratio of the level of monopoly profits achievable through a monopoly over L to the level of monopoly profits achievable if the firm integrates downstream into the production of X:

$$R_{\Pi} = \frac{\bar{\Pi}}{\Pi} = \frac{(1 - 1/\eta)[1/(1 - 1/\eta) - \delta/(1 + 1/g) - (1 - \delta)/(1 + 1/e)]}{\delta\left(1 - \dfrac{(1 - 1/E)}{(1 + 1/g)}\right)}$$

$$\left(\frac{(1 - 1/\eta)^{g(e+\delta)+e(1-\delta)}}{(1 - 1/E)^{\delta g(1+e)}(1 + 1/e)^{e(1-\delta)(1+g)}}\right)^{(\eta-1)/[\eta(\delta e+g+1-\delta g)+g(\delta+e)+e(1-\delta)]} > 1 \qquad (6.24)$$

where g is the elasticity of the marginal-cost curve for the monopolized input.

As $g \to \infty$, Equation (6.24) reduces to Equation (6.23); and as $g \to 0$, Equation (6.24) reduces to Equation (6.22). Thus if a union takes all gains in increased employment, the percentage increase in employment is equal to the percentage increase in profits made by an integrating firm with constant costs for the monopolized input. And if a union takes all gains in earnings per worker, the percentage increase in earnings per worker is equal to the percentage increase in profits by an integrating firm with a fixed supply of the monopolized input.

Effect of Vertical Control on the Price of the Final Product

Using Equations (6.3) and (6.9), we can solve for the ratio of the price of the final product after vertical control to the price of the final product before vertical control.

$$R_{P_x} = \frac{\overline{P}_x}{P_x} = \left(\frac{\overline{P}_l}{P_l}\right)^{\delta} \left(\frac{\overline{P}_k}{P_k}\right)^{(1-\delta)} \left(\frac{1}{(1-t_x)}\right) \tag{6.25}$$

Using Equation (6.4) and the constant-shares (after tax) characteristic of the Cobb-Douglas production function, we can derive:

$$P_k = \left[\frac{(1-\delta)P_l L}{\delta H}\right]^{1/(1+e)} \tag{6.26}$$

and

$$\overline{P}_k = \left[\frac{(1-\delta)\overline{P}_l \overline{L}}{\delta H}\right]^{1/(1+e)} \tag{6.27}$$

If we substitute P_k from (6.26), $\overline{P}_k$ from (6.27), P_l from (6.5), $\overline{P}_l$ from (6.10), and t_x from (6.12) into equation (6.25):

$$R_{P_x} = \left[\frac{L}{\overline{L}}\right]^{\delta(1+e)/[\eta+e+\delta e(\eta-1)]} \left[\frac{(1+1/e)}{(1-1/\eta)}\right]^{e(1-\delta)/[\eta+e+\delta e(\eta-1)]} \tag{6.28}$$

If the union takes all gains from vertical control in increased earnings per worker, $L = \overline{L}$, and:

$$R_{P_x:L=\overline{L}} = \left[\frac{(1+1/e)}{(1-1/\eta)}\right]^{e(1-\delta)/[\eta+e+\delta e(\eta-1)]} > 1 \tag{6.29}$$

If the union takes all gains from vertical control in increased employment $W = P_l$, and:

$$R_{P_x:W=P_l} = \left[\frac{(1-1/E)^{\delta(1+e)}(1+1/e)^{e(1-\delta)}}{(1-1/\eta)^{(\delta+e)}}\right]^{1/[\eta+e-\delta(\eta-1)]} \lesseqgtr 1 \tag{6.30}$$

In Appendix A, Equation (A.16), we derived the ratio, for $\sigma = 1$, of the price of the final product after vertical control by a firm, to the price of the final product before vertical control by a firm:

$$R_{P_x}_{\sigma=1} = \left[\frac{(1-1/E)^{\delta g(1+e)}(1+1/e)^{e(1-\delta)(g+1)}}{(1-1/\eta)^{g(e+\delta)+e(1-\delta)}} \right]^{1/[\eta(\delta e+g+1-\delta g)+g(\delta+e)+e(1-\delta)]} \tag{6.31}$$

where g was the elasticity of the marginal-cost function for the monopolized input. As $g \to 0$, Equation (6.31) reduces to Equation (6.29). As $g \to \infty$, Equation (6.31) reduces to Equation (6.30). Thus if a utility-maximizing union takes all gains in increased wages, the effect on the price of the final product is the same as if the unit exerting vertical control were a profit-maximizing firm with a fixed supply of the monopolized input. Similarly, vertical control by a utility-maximizing union with a vertical wage-preference path has the same effect on the price of the product as does vertical control by a firm with constant marginal costs in the production of the monopolized input.

Effect of Vertical Control on the Price and Quantity of Capital

Since $\partial R_{P_x}/\partial g < 0$ in Equation (6.31), the price increase resulting from union vertical control will be greater the more the union chooses to take its gains from vertical control in the form of increased earnings rather than increased employment—a result to be expected. What is perhaps less expectable is that it is possible, though unlikely, that vertical control by unions will result in a *fall* in the price of the final product if the supply of K is sufficiently inelastic. To take an extreme case, if $e = 0$, $g \to \infty$, (that is, fixed supply of the cooperant input K, and constant marginal costs for the monopolized input L) then Equation (6.31) reduces to:

$$R_{P_x : W=P_l}_{e=0} = \delta^{\delta/[\delta+\eta(1-\delta)]} < 1 \tag{6.32}$$

In essence, with $e < \infty$, vertical control by the union enables the union effectively to monopsonize nonlabor inputs. If the gain from such monopsonization is sufficiently large, some of that gain may be passed on to consumers of the final product.

In contrast to consumers of the final product, capital (or other cooperant input) suppliers always lose as a result of union vertical control. If the union takes all gains in increased earnings, the effect on the quantity of K is:

$$R_{K:L=\bar{L}} = \left(\frac{\bar{K}}{K}\right)_{L=\bar{L}} = \left[\frac{(1-1/\eta)}{(1+1/e)}\right]^{e\eta/[\eta+e+\delta e(\eta-1)]} < 1 \qquad (6.33)$$

and the effect on the rate of return to capital in the industry is:

$$R_{P_k:L=\bar{L}} = \left[\frac{\bar{P}_k}{P_k}\right]_{L=\bar{L}} = \left[\frac{(1-1/\eta)}{(1+1/e)}\right]^{\eta/[\eta+e+\delta e(\eta-1)]} < 1 \quad (6.34)$$

If the union takes all gains in increased employment:

$$R_{K:W=P_l} = \left(\frac{\bar{K}}{K}\right)_{W=P_l}$$

$$= \left[\frac{(1-1/\eta)^{\eta}}{(1-1/E)^{\delta(\eta-1)}(1+1/e)^{\delta+\eta(1-\delta)}}\right]^{e/[\eta+e-\delta(\eta-1)]} < 1 \qquad (6.35)$$

$$R_{P_k:W=P_l} = \left(\frac{\bar{P}_k}{P_k}\right)_{W=P_l}$$

$$= \left[\frac{(1-1/\eta)^{\eta}}{(1-1/E)^{\delta(\eta-1)}(1+1/e)^{\delta+\eta(1-\delta)}}\right]^{1/[\eta+e-\delta(\eta-1)]} < 1 \qquad (6.36)$$

While capital suppliers always lose as a result of union vertical control, their losses are lessened if the union takes its gains in increased employment ($R_{P_k:L=\bar{L}} > R_{P_k:W=P_l}$).

As expected, Equations (6.34) and (6.36) also result as $g \to 0$ and as $g \to \infty$, respectively, in Equation (A.18) of Appendix A.

The effects of optimal vertical control by a union on the labor, capital, and output markets are illustrated in Figure 6–2, which assumes $\eta = e = 2$, $\sigma = 1$, and $\delta = 1/4$. For ease of exposition, initial equilibrium input and output prices have been set at unity by assuming $Y = (4/3)^{0.75}$, $Z = 4$, $H = 3$, and $P_l = 1$. Facing the initial demand curve for labor, LL in Figure 6–2 (Equation (6.5)), the union chooses

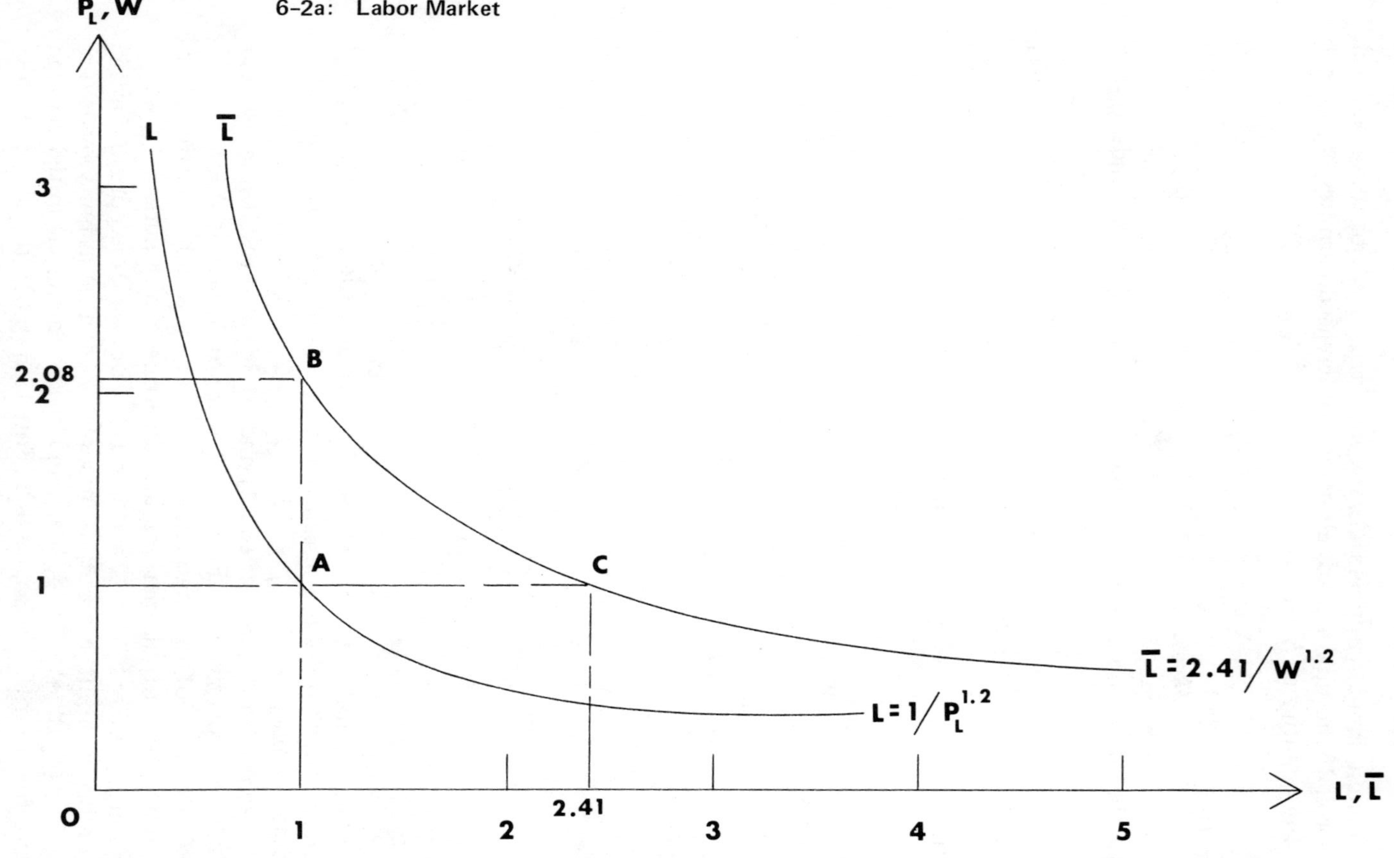

Figure 6-2. Effects of Vertical Control by a Labor Union on the Labor, Capital and Output Markets, Assuming $\eta = e = 2$, $\sigma = 1$, $\delta = 1/4$

6-2b: Capital Market

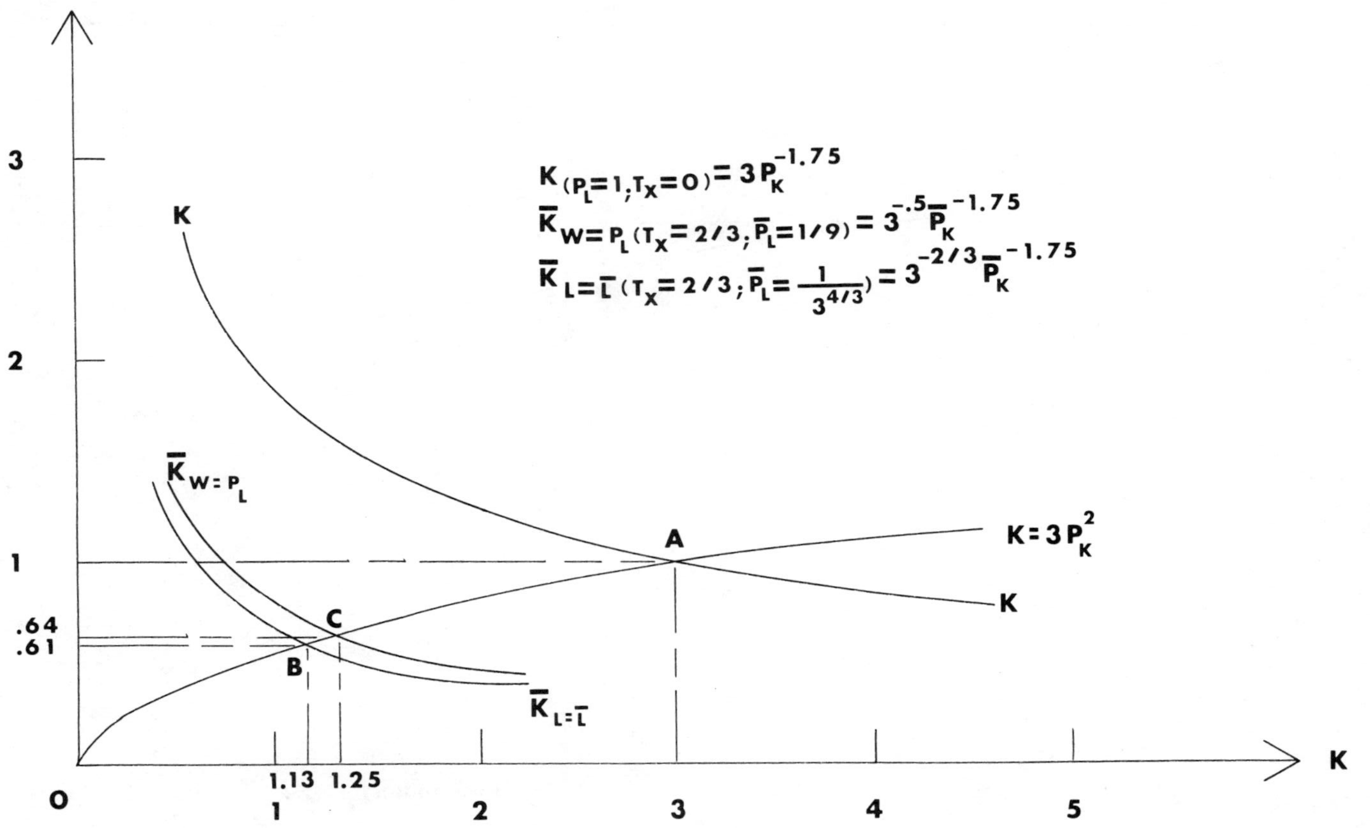

P_K
3
2
1
.64
.61
O
1
2
3
4
5
1.13
1.25
K
$K_{(P_L=1;\,T_X=0)} = 3P_K^{-1.75}$
$\overline{K}_{W=P_L}(T_X=2/3;\,\overline{P}_L=1/9) = 3^{-.5}\overline{P}_K^{-1.75}$
$\overline{K}_{L=\overline{L}}(T_X=2/3;\,\overline{P}_L=\frac{1}{3^{4/3}}) = 3^{-2/3}\overline{P}_K^{-1.75}$
K
$\overline{K}_{W=P_L}$
$K=3P_K^2$
A
K
C
B
$\overline{K}_{L=\overline{L}}$

6-2c: Output Market

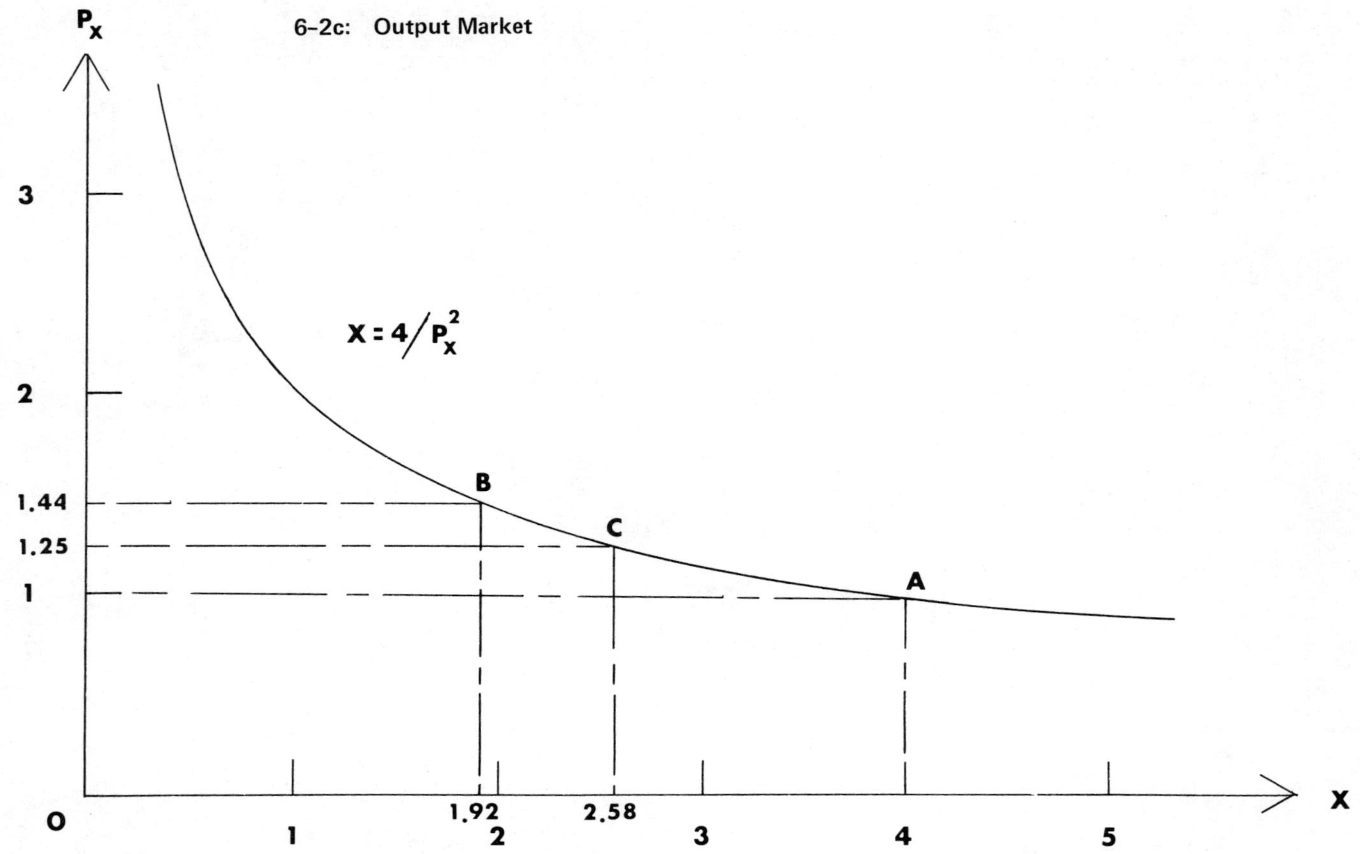

point a, resulting in $P_l = P_k = P_x = 1$. With an optimal tax ($t_x = 2/3$, from Equation (6.12)), the labor-demand curve, with earnings per worker from wages and tax revenue on the vertical axis, shifts out to $\overline{LL}$ (Equation (6.14)). Since, ceteris paribus, the output effect of a royalty would reduce the quantity of labor demanded, a reduction in the wage rate is necessary if the quantity of labor demanded is to remain constant or increase after vertical control. In this example, if the wage rate is reduced to $P_l = 3^{-4/3} \cong 0.23$, the output and substitution effects on the quantity of labor demanded will just balance the output effect of the royalty on the quantity of labor demanded. Since the gain in royalty revenue more than compensates for the fall in wage income, the net result is a movement to point b in Figure 6–2a, with a 108 percent increase in earning per worker at the same level of employment (Equation (6.22)). In the capital market (Figure 6–2b), the net effect of the royalty and the lower wage rate is a leftward shift in the demand schedule for capital,[15] resulting in a 39 percental fall in the price of the cooperant input (Equation (6.34)) and a 62 percent reduction in the quantity demanded (Equation (6.33)). In the output market (Figure 6–2c), the net effect of the output royalty and the reduction in both input prices is a 44 percent increase in the price of the final product (Equation (6.29)).

Alternatively, if the union takes all the gains from vertical control in increased employment, with no change in earnings per worker, it can move to point c in Figure 6–2a by further reducing the wage rate to $P_l = 1/9 \cong 0.11$. As compared with the situation before vertical control, this would result in a 140 percent increase in employment, with no change in earnings per worker (Equation (6.23)); a 36 percent reduction in the price of capital (Equation (6.36)) and a 68 percent fall in the quantity of capital demanded (Equation (6.35)), and a 25 percent increase in the price of the final product (Equation (6.30)).

GENERALIZATION TO A CES PRODUCTION FUNCTION

The model can be further generalized by the substitution of a general CES production function of the form

$$X = Y\left[\delta L^{(\sigma-1)/\sigma} + (1-\delta)K^{(\sigma-1)/\sigma}\right]^{\sigma/(\sigma-1)} \quad Y > 0,\ 0 < \delta < 1,\ 0 < \sigma < \infty \tag{6.37}$$

in place of the Cobb-Douglas production function. If the union has a vertical wage-preference path, the correspondence between the effects of vertical control by a union, and the effects of vertical control by a profit-maximizing firm with fixed supply of the monopolized input, still holds. The analogy between a union taking all gains in increased employment and a firm with constant marginal costs for the monopolized input, however, breaks down with $\sigma \neq 1$. This latter identity held in the $\sigma = 1$ case because the constant-shares characteristic of Cobb-Douglas meant that, with constant η and e, the elas-

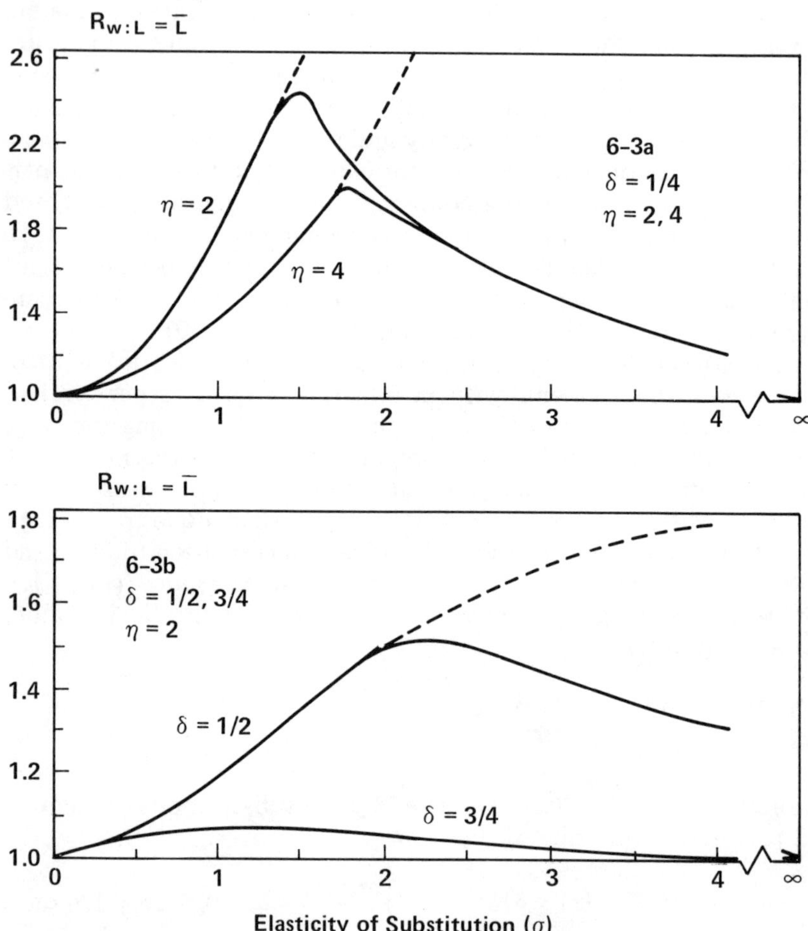

Figure 6-3. Ratio of Earnings per Worker after Vertical Control to Earnings per Worker before Vertical Control, Holding Employment Constant, as a Function of the Elasticity of Substitution.

ticity of derived demand for labor:

$$E = \frac{\sigma(\eta + e) + k_l e(\eta - \sigma)}{(\eta + e) - k_l(\eta - \sigma)}$$

is the same along the new demand curve after vertical control as along the old demand curve. If $\sigma > 1$, E falls after vertical control, while if $\sigma < 1$, E increases. With $\sigma > \eta$, the fall in E is sufficient to result in a fall in the quantity of the monopolized input sold by a profit-maximizing firm with constant marginal costs (see Chapter 5). Thus with $\sigma > 1$, the effect of a union taking some or all gains in increased employment would correspond to profit-maximization with an implicit marginal-cost schedule that was upward-sloping. With $\sigma < 1$, the implicit marginal-cost curve would be downward-sloping. Thus compared to a firm with constant marginal costs, the union taking some or all of its gains in increased employment will cause a larger increase in the price of the final product if $\sigma < 1$, and a smaller increase in the price of the final product if $\sigma > 1$.

Simulation results for the CES case reveal an expectable pattern. Figure 6–3 shows the relationship between the elasticity of substitution and the effect of vertical control on earnings per worker, holding employment constant, for different values for η and δ. The effect on earnings rises from zero at $\sigma = 0$, reaches a maximum at some $\sigma > 1$ and falls again to zero as σ approaches infinity. The possible gains from vertical control are clearly very sensitive to the values assumed for η and δ. With low values for η and δ, and with σ roughly between 1.0 and 2.0, the gains from vertical control can be substantial, even when, as in these simulation, $e \to \infty$. so no monopsony gain occurs. Note that in three of the four cases, the P_x constraint eventually becomes effective at some $\sigma > 1$, reducing the earnings effect from the values shown by the dashed lines to those shown by the solid lines in Figure 6–3.

NONUNION LABOR CONSTRAINT

In many cases the power of a union to increase labor costs to firms may be effectively constrained by the existence of nonunion labor. If the union forces the cost of unionized labor up too far, new firms using nonunion labor may enter the industry, or existing firms may switch over to nonunion labor.

Suppose that the effective constraint is the possible entry of new nonunion firms rather than the use of nonunion labor by existing firms. Assume also that entry will occur if the price of the final product reaches some level $\hat{P}_x$. The demand curve for union labor before vertical control is then kinked at a corresponding wage rate $\hat{P}_l$, where, from Equation (6.3),

$$\hat{P}_l = \left[\frac{\hat{P}_x Y \delta^{\delta} (1-\delta)^{(1-\delta)}}{P_k^{(1-\delta)}} \right]^{1/\delta} \tag{6.38}$$

For existing firms, $\eta \to \infty$ at $\hat{P}_x$. The elasticity of derived demand for unionized labor at $\hat{P}_l$, however, is not infinite unless $e \to \infty$:

$$\underset{\eta \to \infty}{E} = \frac{1 + \delta e}{1 - \delta} > 1 \tag{6.39}$$

Since unionized firms cannot pass on any increase in labor costs above $\hat{P}_l$ to consumers, any such increase is at the expense of quasi-rents received by unionized capital suppliers. As P_l rises above $\hat{P}_l$, the marginal-cost schedule for X shifts upward for unionized firms, and output by unionized firms falls until P_k falls sufficiently to offset the increase in labor costs.

The kink in the demand curve for unionized labor before vertical control also results in a kink in the demand curve after vertical control, as illustrated in Figure 6-4. Suppose that before vertical control the union has chosen some wage rate greater than $\hat{P}_l$. The union would then be on section DG of its demand curve, above the kink. Over this range, $\eta \to \infty$ for unionized firms. The maximum increase in earnings per worker, holding employment constant, will then be given by the limit of Equation (6.22) as $\eta \to \infty$. Even if the union had chosen a wage rate below $\hat{P}_l$, however, the price of the final product may reach $\hat{P}_x$ before vertical control is fully achieved. Suppose that the union has chosen a wage rate between $\hat{P}_l$ and P_l' on section GJ of its demand curve. The price of X before vertical control would then be less than $\hat{P}_x$, but the price of X will reach $\hat{P}_x$ before vertical control is fully achieved. Vertical control will thus raise the price of the final product, but the increase will be less than that given by Equation (6.19), and the increase in earnings per worker will be correspondingly lessened. The full increase in P_x and W will be possible only if the union had originally chosen a wage rate less than P_l' on section JD' of its demanded curve.

The nonunion labor constraint is effective over a lesser range if the union takes all its gains in increased employment. As before, the constraint is completely effective over the DG range, where the

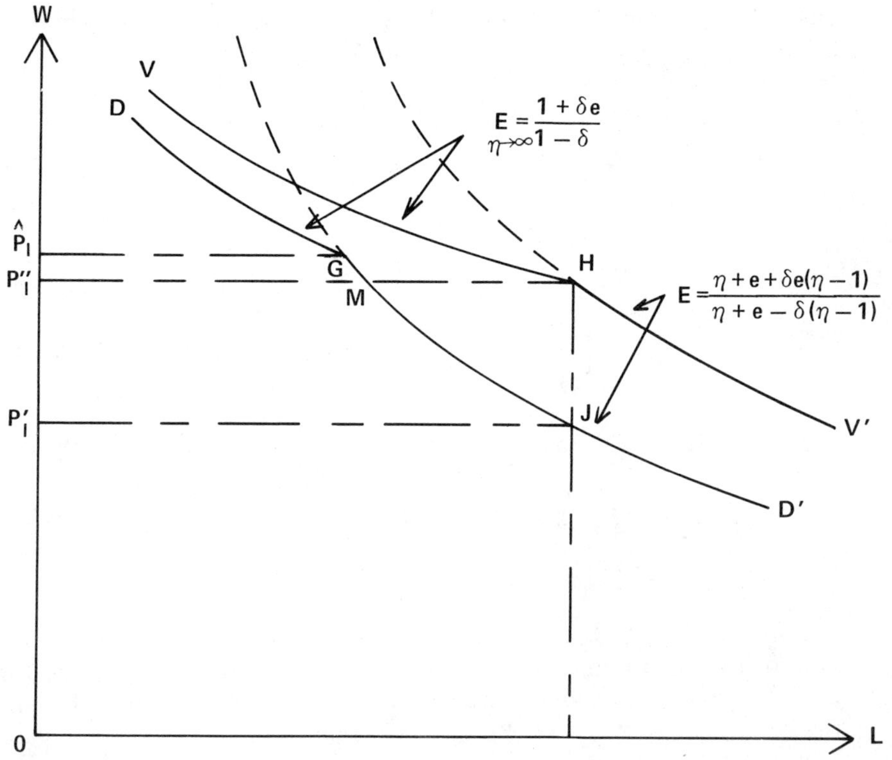

Figure 6-4. Nonunion Labor Constraint: Entrants

maximum increase in employment is given by the limit of Equation (6.23) as $\eta \to \infty$. The range over which the constraint is partially effective, however, is now only GM, and the constraint is completely noneffective over the range MD'. We would therefore expect that nonunion labor poses a lesser threat to unions using vertical control to increase employment.

A clear implication of this analysis is that regulatory or statutory restrictions on entry at the product level, or governmental subsidies, should strongly encourage vertical control by unions in these industries. Removal of such restrictions or subsidies can then be expected to reduce union resistance to, or even result in union support for, mechanization or technical change increasing labor productivity.[16] The U.S. postal and maritime industries may be good examples.

The range over which the nonunion labor constraint is partially effective can be determined explicitly. If the union takes all gains in increased earnings per workers, we can solve for $\hat{P}_l/P_l'$ in Figure 6-4 by setting $R_{px}:L = \bar{L}$ (from Equation (6.29)) equal to $\hat{R}_{px}$:

$$\left[\frac{(1+1/e)}{(1-1/\eta)}\right]^{e(1-\delta)/[\eta+e+\delta e(\eta-1)]} = \left[\frac{\hat{P}_l}{P_l'}\right]^{\delta(1+e)/[\eta+e-\delta(\eta-1)]} \tag{6.40}$$

or:

$$\frac{\hat{P}_l}{P_l'} = \left[\frac{(1+1/e)}{(1-1/\eta)}\right]^{e(1-\delta)/E\delta(1+e)} \tag{6.41}$$

Similarly, if the union takes all gains in increased employment:

$$\frac{\hat{P}_l}{P_l''} = \frac{(1-1/E)(1+1/e)^{e(1-\delta)/\delta(1+e)}}{(1-1/\eta)^{(\delta+e)/\delta(1+e)}} \tag{6.42}$$

The union would be in a worse position if existing firms could switch to nonunion labor when $P_l > \hat{P}_l$. The demand curve for unionized labor is then infinitely elastic at $\hat{P}_l$. If the union has already chosen a wage of $\hat{P}_l$, then vertical control cannot increase earnings per worker, and any increase in employment must come at the cost of a reduction in earnings per worker sufficient to keep the return to the cooperant input constant. In Figure 6-5, *DGD'* is the demand curve for unionized labor before vertical control, and *DGHV'* is the demand curve for labor after vertical control, where the return to capital is constant at $\hat{P}_k$ along segment *GH*. Since the return to the cooperant input is the same at *G* as at *H*, we can solve for $\hat{P}_l/P_l'$ and $\hat{P}_l/P_l''$ by setting $\hat{R}_{pk} = R_{pk}$. Using Equation (6.34):

$$\frac{\hat{P}_k}{P_k} = \left[\frac{P_l'}{\hat{P}_l}\right]^{(E-1)/(1+e)} = \left[\frac{(1-1/\eta)}{(1+1/e)}\right]^{\eta/[\eta+e+\delta e(\eta-1)]} \tag{6.43}$$

or

$$\frac{\hat{P}_l}{P_l'} = \left[\frac{(1+1/e)}{(1-1/\eta)}\right]^{\eta/E\delta(\eta-1)} \tag{6.44}$$

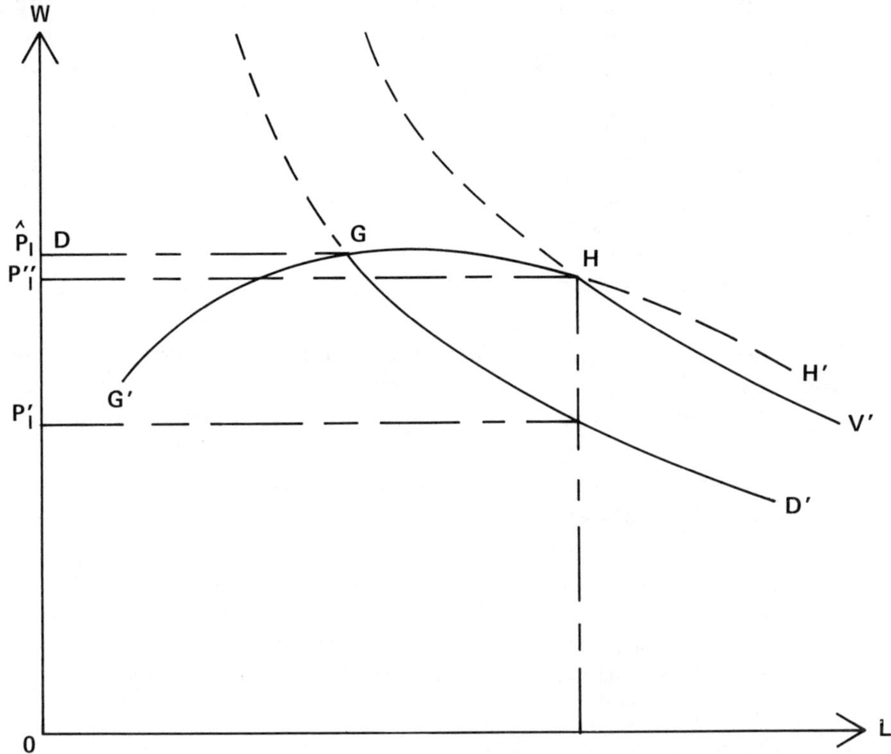

Figure 6-5. Nonunion Labor Constraint: Entrants and Existing Firms.

Similarly, using Equation (6.36):

$$\frac{\hat{P}_l}{P''_l} = \frac{(1 - 1/E)(1 + 1/e)^{[\delta + \eta(1-\delta)]/\delta(\eta-1)}}{(1 - 1/\eta)^{\eta/\delta(\eta-1)}} \tag{6.45}$$

As expected, $\hat{P}_l/P'_l$ and $\hat{P}_l/P''_l$ are greater if existing firms would switch to nonunion labor at $\hat{P}_l$ (Equations (6.44) and (6.45)), than if only new entrants would use nonunionized labor (Equations (6.41) and (6.42)).

As Figure 6-5 shows, the union cannot increase both employment and earnings per worker unless a higher wage rate was achievable before vertical control, but was not chosen due to the consequences for employment. If the union has a sufficiently strong preference for increased earnings per worker (so that the indifference curve through G does not cut the $DGHV'$ curve), vertical control will be useless to the union. An unexploited ability to further raise wages before vertical control would only be unimportant in the unlikely event that a point on section HV' is preferred by the union to any point on section GH.

Since unexploited ability to raise wages is crucial to union vertical control, we now turn to a second possible constraint on a union's ability to raise wages—resistance by employers to union wage demands.

ENFORCEMENT COSTS

Up to this point we have implicitly assumed that the union had the power to choose any wage-employment combination on its derived-demand curve. In many cases, however, a union is forced to strike in order to enforce its desired wage. Enforcing a labor monopoly may thus involve fixed costs over the contract period which the union must take into consideration.

> For some problems, it does no harm to assume that monopolizing is costless. But for others . . . it is essential to assume that monopolizing is an expensive business in which the costs of driving the wage rate above (the competitive level) may in some cases increase rapidly as the wage rate increases. [Lewis, 1959, p. 196].

The cost of enforcing the desired wage rate clearly depends on a number of variables. Employers' resistance to union demands should depend on their perceptions of the extent to which profits will be reduced if they agree to the union demand, as compared to withstanding a strike. These perceptions will also be conditioned by such factors as management's attitude toward the union, their expectations of the effect of this decision on future demands by the union, their estimate of the ability and willingness of the union to undergo a lengthy strike, and the degree to which employers bargain collectively. If a union faces enforcement costs in moving up the demand curve for labor, it can also expect to incur enforcement costs if it attempts vertical control. For our purposes we are interested in any difference in the nature of enforcement costs when the union utilizes a vertical-control strategy.[17]

Vertical control by unions, particularly in the form of work rules, may be especially resisted by firms which believe such rules infringe on the functions and powers of management and hinder rapid adjustment to changing conditions. Agreements that specify both the wage and the quantity of employment may be resisted because they impose particular risks on employers. Where public opinion is an important element in bargaining, union demands that can be interpreted as featherbedding may be difficult to support, and may even lack legitimacy in the eyes of the union. While all these factors may affect the enforcement costs of vertical control, they are difficult to introduce into a general model. The most important determinant of employer resistance, however, is probably the effect of union demands on the level of firm profits. As we have already seen from Equations (6.33) through (6.36), vertical control by a union reduces the equilibrium amount of capital in the industry and, assuming $e < \infty$, reduces the rate of return to capital. In effect, vertical control enables the union to substitute a tax on capital for a tax on labor. The union thus gains both monopoly power over the sale, and monopsony power over the purchase, of the cooperant input. Suppliers of the cooperant input have, therefore, a very strong incentive to resist union vertical control in any form.

In general, therefore, we would expect that vertical control will be attempted mainly by strong unions facing relatively weak opposition. This implies that vertical control would be observed more in competitive industries, where individual employers are less able to resist union pressures, than in an oligopolistic industries, where firms are larger and financially stronger and where the limited number of firms facilitates a unified stand toward the union (see Levinson, 1967). On the other hand, a competitive industry structure implies that entry into the industry is relatively easy, and this may increase the importance of the nonunion labor constraint. Thus, in an industry with high barriers:

> A union, once firmly established within all or a large proportion of the existing firms in the industry, is more able to maintain its jurisdictional control against threat of erosion by the establishment of new nonunion firms and hence (other things equal) can press more aggressively for greater wage adjustments. By contrast, a competitive product market implies a much greater ease of entry of new firms as well as a much higher degree of plant mobility among existing concerns, both of which contribute to a gradual erosion of union jurisdictional control and to a lowered ability to obtain wage gains. [Levinson, 1967, p. 201]

While strong opposition by employers may effectively limit the ability of a union to enforce vertical control, two further points should be considered. First, we have assumed a two-factor model, where K can be a composite of all other inputs. Ceteris paribus, the less elastic the supply of these inputs, the greater is both the union's potential gain from vertical control (Equation (6.22)), and the expected enforcement costs. Unless the firm facing the union is the owner of all the inputs in noninfinitely elastic supply, however, some or all of the losses to cooperant inputs, like losses to consumers, will not be incurred by the firm facing the union, and that firm will have a correspondingly lesser incentive to resist union vertical control. For example, if vertical control by a union in the steel industry would result in a reduction in quasi-rents to owners of iron-ore mines, the resistance by steel firms to union vertical control will not be increased by such losses unless the steel firm owns its own ore fields.

The second point is that limited vertical control can be used to increase utility for the union at no cost to the firm. In Figure 6-6

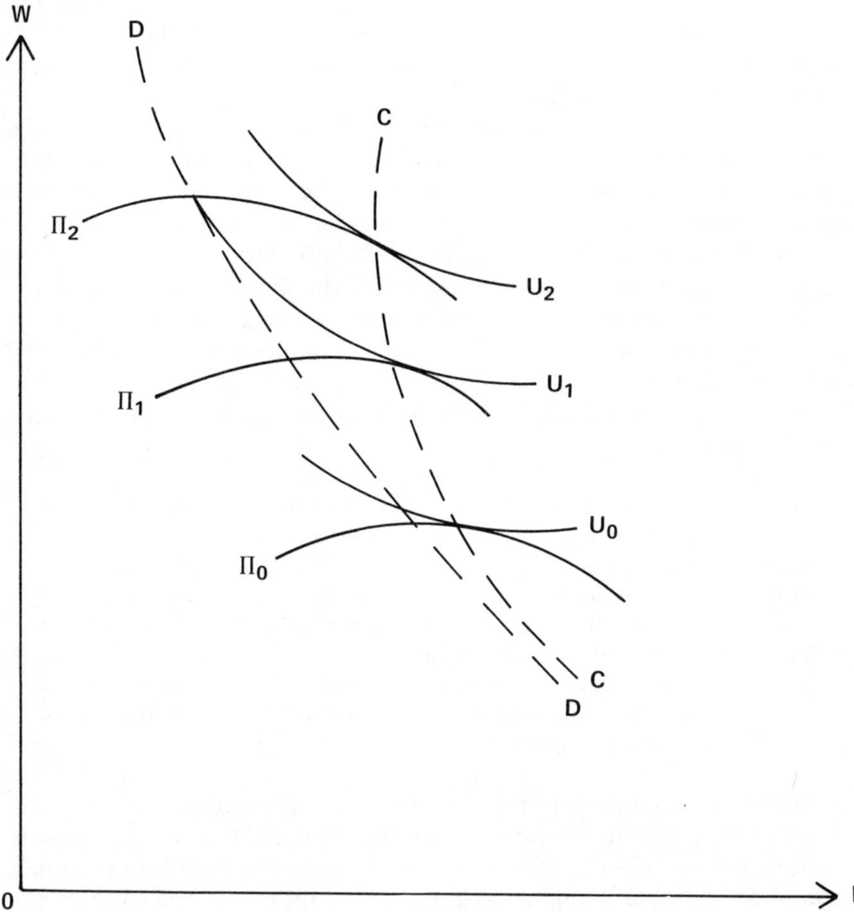

Figure 6-6. Contract Curve for Union and Employer

a set of capital isoprofit curves are drawn. The demand curve for labor, *DD*, is the locus of the high points of each isoprofit curve since, given any wage rate, the level of employment will be chosen that maximizes profits (quasi-rents to capital). Note that unless the union has a fixed-proportions preference mapping, the demand curve for labor is not the contract curve, *CC*.

VERTICAL CONTROL BY THE UNITED MINE WORKERS OF AMERICA

The clearest example of vertical control by a union has been the financing of the United Mine Workers Welfare and Retirement Fund through a royalty on coal output.[18] Royalty payments, which reached $297 million in fiscal 1973/74, have totaled approximately $4 billion since 1950. Over the 1953–1970 period, during which the royalty rate remained at 40¢ per ton, royalties averaged approximately 8.4 percent of the price of coal (f.o.b. mine), 10.9 percent of value-added in coal mines, and 24.1 percent of total wage costs in unionized mines. The UMW has also been relatively successful in raising the wage rates of its members, although at a significant cost in employment. Lewis (1970) estimates that during the 1960s, unionism raised the wage rate of union workers relative to non-union workers by about 65–70 percent, and increased the average wage by about 32–40 percent relative to what wage rates would have been in the absence of the union. During the 1945–1968 period, however, employment (man-days worked) in bituminous coal fell by about 72 percent.

There is general agreement that the elasticity of substitution between labor and capital in bituminous coal production is approximately unity. Maddala (1965, p. 355) estimates $\sigma = 1.04$, while Lewis (1970) estimates $\sigma = 1.15$. Recent work by Goldstein and Smith (1976) shows strong evidence of constant returns to scale, with σ not significantly different from unity for underground mining, and perhaps somewhat greater than unity for surface mining. There is also general agreement that the demand for coal is inelastic. Lewis (1970) assumes that the elasticity of demand for bituminous coal at the mine is in the 0.25 to 0.50 range, while Goldstein and Smith estimate the elasticity of demand for delivered coal to be approximately 0.48 over the 1941–1970 period. Similarly, Reddy's (1975) results using 1971 data for multifuel steam electric-generating plants indicate that the long-run price elasticity of demand for (delivered) steam coal lies in the 0.37 to 0.97 range.

When applied to our model, these estimates imply considerable restraint in the use of vertical control by the UMW. As Equation (6.12) shows, even if $e \to \infty$, the actual royalty rate of 10.9 percent of value-added would have been the optimal rate only if the elasticity of demand for unionized coal at the mine were approximately 9—far higher than any of the available estimates. The low royalty rate may be due to a number of factors.

One possibility is that the elasticity of demand would increase rapidly before the price of coal implied by the "optimal" tax was reached, due to interfuel competition over the upper ranges of the demand schedule. The recent large increases in the price of oil, however, should have shifted any such elastic section significantly upward. A second factor may be the institutional constraint that royalty revenue can be used only for the Welfare and Retirement Fund. The shift in the 1974 contract to a combined output and wage-tax financing formula, however, weakens this argument. A third limiting force may be the threat that a higher output tax might increase the percentage of bituminous coal output produced in nonunion mines significantly above the present 25 to 35 percent level.[19] Finally, the UMW simply may not be fully aware of the advantages it has gained or could gain from its use of an output levy.

Despite its apparent underutilization, the effects of vertical control by the UMW have been quite significant. We begin by separating bituminous coal into underground and surface production.[20] Following Goldstein and Smith (1976), we assume a constant elasticity of demand for all coal at the delivered stage. The split between underground-minded coal, C_u, and surface-minded coal, C_s, is then determined as a function of the relative delivered prices of the two types of coal, $\hat{P}_s$ and $\hat{P}_u$.

$$\frac{C_u}{C_u + C_s} = \alpha \left(\frac{\hat{P}_s}{\hat{P}_u}\right)^{\beta} \tag{6.46}$$

We have no way of knowing the wage rate that would have been set by the union in the absence of the output royalty. We can, however, generate results for any given $P_l/\overline{P}_l$ (the ratio of what the wage rate would have been without the royalty to the actual wage rate with the royalty),[21] and thus trace out the derived-demand curve for labor in the absence of vertical control. Since data on value-added and wages is available only from the Census of Mineral Industries, we are restricted to the years 1954, 1958, 1963, and 1967. A description of the methods used to calculate the parameter values from census data and the derivation of the equations used are provided in

Appendix B. Two assumptions, however, should be noted here. First, we have assumed an infinite elasticity of supply for all cooperant (nonlabor) inputs. To the extent that this elasticity is less than infinite, the quantitative results reported below are an underestimate of the effects of vertical control by the UMW. On the other hand, the only adjustment for the existence of nonunion mines has been to divide the final demand elasticites for underground and surface coal by the fractions of coal produced in unionized underground and surface mines. This assumes that vertical control by the union has not increased the percentage of coal produced in nonunion mines, an assumption that can be expected to result in an overestimate of the effects of vertical control. In the absence of accurate information as to either the elasticity of supply of cooperant inputs or the effect

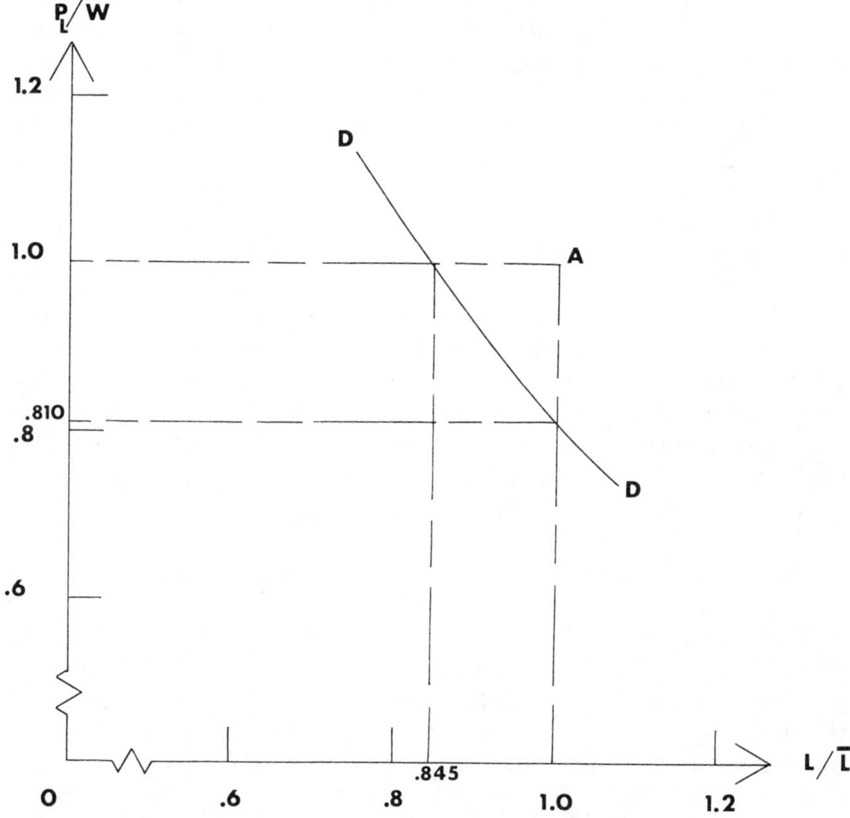

Figure 6-7. The Effect of the Royalty on the Earnings-Employment Level for 1967

of unionization on nonunion shares, it is at least comforting that the two biases act in opposite directions.

The effect of the royalty on the earnings-employment level for 1967 is illustrated in Figure 6-7, where *DD* is the derived-demand curve for union labor in bituminous (underground and surface) coal in the absence of vertical control, and *A* is the actual earnings per worker and employment combination in 1967. If the union had not utilized an output royalty, achieving the actual 1967 level of employment would have required a 19.0 percent cut in earnings per worker. Alternatively, achievement of the actual 1967 level of earnings per worker without the royalty would have resulted in unemployment for 15.5 percent of the 1967 unionized work force.

The effects of vertical control on underground and surface coal production levels, prices, and capital levels depend on the particular point along *DD* the union would have chosen if the UMW Welfare and Retirement Fund had been financed by a wage levy rather than an output royalty. Table 6-1 shows what would have happened if the union had attempted to achieve the actual employment levels in each year without using a royalty. In 1967, for example, earnings per worker would have been 19 percent lower (the net effect of the loss in royalty earnings and an increase of 2 percent in wage rates). While total unionized employment in underground and surface mines would be unchanged, underground-mine employment would have been 1.8 percent lower, and surface-mine employment 11.7 percent higher. The capital stock in underground mines would have been only 0.1 percent higher, but capital in surface mining would have been 13.9 percent greater than the actual stock in 1967. Underground coal production would have been reduced by 0.8 percent, while surface production would have been 13.2 percent higher. Total tonnage (underground and surface, not adjusted for differential BTU content) would have been 3.6 percent higher. Value-added prices would have been 8.3 percent lower for underground coal and 13.6 percent lower for surface coal. Delivered prices would have been 4.8 percent lower for underground coal and 6.6 percent lower for surface coal.

Table 6-2 shows the corresponding effects if the union had attempted to achieve the actual earnings-per-worker levels in each year without using a royalty. It is particularly interesting to note that the resulting fall in employment would have occurred entirely in underground mining, with surface-mining employment actually higher for all years. The results also show that use of an output royalty results in a considerably larger reduction in capital utilization if vertical control is used to increase employment.[22]

Table 6-1. Vertical Control Used To Increase Earnings per Worker ($L = \overline{L}$)

Table 6-2. Vertical Control Used to Increase Employment ($W = P_l$)

	Table 6-1				Table 6-2			
	1954	*1958*	*1963*	*1967*	*1954*	*1958*	*1963*	*1967*
P_l/W	0.853	0.853	0.819	0.810	1.000	1.000	1.000	1.000
$P_l/\overline{P}_l$	1.027	1.021	1.015	1.020	1.203	1.197	1.239	1.259
$L_u/\overline{L}_u$	0.987	0.986	0.981	0.982	0.865	0.864	0.825	0.819
$L_s/\overline{L}_s$	1.136	1.104	1.111	1.117	1.152	1.067	1.017	1.017
$L/\overline{L}$	1.000	1.000	1.000	1.000	0.891	0.888	0.852	0.845
$K_u/\overline{K}_u$	1.013	1.007	0.996	1.001	1.041	1.034	1.022	1.031
$K_s/\overline{K}_s$	1.166	1.128	1.128	1.139	1.386	1.277	1.261	1.281
$C_u/\overline{C}_u$	0.996	0.995	0.989	0.992	0.924	0.936	0.919	0.926
$C_s/\overline{C}_s$	1.154	1.119	1.123	1.132	1.291	1.196	1.179	1.195
$C/\overline{C}$	1.032	1.029	1.036	1.036	1.007	1.007	1.010	1.009
$P_u/\overline{P}_u$	0.913	0.926	0.921	0.917	1.012	1.011	1.017	1.012
$P_s/\overline{P}_s$	0.854	0.875	0.861	0.864	0.907	0.927	0.916	0.921
$\hat{P}_u/\hat{\overline{P}}_u$	0.953	0.959	0.955	0.952	1.006	1.006	1.009	1.007
$\hat{P}_s/\hat{\overline{P}}_s$	0.937	0.945	0.936	0.934	0.961	0.969	0.962	0.963

One intriguing possibility that emerges from these results is that underground coal-mine operators may actually have benefited from the UMW's use of an output royalty. If vertical control has been used to increase employment, Table 6-2 shows that the reduction in the wage rate more than offsets the effect of the output royalty on underground unit costs. Combined with the outward shift of the demand curve for underground coal (due to the increase in the relative price of surface-mined coal), this reduction in underground unit costs results in an approximately 7 percent increase in underground production over the period. If vertical control has been used to increase earnings per worker (Table 6-1), unit costs for underground mines have risen, but the demand shift is still sufficient to result in a marginal increase in underground output. The implication is that as long as the same wage rate and royalty per ton is imposed on all coal mines, underground coal operators as a group (and especially the operators of small underground mines with high labor-output and labor-capital ratios) could well have benefited from the UMW's use of an output royalty.[23]

SUMMARY AND CONCLUSIONS

Restrictive work rules, output taxes, profit-sharing, or other forms of vertical control can be of significant benefit to union members, particularly when the elasticity of demand for the final product, the share of labor in total costs (more precisely, the distribution parameter), and the elasticity of supply of other inputs are all low, while the elasticity of substitution between labor and other inputs is somewhat greater than unity. The effects of such union actions are analytically very similar to the effects of vertical integration, tying arrangements, or other forms of vertical control by firms with market power over a product that can be used in variable proportions as an input by downstream producers. Since estimates of substitution elasticities between capital and labor are usually higher than between commodity and other inputs, however, we would expect vertical control to be more attractive to unions than to firms.

While numerous examples of union vertical control can be observed, the major empirical problem is to explain those cases where vertical control either is not used or is seemingly underutilized. Several explanations are possible. First, the parameter values for σ, η, δ, and e may be such that vertical control would be of little benefit to a particular union. In trucking, for example, the limited degree of vertical control observed may be due to a high elasticity of product demand caused by intermodal competition from railroads (see

Levinson, 1971, p. 76), and a very high elasticity of supply of capital equipment. The result would be similar to the situation depicted in Figure 6-5. A second explanation would involve the threat of entry by non-unionized labor, a problem that has plagued the United Mine Workers. A third reason, strong resistance by employers, has been attributed as the explanation for the 1960 Mechanization and Modernization Agreement in West Coast longshoring (Hartman, 1969, p. 231). In general a union that is unable to move some considerable distance up its derived-demand curve is unlikely to be able to exert a significant degree of vertical control, especially since—as we have seen—vertical control can be particularly expensive to employers. It is interesting to note that there is a close correspondence between unions that have achieved significant wage gains—such as the United Mine Workers and the Air Line Pilots Association (see Lewis, 1963)—and unions that have exerted vertical control.[24]

A last group of explanations could involve uncertainty, non-maximizing behavior, or simply a lack of understanding by unions of the potential gains from vertical control. Ross (1948), for example, has argued that uncertainty about shifts in demand results in unions simply ignoring the employment effects of wage increases. If this is correct,[25] of course, the entire basis for vertical control by unions is eliminated. Uncertainty as to demand shifts may also result in strong resistance by risk-adverse employers to some forms of vertical control—such as wage and employment bargaining—which would effectively impose large fixed costs on employers. Non-maximizing by unions may take the form of satisficing behavior, or an unwillingness to press for "unreasonable" wage or employment levels.[26] In some cases a threshold level of potential unemployment may be necessary before vertical control is attempted. Finally, unions may simply be unaware of the potential gains from vertical control. There is no indication, for example, that the United Mine Workers, either in 1946 or since, has had any real understanding of the superiority of an output royalty to a wage levy as a method of financing the Welfare and Retirement Fund.[27]

Some or all of these factors may explain the degree of vertical control actually observed. On a more normative level it is difficult to make any *a priori* judgments as to welfare effects of vertical control by unions and the desirability or undesirability of public policy to prevent its occurrence.[28] On the one hand, one can regard vertical control by unions as an unwelcome extension of existing monopoly power. On the other hand, in some cases union vertical control—especially when used to increase employment—may be an effective way of improving income distribution,[29] and in a second-best world with unemployment or extensive factor-ratio distortions due to unionization, may even increase efficiency.

NOTES

1. Unions may also perform a productive function as collectors and transmitters of information, providing "a direct channel of communication between workers and management; an alternative mode of expressing discontent than quitting, with consequent reductions in turnover costs and increases in specific training and work conditions; and social relations of production which can mitigate the problems associated with the authority relation in firms" (Freeman, 1976, p. 364). For other works in the "exit-voice" approach to unions, see Williamson (1976) and references cited by both authors.

2. Featherbedding has been broadly defined as "a working rule which causes the firm to hire more labor units of a particular type than it would at the existing wage, assuming technology and social norms to be given" (Weinstein, 1960, p. 379). As an irrelevant aside, the term apparently originated when a yard fireman on the Illinois Central supposedly installed a feather mattress on the left-hand side of his cab sometime during the 1940s (Rehmus, 1971, p. 195).

3. For the argument that the effect of restrictive practices in construction has been relatively minor, however, see Mandelstramm (1965), Bertram and Maisel (1955, p. 66), and Mills (1972, pp. 258–68).

4. For a review of union response to profit-sharing plans, see Helburn (1971).

5. The analysis is very similar to that of Chapter 4, pp. 64–75.

6.

> In the longshore industry, as in other casual-labor-market industries and in seasonal industries in which the guaranteed annual wage has been sought, the chief motive to the lump-of-labor requirement is to force the employer to regularize employment. It appears very unlikely that the union would pick an absolute labor input level so large that the employer would seldom reach a technically efficient output level . . . . The guarantee is successful, in the eyes of the negotiators, if the employers are able to reorganize production so that no idle labor input is required. [Hartmen 1969, p. 217]

It should be noted, however, that employment guarantees are only one of several restrictive rules in longshoring.

7. Possible techniques for spreading work include reduction of hours per employee, high overtime rates, rotation of employment through a union hiring hall, vacations, severence or retirement bonuses or pensions, and the requirement that completely useless ("bogus") work be done. If the elasticity of derived demand is less than unity, work-sharing may result in both a larger number of employees and higher earnings per employee. It is in this sense that a union with control over the workweek could be expected not to choose an inelastic point

on its derived-demand curve. For the debate on this point, see Dunlop (1944, pp. 32-44) and Atherton (1973, pp. 5-30). Nevertheless, while pure work-sharing may ease the internal political problems created when a union moves up its demand curve, it does not shift that demand curve. This conclusion assumes that work-sharing that alters the time vector of labor input does not affect the quality of inputs or constrain the production function (vacations or a reduced workweek, for example, might increase the productivity of workers or, alternatively, might create shift-scheduling problems that would lower the intensity of use of capital). It is interesting to note that, for an unconstrained union exerting vertical control, the proposition that the union will choose a wage where $E > 1$ is replaced by the proposition that the union will choose a wage-employment level where $\eta > 1$.

In the remainder of this chapter, the terms "employment" and "quantity of labor" will be used interchangeably. Strictly speaking, we assume that vertical control does not alter the quantity of labor input per employee. The distinction between labor and employment should, however, be kept in mind.

8.

> The trade union is an economic organization which does not behave economically in the sense of following a maximization principle . . . The ingenuity which some economists have devoted to the question "What does a union try to maximize?" thus seems largely wasted, for the indications are that unions do not try to maximize anything. [Reynolds, 1964, p. 196]

9. The introduction of a utility function for the supplier of a monopolized input eliminates both the profit-maximizing assumption and the marginal-cost function for the monopolized input. This formulation is more intuitively appealing than assuming a marginal-cost function for labor, and union maximization of "profits." As we shall see, however, given any utility function for the union, the same utility-maximizing wage-employment combination can be arrived at by a model that assumes a "profit"-maximizing objective function combined with *some* marginal-cost curve for labor. This mathematical identity with the utility-maximization formulation is very useful.

10. The parallel with the constraints on vertical control by firms is clear. In the firm model of Chapter 5, the vertically integrating firm had two constraints on its choice of a price, $\overline{P}_x$, for the final product after integration. The first constraint was the minimum cost, $\hat{P}_x$, of producing the final good without using the monopolized input. This constraint arose only when the elasticity of substitution, σ, between the monopolized input, A, and all other inputs, B, was greater than unity. The second constraint on the firm was the possibility of an entry price for the monopolized input, $\hat{P}_a$, above which other firms would enter into production of A. With $\hat{P}_a$ less than infinity, $\hat{P}_x$ became the cost of producing X using A at price $\hat{P}_a$. This constraint on the integrated monopolist's choice of $\overline{P}_x$ could be effective even when $\sigma < 1$. In the context of a union, $\hat{P}_x$ becomes the maximum price for X after vertical control due to the possibility of existing

firms or new firms producing X either by using no labor, or by using nonunion labor at some wage $\hat{P}_l$.

11. It is interesting to speculate why firms appear more likely to accept a monopolized input's price as a parameter when that input is a commodity input rather than a labor input. The incentive to resist a given input price is probably a decreasing function of the number of purchasers (usually low for a labor union) and an increasing function of the input's share in total costs (usually high for labor). In addition, multiple pricing for labor is probably easier to maintain because of the difficulty of arbitraging labor services and the legal constraints against price discrimination for commodities. Other factors, such as the perishability of labor services, the political nature of labor monopolies, and the relative impersonality of commodity markets, may also be relevant.

12. The Cobb-Douglas case is presented in detail for two reasons. First, as in the case of the model developed for vertical control by firms, the Cobb-Douglas case permits the derivation of explicit equations for the effect of vertical control. Second, one of the most interesting cases of union vertical control occurs in the coal-mining industry, for which there is strong evidence of constant returns to scale, and an elasticity of substitution between capital and labor of approximately unity.

13. See Karsh and London (1954).

14. See Lewis (1951, pp. 284–85).

15. Since a supply schedule for labor does not exist, we cannot solve for a true demand function for K. For any given wage rate and tax rate, however, a "demand curve" for K can be derived. Note that since we assume $\sigma = 1 < \eta = 2$ in this example, K and L are gross complements, so a reduction in the wage rate, holding the tax rate constant, shifts out the demand curve for K.

16. As an aside, it can be shown that in the absence of union vertical control, labor's benefit from technical change that increases labor producticity is an increasing function of E, and that if $E < 1$, unions can be expected to resist even a costless technical change that increases labor productivity (see Warren-Boulton, 1977b). If the $\hat{P}_x$ constraint is effective, however, unions will always welcome such technical change since, as Equation (6.39) shows, $E > 1$. If the government either subsidizes the unionized sector or restricts entry by nonunion firms, $\hat{P}_x$ is increased and unions can be expected to reduce their support for, or even actively oppose, technical change that increases labor productivity.

17. A general discussion of bargaining theory would be beyond the scope of this chapter. See, for example, Pen (1959), Shackle (1964), Cartter and Marshall (1972), de Menil (1971), or Coddington (1968). As Atherton (1973, p. 5) points out, three kinds of theory are needed to deal with collective bargaining: a theory of the employer's "aims," which can be thought of as a preference ordering over the various outcomes that might be achieved, and which involves application of the theory of the firm; a theory of the union's preference orderings over the same list of possible outcomes; and a theory that will predict the outcome. We have been concerned in this chapter essentially with the first two of these areas. However, unless the bargaining position of employers is very weak (as we have generally assumed in this chapter) a formal integration with bargaining theory would be desirable.

18. From a 5¢-per-ton levy under the 1946 Krug-Lewis Agreement, the royalty rate rose rapidly to 40¢ per ton in 1952, where it remained for nearly twenty years until increased to 60¢ in 1971, and to 80¢ in 1974. The 1974 three-year union contract, however, has changed the financing method to a combined wage and output levy of 74¢ per ton and 90¢ per hour for November 1974 to November 1975, 78¢ per ton and $1.40 per hour for November 1975 to November 1976, and 82¢ per ton and $1.54 per hour for November 1976 to November 1977.

19. It should be noted, however, that increased reliance on an output royalty would improve the relative position of smaller, narrow-seam mines with low output-labor and capital-labor ratios, where the problem of nonunion labor is particularly acute. On the other hand, a higher output levy would be particularly burdensome for surface mining, with its high output-labor ratio and lower price per ton, and might lead to difficulties in maintaining unionization in surface mining.

20. A unitary elasticity of substitution between labor and capital can be safely assumed for both underground and surface production functions. However, since value-added per ton of surface coal is lower than that of underground, the union royalty rate in ad valorem terms is higher for surface than for underground coal ($t_s > t_u$). In addition, labor share in value-added is higher for underground production than for surface ($\delta_u > \delta_s$).

21. We assume the same value of $P_l/\overline{P}_l$ for both underground and surface mining. This assumption, of course, reduces the possible effects from vertical control. It would appear unlikely, however, that the UMW could or would deliberately adjust relative wage rates in surface and underground mines so as to maximize the gains from vertical control.

22. The contrast with the conclusion on page 135 above is worth noting. A finite "optimal" output levy requires that $\eta > 1$. Since we assume $\sigma = 1$, capital and labor will be net complements if $\eta > 1$, so that the conclusion on page 135 holds. If $\eta < 1$, however, as in the UMW case with a "sub-optimal" royalty rate, capital and labor will be net substitutes, and vertical control will result in a larger reduction in the capital stock if the royalty is used to increase employment.

23. Williamson (1968a) has argued that higher wage rates imposed on all mines may be in the interest of the operators of the larger underground coal mines where labor-capital ratios are significantly lower than in the smaller underground mines. The introduction of surface mines as a third sector with the lowest labor-capital ratios would weaken and perhaps reverse this conclusion. A comparison of Tables 6-1 and 6-2, however, indicates that Williamson's proposition is correct for surface-mine operators.

24. Unions that have used vertical control mainly to increase employment, of course, may not show such a correspondence. Examples might include the railroad and maritime unions. For maritime unions, however, the relevant comparison is with wages of non-U.S. seamen. The seamen's union has encountered especially limited employer resistance to vertical control because of the subsidy to U.S. shipping, which effectively removes most of the incentive for U.S. shippers to restrain labor costs (see Goldberg, 1971, pp. 304-15).

25. For a rebuttal of this proposition, see Shultz and Myers (1950).

26. Using vertical control to increase employment, however, can be a method of "increasing the income of the memberships, assuming that the members have been experiencing some unemployment, without creating a wage that appears unfairly high" (Rees, 1962, p. 82).

27. See the *Monthly Labor Review*, June 1946, for a description of the original negotiations. The same issue of the *Review* contains a discussion of welfare provisions for miners in other countries. Of the six countries examined, welfare funds were financed by payroll and employer deductions in Belgium; by a royalty on coal in Great Britain, British India and New Zealand; a combination of royalty and percentage of earnings in Spain; and by an absolute per-capita levy in the Netherlands. The UMW in 1946 must have been aware of the methods used to finance welfare funds in other countries. The fact that such funds were financed both by royalty payments and by payroll deductions may have resulted in John L. Lewis's apparent indifference between financing methods. The situation does not appear to have improved significantly since 1946. The *United Mine Workers Journal* recently reported that "some union officials have raised questions about whether a production-based royalty is the best method of financing Fund benefits. Few other industries tie their benefit programs to production by workers. Instead, they are negotiated through various per-member payments by the companies . . . ." *United Mine Workers Journal* (June 1-15, 1973, p. 20).

28. Elimination of vertical control by unions would require a rather drastic revision or reinterpretation of antitrust law. The Supreme Court decision in *United Mine Workers* v. *Pennington*, 85 S. Ct. 1585 (1965) clearly indicates that vertical control by unions is not in violation of the antitrust laws unless the union explicitly agrees with one set of employers to impose the same conditions on other employers.

29. It is interesting that in a world with competitive product markets, Cobb-Douglas production and utility functions, and proportional income taxes, wage levies by unions cannot alter labor's relative share. Vertical control by unions, however, can be expected to increase labor's relative share. In general, the effect on nonunion workers of vertical control by unions could be expected to be less damaging than the effect of wage levies. For discussions of the effects of unionization in a general equilibrium framework, see Johnson and Mieszkowski (1970) and Jones (1971).

 Chapter 7

Summary and Conclusions

Table 7-1 presents a list of the incentives for vertical control (on the vertical axis) and the different forms of vertical control (on the horizontal axis). If a form of vertical control is a possible response to a particular incentive, an X is marked in the corresponding position.[1]

The designation of possible combinations is somewhat arbitrary. Take tying arrangements, for example. For some incentives, such as price discrimination, the combination is both theoretically clear and has often been observed in practice. Other incentives seem extremely unlikely. It is hard to imagine, for example, how market power at another level would lead a competitive firm to use a tying arrangement. Some combinations, however, may be possible in theory but unlikely in practice, while others could even be counterproductive. For example, it has been argued that tying arrangements can facilitate oligopolistic pricing, either by preventing the disruption of an oligopolistic pricing structure in a second market or by reducing price instability. In different situations, however, a tying arrangement may facilitate hidden price reductions and thus increase the costs of policing an oligopolistic pricing arrangement.

What is immediately clear, however, is that each form of vertical control can have several alternative explanations, although only vertical integration is a possible response to every incentive. The single exception would seem to be setting maximum resale prices, for which the only clear incentive is to eliminate successive monopoly and for which a per se legal approach would therefore seem optimal. Peculiarly enough, however, in a 1968 decision[2] the Su-

Table 7-1. Incentives and Forms of Vertical Control

	7-1a: By Competitive Firms								
Form *Motivation*	*Integration*	*Tying Contracts*	*Price/Quantity Contracts*	*Requirements Contracts*	*Exclusive Dealing*	*Resale Price Setting*	*Royalty Contracts*	*Profit-Sharing*	*Work Rules*
Information	X	X	X	X	X		X	X	
Control	X	X	X		X				
Externalities	X	X	X		X	X (Min.)			X
Risk Aversion	X	X		X			X	X	
Market Power at Vertically Related Level Only	X								
Taxation, Regulation, or Price Controls	X	X							

7–1b: By Firms with Market Power

Form / *Motivation*	*Integration*	*Tying Contracts*	*Price/Quantity Contracts*	*Requirements Contracts*	*Exclusive Dealing*	*Resale Price Setting*	*Royalty Contracts*	*Profit-Sharing*	*Work Rules*
Successive Monopoly	X		X			X (Max.)		X	
Bilateral Monopoly	X		X					X	
Monopsony	X	X	X				X	X	
Price Discrimination	X	X	X		X		X		X
Entry Barriers	X	X		X	X				
Oligopolistic Discipline	X	X		X		X (Min.)			
Variable Proportions	X	X	X				X	X	X

preme Court declared setting maximum resale prices to be per se illegal. Thus in the one instance where policy reliance on the form of vertical control could be useful, the court appears to have made the wrong decision.

In general, however, basing policy on the form of vertical control rather than its motivation is not an acceptable policy shortcut. It is essential to know the particular incentive (or, in some cases, the group of incentives) behind vertical control in any particular case. Since identifying the form of vertical control is usually much easier than identifying the incentive, this makes the task of policymakers much more difficult—a consideration that probably explains much of the observed emphasis on form over content in this area.

Unfortunately this task is not necessarily finished once the incentive is determined. Different forms of vertical control can be close substitutes for achieving any particular goal. All we can assume is that the particular form chosen is the most profitable to the firm or union, and that if that form is proscribed, profits or utility will fall. If vertical control is used only to reduce costs (by improving information flows or control, internalizing externalities, reducing risk, or eliminating market power at a related level) we can—under most objective functions for policy—generally assume that the form chosen is both privately and socially optimal.

For a second group of incentives, however, we may decide that while the results are desirable, the privately optimal form is not the socially optimal form. For example, it could be desirable to prevent a merger aimed at eliminating successive or bilateral monopoly, even though the result would be an improvement over the present situation, if mutual integration by entry is a likely and preferable alternative.

Finally, even if the incentive for vertical control in a particular case is believed to have socially undesirable results, proscribing the form chosen may not improve the situation. We need to know what is likely to occur if the practice is forbidden. If a firm is prevented from using a tying arrangement to price discriminate, for example, it may resort to integration or some other form of vertical control. While we can assume that the tying arrangement was the most profitable alternative, we do not know *a priori* if it was more profitable because it enabled greater capture of consumer surplus or because it involved lower transaction costs.[3] Ideally, before a decision is made, the firm's ranking of alternative forms should be known, and a social evaluation of alternative states made. Some or all of these alternatives may then also be proscribed, although some alternative forms may be difficult to prevent.

In practice such an ideal approach may be excessively expensive or even impossible. In most cases identification of the incentive or class of incentives for vertical control may be the most that can be expected. This task is enormously simplified when a process of elimination can be used. In particular, a necessary condition for a large number of incentives is the existence of either horizontal market power or government policies that indirectly foster vertical control. If the firm is in a competitive industry where government policies are neutral toward vertical control, the only remaining incentives involve increased efficiency.[4] Under most definitions of the goals of public policy, this implies that whatever form of vertical control is chosen under these conditions is the socially optimal form, and no intervention is necessary. If horizontal market power is clearly present, however, or if the industry is regulated or subject to price controls or certain kinds of taxes, vertical control cannot be simply assumed desirable, and further information is necessary. Since the policy decision in such cases will depend heavily on the objectives of public policy and the range of possible policy alternatives, we turn now to a brief discussion of alternative objective functions and the use of second-best policies.

THE OBJECTIVES OF PUBLIC POLICY

Unless otherwise stated, we have implicitly assumed that the objective of public policy is to maximize economic welfare, which is defined as an equally weighted combination of consumers' surplus and producers' surplus, including any monopoly profits. The choice of an objective function, however, is a value judgment that must ultimately be left to the individual. Alternative views of the objectives of public policy can have a considerable effect on the determination of general policy guidelines and on the degree of preference for an active interventionist policy approach. Differing conclusions can also result, however, from different assumptions or beliefs on questions of fact.

Vertical control can have economic effects on four groups: (1) the economic unit exerting vertical control; (2) consumers of the final product; (3) other economic units such as input suppliers or competing firms, and (4) taxpayers. Let us define the effect of vertical control on the firm or union exerting vertical control as the change in quasi-rents or profits ($\Delta\pi$); the effect on consumers as the change in consumers' surplus due to any changes in final-product price or quality (ΔCS); the effect on other producing units as the change in their quasi-rents or profits (ΔR); and the effect on taxpayers as the change in tax revenue or intervention costs (ΔT). We can then define the aggregate welfare effect of vertical control as:

$$\Delta W = \alpha\Delta\pi + \beta\Delta CS + \gamma\Delta R + \delta\Delta T$$

where a, β, γ, and δ are weights resulting from individual value judgments.

The one component of ΔW we can reasonably assume to be always positive is $\Delta\pi$, at least for profit- (or utility-) maximizing economic units. Thus any value judgments or factual beliefs that reduce $\alpha\Delta\pi$, ceteris paribus, will make an interventionist public policy approach more attractive. On the one hand, a value judgment can be made that the objective of public policy should be to protect "other" units against any possible negative effects. The implicit statement is thus that $\alpha = 0$. A low value for α may also result from a belief that $\Delta\pi$ will accrue mainly to high-income groups, combined with a preference for more egalitarian income distribution. In some cases, however, income-distribution considerations may lead to relatively high values for α, as when the economic unit exerting vertical control is a labor union in a low-wage industry, especially if significant unemployment is present. Assuming a higher α for union vertical control, however, may often be difficult to justify. The desirability of an income transfer from electric-power consumers to mine workers, or from airline passengers to pilots, for example, is not obvious. One can at least argue that if income-distribution considerations are deemed relevant, they should be both explicit and adequately investigated empirically. In addition, some justification is required for altering income distribution through antitrust actions rather than through more direct methods.

The perceptions of both α and $\Delta\pi$ can also be affected by arguments relating to the "dissipation" of monopoly profits. In simplest terms, the argument is often made that an increase in monopoly profits will cause an increase in costs. The mechanism may be either managerial discretion,[5] X-inefficiency,[6] transaction costs,[7] or competition to obtain or defend market power.[8] In some cases, however, these costs to the firm may be socially desirable expenditures. For example, suppose that expenditure on research and development is suboptimal due to difficulties in capturing the full return to investment in information.[9] If vertical control can be used to increase the return to such investments, improved resource allocation may result.

Attitudes toward public policy in this area can also be strongly influenced by beliefs about the general extent and durability of horizontal market power. Most of the really significant present cases of market power appear to be due to government actions—either directly in the form of patents or indirectly as a result of regulatory actions that either explicitly prevent entry or impose large barriers to entry. In addition, large areas of economic activity are exempted from the antitrust laws. In the absence of government barriers to competition, market power may be a relatively temporary phenomenon.[10] In addition, in nonexempted areas, past antitrust actions have hopefully helped reduce horizontal market power. This implies, first, that unsanctioned horizontal market power is not likely to be a major force for vertical control, and second, if vertical control does increase monopoly profits, this increase in monopoly profits may either encourage entry or provide a signal to the antitrust authorities that actions to reduce horizontal market power are indicated. Thus even if the effect on profits is a significant component of the total welfare effect, this component may be transformed over time into increased consumers' surplus.

Implicit in the discussion so far is a "procompetitive" view of policy objectives, where a major emphasis is placed on the benefits or costs to consumers. The history of policy in the vertical control area, however, has often seen the surfacing of a "procompetitor" viewpoint. The concern here is that vertical control by one economic unit may place competing economic units at a disadvantage. If this concern is based on the belief that vertical control may increase entry barriers without increasing efficiency,[11] this view is consistent with a concern for consumer welfare. The conflict arises when vertical control increases efficiency or facilitates avoidance of oligopolistic restraints. If vertical control increases efficiency, but the benefits are greater (or costs less) to some firms than to others, these other firms will be at a competitive disadvantage. Similarly, if integration or tying arrangements are used to disguise price reductions or quality improvements, the firm's rivals will be "damaged". To regard such effects as an increase in entry barriers, however, seems to be a distortion of the concept, even though vertical control in such situations may discourage entry or even result in the exit of some firms. In terms of our welfare equation, the procompetitor approach implies a relatively large value for γ, and a uniquely low value for β, the value weight given to the welfare of consumers.

A procompetitor approach must, therefore, be based on some noneconomic rationale such as that presented by Judge Learned Hand in the *Alcoa* case:

> It is possible, because of its indirect social or moral effect, to prefer a system of small producers, each dependent for his success upon his own

> skill or character, to one in which the great mass of those engaged must accept the direction of the few . . . . Throughout the history of these statutes it has been constantly assumed that one of their purposes was to perpetuate and preserve, for its own sake and in spite of possible costs, an organization of small units which can effectively compete with each other.[12]

To an economist this is an externalities argument, since if the benefits from independence or small size accrue to those directly involved there is no need for intervention.[13] Even if some benefits are external, however, one would like to see some estimate of the benefits and costs of intervention; some determination of who gains and who loses; and some justification for the use of antitrust policy rather than alternative methods—such as selective subsidies to small business—which would make the costs more visible and allow a less random distribution of those costs.

A final consideration is the cost of intervention to both government and private parties. While intervention may increase rents to economists, lawyers, and the copying industry, most of such costs must be considered deadweight losses. This author is unaware of any data on the total cost of antitrust intervention and remedies imposed, or on the distribution of these costs between shareholders, consumers, and taxpayers. It seems clear, however, that the costs incurred by the government are only a small share of the total costs of intervention.[14] If these costs are significant, clear guidelines by the courts or the antitrust authorities become more desirable.

POLICY TOWARD VERTICAL CONTROL AS A SECOND-BEST APPROACH

All of the possible objectives of public policy toward vertical control can be achieved by alternative policy instruments. If these instruments are superior to vertical antitrust intervention, such intervention becomes a second-best approach that requires some justification. Since a unified and coordinated public policy may in practice be impossible, second-best policies may be unavoidable. Thus a preference for income redistribution or a belief in small-business externalities, for example, may influence antitrust action even though taxation or subsidy instruments may be far better suited to these tasks. Similarly, if regulation, taxation, or price-control policies must be taken as given to antitrust policymakers, second-best alternatives involving prevention of certain kinds of vertical control induced by these policies may be defensible, though hardly optimal.

But within the antitrust area there is no reason why second-best policies should be pursued. In particular, we have argued that horizontal market power is the major prerequisite for undesirable effects from vertical control. A defense of interventionist policies toward vertical control thus requires not only a clear demonstration of the existence of horizontal market power, but also a demonstration that direct action to eliminate that market power is not the first-best approach.

This requirement would be satisfied for two broad groups of cases. The first is where horizontal market power is deemed desirable or inevitable. Examples include investment in information (patents), labor unions, and cases of increasing returns to scale. In such cases, if vertical control is an undesirable extension of market power it may be possible to prevent vertical control, even though the basic condition of horizontal market power cannot be altered. The most relevant incentives for vertical control for such cases would be price discrimination and downstream variable proportions. The second broad group of cases involves situations where horizontal market power can be easiest attacked through policies toward vertical control. This would require demonstration that proscribing vertical control could significantly reduce entry barriers at relatively low cost (including both efficiency and transaction costs) in an industry where horizontal divestiture would be relatively expensive. There is some evidence that these conditions held in the metal container industry,[15] for example, and may hold in the automobile industry.[16]

For individuals such as myself, with a consumer-oriented, procompetitive view of antitrust objectives and a strong preference for first-best policies, some general conclusions are possible. First, a per se illegal approach to any form of vertical control is undesirable. Intervention can be desirable if horizontal market power is present, but each case should be examined on its own merits. Second, present policy toward vertical control appears excessively restrictive. There has been too little regard for the efficiency incentives for vertical control, and too much emphasis on an amorphous concept of "foreclosure." For vertical mergers the Justice Department's merger guidelines appear excessively restrictive, with a virtually per se prohibition for certain classes of mergers and a refusal to consider efficiency as a defense unless "exceptional circumstances" are present.[17] A rejection of efficiency considerations, and even a procompetitor bias against efficiency, has emerged in several court decisions, notably the *Brown Shoe Case.*[18] Present policy toward tying arrangements and other forms of vertical control,[19] including even resale price maintenance,[20] is open to similar criticisms.

Implicit in this argument for a more flexible policy, however, is the belief that the antitrust authorities and the courts are able to analyze accurately cases of vertical control and to carry out appropriate remedies. It is hoped that this book will be of some assistance in that task.

NOTES

1. For the corresponding discussions in the text, see the cross-reference listings in the index.

2. See *Albrecht v. Herald Co.* 390 U.S. 148 (1968).

3. For a more extended discussion of this case, see the section in Chapter 4, "Public Policy Toward Vertical Control . . . . "

4. This conclusion is subject to the caveat that vertical control by one firm in a competitive industry could increase costs to other firms if uncertainty and price rigidity are present (see the discussion in Chapter 2 under "Information Costs" and "Conclusions"). In such cases, however, several forms of vertical control—notably integration, long-term supply contracts, or even inventories—can be close or even perfect substitutes. In practice, it may be impossible to prevent the use of some of these alternative forms, and thus little or nothing will be gained from intervention.

5. See Williamson (1964); Masson (1971); Grabowski and Mueller (1972).

6. See Leibenstein (1966; 1969) and the exchange in the *Quarterly Journal of Economics*, May 1972. For a recent empirical estimate of the effect of competition on unit costs, see Primeaux (1977).

7. For a discussion of the effects of transaction costs on vertical control used to avoid successive monopoly or facilitate price discrimination, see the sections in Chapter 4, "Taxonomy of Market Structures" and "Public Policy Toward Vertical Control . . . . "

8. See Tullock (1967), Krueger (1974); Posner (1975).

9. But see the discussion in Chapter 2 under "Information Costs."

10. See Brozen (1970), and the discussion in the *Journal of Law and Economics*, October 1971.

11. As noted in Chapter 4 under "Entry Barriers," this would require: (1) that vertical control by the initiating firm will force other firms (including potential entrants) either to follow suit or suffer losses; (2) that either these other firms face higher prices for the factors required for vertical control, or vertical control by these firms would involve operation at less than minimum efficient scale at vertically-related levels, so that vertical control would be more expensive for these firms than for the initiating firm; and, (3) that this increase in costs to other firms leads to a price increase greater than the increase in unit costs to the initiating firm.

12. *United States* v. *Aluminum Company of America*, 148 F., 2d 416, 427, 429 (2d Cir. 1945). For a similar judicial statement, see Justice Douglas's dissent in *United States* v. *Columbia Steel Company*, 334 U.S. 495 (1948). The procompetitor viewpoint has been heavily criticized, notably by Bork and Bowman

(1965) and by Liebeler (1968). For a partial defense, see Blake and Jones (1965).

13. The common observation that small businesses often earn less than a "normal" rate of return is consistent with the idea that operators of such businesses place a positive value on their independence.

14. See Neale (1970, pp. 383–84). A similar tendency to shift the cost of government regulatory intervention onto shareholders and consumers has been emphasized by Weidenbaum (1975, 1977).

15. See McKie (1955; 1959).

16. For exclusive dealing, see Pashigian (1961) and Scherer (1970); for upstream vertical integration, see Crandall (1968b), but see also Zelenitz (1975).

17. U.S. Department of Justice, Merger Guidelines, May 30, 1968 (mimeo.). Reprinted in Neale (1970, pp. 494–505).

18. *Brown Shoe Co.* v. *U.S.*, 370 U.S. 294 (1962). For a strong criticism of the Court's decision, see Peterman (1975a), who concludes, "In a broad sense, the cause of the merger's illegality was its efficiency" (p. 143).

19. For franchising, for example, see Peterman's (1975b) analysis of *F.T.C.* v. *Brown Shoe Co.*, 384 U.S. 316 (1966). For a discussion of the legal and economic issues relating to vertical restrictions on intrabrand competition, see American Bar Association (1977) and the Antitrust Law Journal, Vol. 44, Issue 3, (1974–75).

20. For an analysis of resale price maintenance (RPM), see Telser (1960). The efficiency argument for allowing noncolluding manufacturers to impose minimum resale prices centers on the free-rider problem associated with provision of the optimal amount of services provided at the retail level (see "Ownership Externalities" in Chapter 4, above). Note that empirical findings that prices are higher with RPM are irrelevant, since services provided are presumably also higher. For a recent legal review of RPM, see Givens and Worsinger (1977).

Appendix A

Derivation of R with $\sigma = 1$

Assume: A Cobb-Douglas production function for the final product:

$$X = YA^{\delta}B^{(1-\delta)} \qquad Y > 0 \tag{A.1}$$

constant elasticity of demand for the final product:

$$X = Z/P_x{}^{\eta} \qquad Z > 0, \eta > 1 \tag{A.2}$$

constant elasticity of supply for the cooperant input:

$$B = CP_b^e \qquad C > 0 \tag{A.3}$$

and a constant-elasticity marginal-cost schedule for the monopolized input:

$$A = DM_a{}^g \qquad D > 0 \tag{A.4}$$

Using the factor efficiency conditions in the X industry:

$$\frac{A}{B} = \frac{\delta P_b}{(1-\delta)P_a} \tag{A.5}$$

we can solve for the price of the final product set by competitive X firms:

$$P_x = \frac{P_a{}^{\delta} P_b{}^{(1-\delta)}}{Y\delta^{\delta}(1-\delta)^{(1-\delta)}} \tag{A.6}$$

Since A is monopolized:

$$P_a = \frac{M_a}{(1 - 1/E)} \tag{A.7}$$

where:

$$E = \frac{\eta + e + \delta e(\eta - 1)}{\eta + e - \delta(\eta - 1)}$$

Using (A.5), (A.7), (A.4) and (A.3) in turn:

$$B = \frac{A(1-\delta)P_a}{\delta P_b} = \frac{A(1-\delta)M_a}{\delta(1-1/E)P_b} = \frac{D(1-\delta)M_a{}^{(1+g)}}{\delta(1-1/E)P_b}$$

$$= \frac{D(1-\delta)M_a{}^{(1+g)}C^{(1/e)}}{\delta(1-1/E)B^{(1/e)}}$$

or,

$$B = \left[\frac{D(1-\delta)M_a{}^{(1+g)}C^{(1/e)}}{\delta(1-1/E)}\right]^{e/(e+1)} \tag{A.8}$$

Substituting (A.8), (A.4), and (A.2) into (A.1)

$$\frac{Z}{P_x{}^{\eta}} = Y(DM_a{}^{g})^{\delta}\left(\frac{D(1-\delta)M_a{}^{(1+g)}C^{(1/e)}}{\delta(1-1/E)}\right)^{e(1-\delta)/(e+1)}$$

or,

$$M_a = \left(\frac{Z^{(e+1)}[\delta(1-1/E)]^{e(1-\delta)}}{Y^{(e+1)}C^{(1-\delta)}D^{(\delta+e)}(1-\delta)^{e(1-\delta)}P_x{}^{\eta(e+1)}}\right)^{1/[g(\delta+e)+e(1-\delta)]} \tag{A.9}$$

We can solve for P_b in the same manner:

$$P_b = \left(\frac{Z^{g+1}(1-\delta)^{\delta g}}{Y^{(g+1)} C^{(g+1-\delta)} D^{\delta} [\delta(1-1/E)]^{\delta g} P_x{}^{\eta(g+1)}} \right)^{1/[g(\delta+e)+e(1-\delta)]} \tag{A.10}$$

Substituting (A.10), (A.9) and (A.7) into (A.6), and clearing:

$$P_x = \left[\frac{Z^{\delta(e-g)+g+1}}{Y^{(e+1)(g+1)} C^{(1-\delta)(g+1)} D^{\delta(e+1)} (1-\delta)^{e(1-\delta)(g+1)} [\delta(1-1/E)]^{\delta g(1+e)}} \right]^{1/[\eta(\delta e+g+1-\delta g)+g(\delta+e)+e(1-\delta)]} \tag{A.11}$$

After vertical integration, the firm sets marginal revenue equal to marginal cost in the X market:

$$\overline{P}_x = \frac{\overline{M}_a{}^{\delta} \overline{M}_b{}^{(1-\delta)}}{Y \delta^{\delta} (1-\delta)^{(1-\delta)} (1-1/\eta)} \tag{A.12}$$

where

$$\overline{M}_b = \overline{P}_b(1 + 1/e)$$

As before, we can solve for $\overline{M}_a$ and $\overline{M}_b$:

$$\overline{M}_a = \left[\left(\frac{Z}{\overline{P}_x{}^{\eta} Y} \right)^{(e+1)} \left(\frac{\delta(1+1/e)}{(1-\delta)C^{1/e}} \right)^{e(1-\delta)} \left(D^{-(\delta+e)} \right) \right]^{1/[g(\delta+e)+e(1-\delta)]} \tag{A.13}$$

$$\overline{M}_b = \left[\left(\frac{Z}{\overline{P}_x{}^{\eta} Y} \right)^{(g+1)} \left(\frac{(1+1/e)}{C^{(g+1+\delta)}} \right)^{e(g+1-\delta)} \left(\frac{1-\delta}{\delta D^{1/g}} \right)^{\delta g} \right]^{1/[g(\delta+e)+e(1-\delta)]} \tag{A.14}$$

Substituting (A.13) and (A.14) into (A.12) and clearing:

$$\overline{P}_x = \left[\frac{Z^{\delta(e-g)+g+1}(1+1/e)^{e(1-\delta)(g+1)}}{Y^{(e+1)(g+1)} C^{(1-\delta)(g+1)} D^{\delta(e+1)} (1-\delta)^{e(1-\delta)(g+1)} \delta^{\delta g(e+1)} (1-1/\eta)^{g(e+\delta)+e(1-\delta}} \right]^{1/[\eta(\delta e+g+1-\delta g)+g(\delta+e} \tag{A.15}$$

Thus, from (A.11) and (A.15):

$$\underset{\sigma=1}{R} = \left[\frac{(1-1/E)^{\delta g(1+e)}(1+1/e)^{e(1-\delta)(g+1)}}{(1-1/\eta)^{g(e+\delta)+e(1-\delta)}}\right]^{1/[\eta(\delta e+g+1-\delta g)+g(\delta+e)+e(1-\delta)]} \quad \text{(A.16)}$$

Equations (A.11), (A.13) and (A.14) in the text are then derived by substitution of particular values for g or e into equation (A.16) above.

It is useful (see Chapter 6) also to present here the expressions for the effect of vertical control on monopoly profits:

$$R_{\Pi} = \frac{\overline{\Pi}}{\,} = \frac{(1-1/\eta)[1/(1-1/\eta)-\delta/(1+1/g)-(1-\delta)/(1+1/e)]}{\delta[1-(1-1/E)/(1+1/g)]}$$

$$\left[\frac{(1-1/\eta)^{g(e+\delta)+e(1-\delta)}}{(1-1/E)^{\delta g(1+e)}(1+1/e)^{e(1-\delta)(1+g)}}\right]^{(\eta-1)/[\eta(\delta e+g+1-\delta g)+g(\delta+e)+e(1-\delta)]} \quad \text{(A.17)}$$

and the effect of vertical control on the price of the cooperant input:

$$R_{P_b} = \frac{\overline{P}_b}{P_b} = \left[\frac{(1-1/E)}{(1+1/e)}\right]^{\delta g/[g(\delta+e)+e(1-\delta)]}$$

$$\times \left[\frac{(1-1/\eta)}{(1-1/E)^{\delta g(1+e)/g(e+\delta)+e(1-\delta)}(1+1/e)^{e(1-\delta)(1+g)/g(e+\delta)+e(1-\delta)}}\right]^{\eta(1+g)/\eta(\delta e+g+1-\delta g)+g(\delta+e)+e(1-\delta)}$$

(A.18)

 *Appendix B*

The United Mine Workers' Royalty

The purpose of this appendix is to determine what the derived-demand function for unionized labor would have been if the United Mine Workers (UMW) had not used an output royalty to finance its Welfare and Retirement Fund (see Chapter 6, above). In our discussion of optimal union vertical control, we treated the output tax as an endogenous variable. The optimal tax was determined and then used to derive the new labor demand function as a function of $\overline{P}_l$, the nominal (that is, excluding royalty revenue) wage rate. As discussed in the text to Chapter 6, however, the UMW has clearly chosen a suboptimal output royalty. In this appendix, therefore, we take the royalty rate and the observed nominal wage rate, $\overline{P}_l$, as given, and solve for the derived-demand function for labor in the *absence* of an output royalty.

If the coal mining industry produced one homogeneous output using a single production process, the derivation would be relatively simple. Unfortunately, underground and surface coal mining must be treated as two separate processes. A unitary elasticity of substitution between labor and capital can be safely assumed for both underground and surface production functions. However, since value-added per ton of surface coal is lower than that of underground coal, the union royalty rate in ad valorem terms is higher for surface than for underground coal ($t_s > t_u$). In addition, labor share in value-added is higher for underground production than for surface ($\delta_u > \delta_s$). We do not know what wage rate, P_l, would have been set by the union in the absence of an output royalty. However, we know $\overline{P}_l$, and we assume (see note 21 to Chapter 6, above) the same $(\overline{P}_l/P_l)$

ratio in both underground and surface mining. On the demand side, we assume a constant elasticity of demand for all coal at the delivered stage, with the relative share of underground and surface coal determined by their relative prices. The approach used is first to estimate the effects of the royalty on demand at the mine separately for each sector, and then allow for cross-demand effects between underground and surface coal.

We begin by solving for the effect on employment in each sector, before demand cross-effects, as a function of $(\overline{P}_l/P_l)$. From the constant-shares characteristic of the Cobb-Douglas production functions.

$$P_l L_u = \delta_u P_u C_u \tag{B.1}$$

$$\overline{P}_l \overline{L}_u = (1 - t_u)\overline{P}_u \overline{C}_u \tag{B.2}$$

$$P_l L_s = \delta_s P_s C_s \tag{B.3}$$

$$P_l L_s = (1 - t_s)\delta_s \overline{P}_s \overline{C}_s \tag{B.4}$$

where:

P_l = wage rate before royalty

L_u = underground employment before royalty

C_u = underground coal output before royalty

δ_u = labor share in underground production

t_u = royalty rate as a proportion of value added in underground mining

and values subscripted with an s refer to surface mining, and bars over variables indicate values after the royalty is imposed.

From (B.1) and (B.2):

$$\frac{\overline{L}_u}{L_u} = \frac{(P_l/\overline{P}_l)(1 - t_u)\overline{P}_u \overline{C}_u}{P_u C_u} \tag{B.5}$$

From (B.3) and (B.4):

$$\frac{\overline{L}_s}{L_s} = \frac{(P_l/\overline{P}_l)(1 - t_s)\overline{P}_s \overline{C}_s}{P_s C_s} \tag{B.6}$$

BEFORE CROSS-EFFECTS

We assume a constant elasticity of demand at the mine for unionized underground coal (before cross-effects), η_u, which is approximated by:

$$\eta_u = \frac{\eta}{k_u S_u} \tag{B.7}$$

where:

η = "overall" elasticity of demand for all delivered coal

k_u = ratio of value-added per ton to delivered price per ton, for underground coal.

S_u = share of underground coal output from unionized mines

Using similar notation:

$$\eta_s = \frac{\eta}{k_s S_s} \tag{B.8}$$

With constant η_u and η_s:

$$\frac{\overline{P}_u \overline{\overline{C}}_u}{P_u C_u} = \left(\frac{\overline{P}_u}{P_u}\right)^{(1-\eta_u)} \tag{B.9}$$

$$\frac{\overline{P}_s \overline{\overline{C}}_s}{P_s C_s} = \left(\frac{\overline{P}_s}{P_s}\right)^{(1-\eta_s)} \tag{B.10}$$

where double bars over quantity variables refer to quantities before cross-effects. (Since prices are not affected by cross-effects, single bars on price variables have been retained for notational convenience.)

Since.

$$\frac{\overline{P}_u}{P_u} = \frac{(\overline{P}_l/P_l)^{\delta_u}}{(1-t_u)} \tag{B.11}$$

$$\frac{\overline{P}_s}{P_s} = \frac{(\overline{P}_l/P_l)^{\delta_u}}{(1-t_u)} \tag{B.12}$$

we can substitute (B.11) into (B.9) and then into the before-cross-effect version of (B.5) to get:

$$\frac{\overline{\overline{L}}_u}{L_u} = (1-t_u)^{\eta_u}\left(\frac{\overline{P}_l}{P_l}\right)^{-E_u} \tag{B.13}$$

where:

$$E_u = 1 + \delta_u(\eta_u - 1)$$

Using a similar notation and derivation for surface coal:

$$\frac{\overline{\overline{L}}_s}{L_s} = (1-t_s)^{\eta_s}\left(\frac{\overline{P}_l}{P_l}\right)^{-E_s} \tag{B.14}$$

In addition, from substituting (B.11) into (B.9) we observe that:

$$\frac{\overline{\overline{C}}_u}{C_u} = \frac{(1-t_u)^{\eta_u}}{(\overline{P}_l/P_l)^{\delta_u\eta_u}} \tag{B.15}$$

and, substituting (B.12) into (B.10)

$$\frac{\overline{\overline{C}}_s}{C_s} = \frac{(1-t_s)^{\eta_s}}{(\overline{P}_l/P_l)^{\delta_s\eta_s}} \tag{B.16}$$

CROSS-EFFECTS

Following Goldstein and Smith (1976), we assume:

$$\frac{C_u}{C_u + C_s} = \alpha\left(\frac{\hat{P}_s}{\hat{P}_u}\right)^{\beta} \tag{B.17}$$

where:

$\hat{P}_u$ = delivered price of underground coal

$\hat{P}_s$ = delivered price of surface coal

Thus:

$$\frac{\Delta[C_u/(C_u + C_s)]}{C_u/(C_u + C_s)} = \beta\left[\frac{\Delta(\hat{P}_s/\hat{P}_u)}{\hat{P}_s/\hat{P}_u}\right] \tag{B.18}$$

or, since $\bar{C}_u + \bar{C}_s = \bar{\bar{C}}_u + \bar{\bar{C}}_s$:

$$\bar{C}_u/\bar{\bar{C}}_u - 1 = \beta\left[\frac{\hat{P}_s/\hat{\hat{P}}_u - \hat{P}_s/\hat{P}_u}{\hat{P}_s/\hat{P}_u}\right] \tag{B.19}$$

Since:

$$\hat{P}_u = \frac{P_u}{k_u} \tag{B.21}$$

$$\hat{P}_s = \frac{P_s}{k_s} \tag{B.20}$$

we can substitute (B.20), (B.21), (B.11), and (B.12) into (B.19):

$$\frac{\bar{\bar{C}}_u}{\bar{C}_u} = \frac{1}{(D+1)} \tag{B.22}$$

where:

$$D = \beta\left[\frac{1 + k_s\ [(\bar{P}_l/P_l)^{\delta_s}/(1-t_s)] - 1}{1 + k_u\ [(\bar{P}_l/P_l)^{\delta_u}/(1-t_u)] - 1} - 1\right] \tag{B.23}$$

In a similar fashion, we can solve for the ratio of surface-coal output before cross-effects, to surface-coal output after cross-effects:

$$\frac{\bar{\bar{C}}_s}{\bar{C}_s} = \frac{(\bar{C}_u/\bar{C}_s)D}{D+1} + 1 \tag{B.24}$$

Employment Effects

Since.

$$L_u \equiv \bar{L}_u\left(\frac{L_u}{\bar{\bar{L}}_u}\right)\left(\frac{\bar{\bar{L}}_u}{L_u}\right) = \bar{L}_u\left(\frac{L_u}{\bar{\bar{L}}_u}\right)\left(\frac{\bar{\bar{C}}_u}{\bar{C}_u}\right) \tag{B.25}$$

we can substitute (B.13) and (B.22) into (B.25) to determine the quantity of labor demanded in underground mining in the absence of an output royalty:

$$L_u = \frac{\bar{L}_u(\bar{P}_l/P_l)^{E_u}}{(1-t_u)^{\eta_u}(D+1)} \tag{B.26}$$

In a similar fashion, we can solve for the amount of labor in surface mining in the absence of the royalty:

$$L_s = \frac{\bar{L}_s(\bar{P}_l/P_l)^{E_s}}{(1-t_s)^{\eta_s}}\left[\frac{(\bar{C}_u/\bar{C}_s)D}{D+1} + 1\right] \tag{B.27}$$

The aggregate effect on employment is then given by:

$$\frac{L}{\bar{L}} \equiv \frac{L_u + L_s}{\bar{L}_u + \bar{L}_s} \tag{B.28}$$

Earnings Effects

To get the effects on earnings per worker, we define the earnings per worker after the royalty as:

$$W = P_l + \frac{t_s\bar{P}_s\bar{C}_s + t_u\bar{P}_u\bar{C}_u}{\bar{L}_u + \bar{L}_s} \tag{B.29}$$

Using the constant (after-tax) share of labor:

$$\frac{W}{P_l} = \left(\frac{\bar{P}_l}{P_l}\right)\left[1 + \frac{t_s\bar{L}_s/\,\delta_s(1-t_s) \;+\; t_u\bar{L}_u\,/\delta_u(1-t_u)}{\bar{L}_u + \bar{L}_s}\right] \tag{B.30}$$

Output Effects

Using (B.22) and (B.15) to get the final effect on underground output.

$$\frac{C_u}{\bar{C}_u} \equiv \left(\frac{C_u}{\bar{\bar{C}}_u}\right)\left(\frac{\bar{\bar{C}}_u}{\bar{C}_u}\right) = \frac{(\bar{P}_l/P_l)^{\delta_u\eta_u}}{(1-t_u)^{\eta_u}(D+1)} \tag{B.31}$$

Similarly, we can solve for the effect of the royalty on surface output:

$$\frac{C_s}{\overline{C}_s} = \frac{(\overline{P}_l/P_l)^{\delta_s \eta_s}}{(1-t_s)^{\eta_s}} \left[\frac{D(\overline{C}_u/\overline{C}_s)}{D+1} + 1\right] \tag{B.32}$$

Delivered Prices Effects

The effects of the royalty on output prices at the mine have already been given by (B.11) and (B.12). To get the corresponding effects on delivered prices, we can substitute (B.20) and (B.21) into (B.11) and (B.12):

$$\frac{\hat{P}_u}{\overline{\hat{P}}_u} = \frac{1}{k_u[(\overline{P}_l/P_l)^{\delta_u}/(1-t_u)-1]+1} \tag{B.33}$$

$$\frac{\hat{P}_s}{\overline{\hat{P}}_s} = \frac{1}{k_s\,[\,(\overline{P}_l/P_l)^{\delta_s}/(1-t_s)-1]+1} \tag{B.34}$$

Capital Effects

We assume that K is available in infinitely elastic supply (see Chapter 6, above). Using the constant-shares characteristic and Equations (B.9) and (B.11), we solve for the underground capital ratio before cross-effects:

$$\frac{K_u}{\overline{\overline{K}}_u} = \frac{P_u C_u}{(1-t_u)\overline{P}_u\overline{\overline{C}}_u} = \frac{(\overline{P}_l/P_l)^{\delta_u(\eta_u-1)}}{(1-t_u)^{\eta_u}} \tag{B.35}$$

Similarly, using the constant-shares characteristic and Equations (B.10) and (B.12), we can solve for the surface capital ratio before cross-effects:

$$\frac{K_s}{\overline{\overline{K}}_s} = \frac{P_s C_s}{(1-t_s)\overline{P}_s\overline{\overline{C}}_s} = \frac{(P_l/P_l)^{\delta_s(\eta_s-1)}}{(1-t_s)^{\eta_s}} \tag{B.36}$$

Since:

$$\frac{K_u}{\overline{K}_u} \equiv \left(\frac{K_u}{\overline{\overline{K}}_u}\right)\left(\frac{\overline{\overline{K}}_u}{\overline{K}_u}\right) = \frac{K_u}{\overline{\overline{K}}_u}\;\frac{\overline{\overline{C}}_u}{\overline{C}_u} \tag{B.37}$$

we can substitute (B.35) and (B.22) into (B.37) to get the complete effect of the royalty on capital levels in underground coal:

$$\frac{K_u}{\overline{K}_u} = \frac{(\overline{P}_l/P_l)^{\delta_u(\eta_u - 1)}}{(1 - t_u)^{\eta_u}(D + 1)} \tag{B.38}$$

Similarly, since:

$$\frac{K_s}{\overline{\overline{K}}_s} \equiv \left(\frac{K_s}{\overline{\overline{\overline{K}}}_s}\right)\left(\frac{\overline{\overline{\overline{K}}}_s}{\overline{\overline{K}}_s}\right) = \left(\frac{K_s}{\overline{\overline{\overline{K}}}_s}\right)\left(\frac{\overline{\overline{C}}_s}{\overline{C}_s}\right) \tag{B.39}$$

we can substitute (B.36) and (B.24) into (B.39) to get the complete effect of the royalty on capital levels in surface coal mining:

$$\frac{K_s}{\overline{K}_s} = \left[\frac{(\overline{P}_l/P_l)^{\delta_s(\eta_s - 1)}}{(1 - t_s)^{\eta_s}}\right] \left[\frac{(\overline{C}_u/\overline{C}_s)D}{D + 1} + 1\right] \tag{B.40}$$

Thus for any given $(\overline{P}_l/P_l)$, we can determine the effect of the output royalty on earnings per worker, employment in underground and surface mining, aggregate employment, output in each sector, aggregate ouptut, and capital levels in each sector.

DATA

We need estimates for the following parameters: δ_u, δ_s, t_u, t_s, η, k_u, k_s, S_u, S_s, β, $\overline{C}_u$, $\overline{C}_s$, $\overline{L}_u$, $\overline{L}_s$. We used Goldstein and Smith's (1976) estimate for overall demand elasticity of $\eta = 0.48$, and their estimate for the cross-effect parameter of $\beta = 1.7$. Our best estimates of un-ionized shares in each sector, from union and other sources, was

Table B-1. Estimated Parameter Values: Bituminous Coal.

Parameter	*1967*	*1963*	*1958*	*1954*
δ_u	0.4696	0.4965	0.5586	0.6518
δ_s	0.3231	0.3341	0.3873	0.4135
t_u	0.0914	0.0855	0.0850	0.1023
t_s	0.1406	0.1431	0.1321	0.1551
C_u	310.1	219.258	243.048	279.818
C_s	139.9	117.883	90.924	82.174
L_u	84.1	88.532	129.175	170.392
L_s	13.0	14.865	17.439	16.871
k_u	0.5525	0.5532	0.5339	0.5202
k_s	0.4483	0.4265	0.4090	0.3909

S_u = 0.94 and S_s = 0.56. The remaining parameter values were estimated from the bituminous coal section of the *Census of Mineral Industries* for 1954, 1958, 1963 and 1967, and are shown in Table B-1.

The demand for labor as a function of the wage rate in the absence of an output royalty was then traced out. The results for 1967 are shown in Figure 6–7 in Chapter 6. The $(\bar{P}_l/P_l)$ ratios corresponding to two points, $W = P_l$ and $L = \bar{L}$, were then found and used to determine the effects on output and capital levels for those two points. The results are shown in Tables 6–1 and 6–2 in Chapter 6.

Bibliography

American Bar Association. 1977. Antitrust Section, Monograph No. 2. *Vertical restrictions limiting intrabrand competition.*

Adams, Walter, and Dirlam, Joel B. 1964. Steel imports and vertical oligopoly power. *American Economic Review* 54 (September): 626–55.

Adams, Walter. 1964. Vertical power, dual distribution, and the squeeze: A case study in steel. *Antitrust Bulletin* 9 (June–July): 493–508.

Adelman, Morris A. 1949. Integration and antitrust policy. *Harvard Law Review* 63: 27–77.

_________. 1972. *The world petroleum market.* Baltimore: Johns Hopkins University Press, 1972.

Alchian, Armen A., and Demsetz, Harold. 1972. Production, information costs, and economic organization. *American Economic Review* 62 (December): 777–95.

Alchian, Armen A. 1970. Information costs, pricing, and resource unemployment. In *Microeconomic foundations of employment and inflation theory,* ed. Edmund S. Phelps, et al., pp. 27–52. New York: W. W. Norton & Company.

American Telephone and Telegraph Co. 1969. *Vertical integration in the Bell System: A systems approach to technological and economic imperatives of the telephone network.* President's Task Force on Communications Policy, Staff Paper 5, Part 2, Appendix C, PB-184-418.

_________. 1974. *Hearings on the Industrial Reorganization Act S. 1167: Bell System statements and rebuttals, 1974.*

Archer, S. H., and Farber, L. G. 1966. Firm size and the cost of externally secured capital. *Journal of Finance* 21 (March): 69–83.

Arrow, Kenneth J. 1962. Economic welfare and the allocation of resources for invention. In *The rate and direction of inventive activity: Economic and social factors.* Princeton: Universities—National Bureau of Economic Research Conference Series.

_________.1975. Vertical integration and communication. *Bell Journal of Economics* 6 (Spring): 173–83.

Arrow, K.; Chenery; H. B., Minhas, B.; and Solow, R. S. 1961. Capital-labor substitution and economic efficiency. *Review of Economics and Statistics* 42 (August): 225-50.

Atherton, Wallace N. 1973. *Theory of union bargaining goals.* Princeton: Princeton University Press.

Averch, Harvey, and Johnson, Leland L. 1962. Behavior of the firm under regulatory constraint. *American Economic Review* 52 (December): 1052-69.

Bailey, Elizabeth E. 1973. *Economic theory of regulatory constraint.* Lexington, Mass.: Lexington Books, D. C. Heath and Company.

Bain, Joe S. 1956. *Barriers to new competition: Their character and consequences in manufacturing industries.* Cambridge, Mass.: Harvard University Press.

Baitsell, John M. 1966. *Airline industrial relations: Pilots and flight engineers.* Boston: Divison of Research, Graduate School of Business Administration, Harvard University.

Balassa, B., Guisinger, S. E.; and Schydlowsky, D. M. 1970. The effective rates of protection and the question of labor protection in the United States: A comment. *Journal of Political Economy* 78 (September/October): 1150-62.

Barzel, Yoram. 1968. Optimal timing of innovations. *Review of Economics and Statistics* 50 (August): 348-55.

Bator, Francis, M. 1958. The anatomy of market failure. *Quarterly Journal of Economics* 72 (August): 351-79.

Baumol, William J., and Klevorick, Alvin K. 1970. Input choices and rate-of-return regulation: An overview of the discussion. *Bell Journal of Economics and Management Science* 1 (Autumn): 162-90.

Baumol, William J., and Malkiel, Burton G. 1967. The firm's optimal debt-equity combination and the cost of capital. *Quarterly Journal of Economics* 81 (November): 547-78.

Berkowitz, Monroe. 1954. The economics of trade union organization and administration. *Industrial and Labor Relations Review* 7 (July): 575-92.

Berry, Charles H. 1970. Economic Policy and the Conglomerate Merger. *St. John's Law Review* 44 (Spring): 266-81.

Bertram, Gordon, W., and Maisel, Sherman J. 1955. *Industrial relations in the construction industry.* Berkeley: University of California Institute of Industrial Relations.

Blake, Harlan M., and Jones, William K. 1965a. In defense of antitrust. *Columbia Law Review* 65 (March): 377-400.

_______. 1965b. Toward a three-dimensional antitrust policy. *Columbia Law Review* 65 (March): 422-66.

Blois, K. J. 1972. Vertical quasi-integration. *Journal of Industrial Economics* 20 (July): 253-72.

Bork, Robert H. 1951. Vertical integration and the Sherman Act: The legal history of an economic misconception. *University of Chicago Law Review* 22 (Autumn): 157-201.

_______. 1965. Contrasts in antitrust theory: I. *Columbia Law Review* 65 (March): 401-16.

_______. 1966. The rule of reason and the per se concept: Price fixing and market division II. *Yale Law Journal* 75 (January): 373-475.

________. 1967. A reply to Professors Gould and Yamey. *Yale Law Journal* 76 (March): 731-43.

________. 1968. Resale price maintenance and consumer welfare. *Yale Law Journal* 77 (April): 950-55.

________. 1969. Vertical integration and competitive processes. In *Public policy toward mergers*, ed. J. Fred Weston and Sam Peltzman, pp. 139-49. Pacific Palisades, California: Goodyear Publishing Co.

Bork, Robert H., and Bowman, Ward S., Jr. 1965. The crisis in antitrust. *Columbia Law Review* 65 (March): 363-76.

Bowley, A. L. 1928. Bilateral monopoly. *Economic Journal* 38 (December): 651-59.

Bowman, Ward S., Jr. 1957. Tying arrangements and the leverage problem. *Yale Law Journal* 67 (November): 19-36.

________. 1965. Contrast in antitrust theory: II. *Columbia Law Review* 65 (March): 417-21.

________. 1973. *Patent and antitrust law: A legal and economic appraisal.* Chicago: University of Chicago Press.

Braeutigam, Ronald R. 1974. A comment on ITT v. GTE. Paper presented at Telecommunications Policy Research Conference, Airlie House, Va., April 1974.

Breyer, Stephen, and MacAvoy, Paul W. 1974. *Energy regulation by the Federal Power Commission.* Washington, D.C.: Brookings Institution.

Bronfenbrenner, M. 1961. Notes on the elasticity of derived demand. *Oxford Economic Papers* 13 (October): 254-61.

Brozen, Yale. 1970. The Antitrust Task Force deconcentration recommendation. *Journal of Law and Economics* 13 (October): 279-92.

Burstein, Meyer L. 1960a. The economics of tie-in sales. *Review of Economics and Statistics* 42 (February): 68-73.

________. 1960b. A theory of full-line forcing. *Northwestern University Law Review* 55 (February): 62-95.

Canes, Michael E. 1976. The vertical integration of oil firms. In *Resource allocation and economic policy*, ed. Meyer L. Burstein and Michael Allingham. London: Macmillan.

Carlton, Dennis W. 1976. Vertical integration in competitive markets under uncertainty. Massachusetts Institute of Technology, Department of Economics Working Paper Number 174.

________. 1977. Uncertainty, production lags, and pricing. *American Economic Review* 67 (February): 244-49.

Cartter, Allan M. 1959. *Theory of wages and employment.* Homewood, Illinois. Richard D. Irwin.

Cartter, Allan M., and Marshall, F. Ray. 1972. *Labor economics: Wages, employment, and trade unionism.* Homewood, Ill.: Richard D. Irwin.

Caves, Richard. 1962. *Air transport and its regulators.* Cambridge, Mass.: Harvard University Press.

Chamberlain, Neil W., and Cullen, Donald E. 1971. *The labor sector.* New York: McGraw-Hill.

Cheung, Stephen N. S. 1974. A theory of price control. *Journal of Law and Economics* 18 (April): 53-72.

Christenson, C.L. 1962. *Economic redevelopment in bituminous coal.* Cambridge, Mass.: Harvard University Press.

Coase, Ronald H. 1937. The nature of the firm. *Economica* 4 (November): 386-405.

________. 1960. The problem of social cost. *Journal of Law and Economics* 3 (October): 1-44.

Coddington, Alan. 1968. *Theories of the bargaining process.* London: Allen and Urwin.

Comanor, William S. 1967. Vertical mergers, market power, and the antitrust laws. *American Economic Review* 57 (May): 254-68.

________. 1968. Vertical territorial restrictions: White Motor and its aftermath. *Harvard Law Review* 81 (May): 1419-38.

Countryman, Vern. 1948; 1949. The organized musicians. *Chicago Law Review* 16, Part I (1948); 56-85; Part II (1949): 239-97.

Courville, Leon. 1974. Regulation and efficiency in the electric utility industry. *Bell Journal of Economics and Management Science* 5 (Spring): 53-74.

Cowan, Donald D., and Waverman, Leonard. 1971. The interdependence of communications and data processing: Issues in economics of integration and public policy. *Bell Journal of Economics and Management Science* 2 (Autumn): 657-77.

Cox, Charles C. 1976. Futures trading and market information. *Journal of Political Economy* 84 (December): 1215-38.

Crandall, Robert W. 1968a. Vertical integration and the market for repair parts in the United States automobile industry. *Journal of Industrial Economics* 16 (July): 212-34.

________. 1968b. *Vertical integration in the United States automobile industry.* Unpublished Ph.D. dissertation, Northwestern University.

Dayan, D. 1972. *Vertical integration and monopoly regulation.* Unpublished Ph.D. dissertation, Princeton University.

De Chazeau, Melvin G., and Kahn, Alfred E. 1959. *Integration and competition in the petroleum industry.* Petroleum Monograph Series, Vol. 3. New Haven: Yale University Press.

De Menil, George. 1971. *Bargaining: Monopoly power versus union power.* Cambridge, Mass.: MIT Press.

Demsetz, Harold, 1969. Information and efficiency: Another viewpoint. *Journal of Law and Economics* 12 (April): 1-22.

________. 1976. Economics as a guide to antitrust regulation. *Journal of Law and Economics* 19 (August): 371-84.

Director, Aaron, and Levi, Edward H. 1956. Law and the future: Trade regulation. *Northwestern University Law Review* 51 (May/June): 281-96.

Dunlop, John T. 1944; 1950. *Wage determination under trade unions.* New York: Macmillan, 1944; Augustus M. Kelley, 1950.

Edwards, Edgar O. 1950. The analysis of output under discrimination. *Econometrica* 82 (April): 163-72.

Elzinga, Kenneth G. 1970. Predatory pricing: The case of the gunpowder trust. *Journal of Law and Economics* 13 (April): 223-40.

Erickson, Edward W., Millsaps, Stephen W., and Spann, Robert M. 1974.

Oil supply and tax incentives. *Brookings Papers on Economic Activity* No. 2: 449–78.

Fama, Eugene F., and MacBeth, James D. 1973. Risk, return and equilibrium: Empirical tests. *Journal of Political Economy* 81 (May/June): 607–36.

Fellner, W. 1947. Prices and wages under bilateral monopoly. *Quarterly Journal of Economics* 61 (August): 503–509.

Foran, Terry G. 1976. Market structure and derived demand. *Economica* 43 (February): 83–87.

Freeman, R. B. 1976. Individual mobility and union voice in the labor market. *American Economic Review* 66 (May): 361–68.

Galbraith, John K. 1956. *American capitalism: The concept of countervailing power.* Boston: Houghton Mifflin.

Givens, Richard A., and Worsinger, Laura P. 1977. Vertical restraints after repeal of fair trade. Mimeo.

Goldberg, Joseph P. 1971. Modernization in the maritime industry: Labor management adjustments to technological change. In *Collective bargaining and technological change in American transportation*, ed. Harold M. Levinson et al., pp. 243–419. Evanston, Ill.: The Transportation Center at Northwestern University.

Goldstein, Morris, and Smith, Robert S. 1976. The predicted impact of the black lung benefits program on the coal industry. In *Evaluating the labor market effects of social programs*, ed. O. Ashenfelter, pp. 133–82. Princeton: Industrial Relations Section of Princeton University.

Gordon, Donald R., and Hynes, Allan. 1970. On the theory of price dynamics. In *Microeconomic foundations of employment and inflation theory*, ed. Edmund S. Phelps et al., pp. 369–93. New York: W. W. Norton.

Gort, Michael. 1962. *Diversification and integration in American industry.* Princeton: Princeton University Press.

Gould, J. R., and Preston, L. E. 1965. Resale price maintenance and retail outlets. *Economica* 32 (August): 302–12.

Gould, J. R., and Yamey, B. S. 1967. Professor Bork on vertical price fixing. *Yale Law Journal* 76 (March): 722–30.

________. 1968. Professor Bork on vertical price fixing: A rejoinder. *Yale Law Journal* 77 (April): 936–49.

Grabowski, Henry G., and Mueller, Dennis C. 1972. Managerial and stockholder welfare models of firm expenditure. *Review of Economics and Statistics* 54 (February): 9–24.

Green, Jerry R. 1974. Vertical integration and assurance of markets. Harvard Institute of Economic Research, Discussion Paper Number 383.

Greenhut, M. L., and Ohta, H. 1976a. Joan Robinson's criterion for deciding whether market discrimination reduces output. *Economic Journal* 86 (March): 96–97.

________. 1976b. Related market conditions and interindustrial mergers. *American Economic Review* 66 (June): 267–77.

Haber, William, and Levinson, Hrold. 1956. *Labor relations and productivity in the residential construction industry.* Ann Arbor: University of Michigan Bureau of Industrial Relations.

Haldi, John. 1974. *Postal monopoly: An assessment of the private express statutes.* Washington, D.C.: American Enterprise Institute for Public Policy Research.

Hall, Marshall, and Weiss, Leonard W. 1967. Firm size and profitability. *Review of Economics and Statistics* 49 (August): 319–31.

Hartman, Paul T. 1969. *Collective bargaining and productivity: The longshore mechanization agreement.* Berkeley: University of California Press.

Harvard Law Review 87 (1973/74): 1720–61. Refusals to deal by vertically integrated monopolists.

Hawkins, E. R. 1950. Vertical price relationships. In *Theory in marketing: Selected essays,* ed. Reavis Cox and Wroe Alderson, pp. 179–92. Chicago: Richard D. Irwin.

Hay, George A. 1973. An economic analysis of vertical integration. *Industrial Organization Review* 1: 188–98.

Helburn, I. B. 1971. Trade union response to profit-sharing plans: 1886–1966. *Labor History* 12 (Winter): 68–80.

Hicks, John R. 1964. *The theory of wages.* 2nd ed. New York: St. Martin's Press.

________. 1961. Marshall's third rule: A further comment. *Oxford Economic Papers* 13 (October): 261–65.

Hilton, George W. 1958. Tying sales and full-line forcing. *Weltwirtschaftliches Archiv* 81: 265–76.

________. 1959. The theory of tax incidence applied to the gains of labor unions. In *The allocation of economic resources: Essays in honor of Bernard Francis Haley,* Stanford: Stanford University Press.

Hirshleifer, Jack. 1970. *Investment, interest and capital.* Englewood Cliffs, N.J.: Prentice-Hall.

________. 1971. The private and social value of information and the reward to inventive activity. *American Economic Review* 61 (September): 561–74.

________. 1973. Where are we in the theory of information? *American Economic Review* 63 (May): 31–39.

Hopkins, George E. 1971. *The airline pilots: A study in elite unionization.* Cambridge, Mass.: Harvard University Press.

Humphrey, David Burras, and Moroney, F. R. 1975. Substitution among capital, labor, and natural resource products in American manufacturing. *Journal of Political Economy* 83 (February): 57–82.

Irwin, Manley R. 1969. Vertical integration and the communications industry: Separation of Western Electric and AT&T. *Antitrust Law and Economics Review* 3 (Fall): 125–38.

________. 1971. *The telecommunications industry: Integration versus competition.* New York: Praeger.

________. 1977. The telephone industry. In *The Structure of American Industry* (5th edition) ed. Walter Adams, pp. 312–33. New York: Macmillan Publishing Co.

Irwin, Manley R., and McKee, Robert E. 1968. Vertical integration and the communication equipment industry: Alternatives for public policy. *Cornell Law Review* 52 (February): 446–72.

Johnson, Harry, G., and Mieszkowski, P. M. 1970. The effects of unionization on the distribution of income: A general equilibrium approach. *Quarterly Journal of Economics* 84 (November): 539-61.

Johnson, P. S. 1973. *Cooperative research in industry: An economic study.* New York: Wiley.

Jones, Ronald W. 1971. Distortions in factor markets and the general equilibrium model of production. *Journal of Political Economy* 79 (May/June): 437-59.

Jordan, Judd L. 1976. Telex v. IBM: Remodeling the crisis in antitrust. *UCLA Law Review* 23 (April): 737-62.

Kahn, Alfred E. 1971. *The economics of regulation: principles and institutions—Vols. I and II.* New York: Wiley.

Kahn, Mark L. 1971. Collective bargaining on the airline flight deck: Adjustments to innovation in a regulated growth industry. In *Collective bargaining and technological change in American transportation,* ed. Harold M. Levinson et al. pp. 421-607. Evanston, Ill.: The Transportation Center at Northwestern University.

Karsh, Bernard, and London, Jack. 1954. The coal miners: A study of union control. *Quarterly Journal of Economics* 68 (August): 415-36.

Kaysen, Carl. 1956. *United States versus United Shoe Machinery Corporation.* Cambridge, Mass.: Harvard University Press.

Killingsworth, Charles C. 1962. The modernization of West Coast longshore work rules. *Industrial and Labor Relations Review* 15 (April): 295-306.

Krueger, Anne O. 1974. The political economy of the rent-seeking society. *American Economic Review* 64 (June): 291-303.

Laffer, Arthur B. 1969. Vertical integration by corporations, 1929-1965. *Review of Economics and Statistics* 51 (February): 91-93.

Laidler, David. 1975. The welfare costs of inflation is neo-classical theory—some unsettled problems. Mimeo.

Lavington, F. 1927. Technical influences on vertical integration. *Economica* 7 (March): 27-36.

Leibenstein, Harvey. 1966. Allocative efficiency vs. X-efficiency. *American Economic Review* 56 (June): 392-415.

________. 1969. Organizational or frictional equilibria, X-efficiency, and the rate of innovation. *Quarterly Journal of Economics* 83 (November): 600-23.

Leontief, W. 1946. The pure theory of the guaranteed annual wage contract. *Journal of Political Economy* 54 (February): 76-79.

Levinson, Harold M. 1967. Unionism, concentration and wage changes; Toward a unified theory. *Industrial and Labor Relations Review* 20 (January): 195-205.

________. 1971. Collective bargaining and technological change in the trucking industry. In *Collective bargaining and technological change in American transportation,* ed. Harold M. Levinson et al., pp. 1-84. Evanston, Ill.: The Transportation Center at Northwestern University.

Lewis, H. Gregg, 1951. The labor monopoly problem: A positive program. *Journal of Political Economy* 59 (August): 277-87.

________. 1959. Competitive and monopoly unionism. In *The Public Stake in Union Power,* ed. Philip D. Bradley, pp. 181-208. Charlottesville: University of Virginia Press.

________. 1963. *Unionism and relative wages in the United States: An empirical enquiry*. Chicago: University of Chicago Press.

________. 1970. Unionism, wages and employment in U.S. coal mining, 1945-68. Mimeo. Abstract in *Western Economic Journal* 8 (September 1970): 318.

Liebeler, Wesley L. 1968. Toward a consumer's antitrust law: The Federal Trade Commission and vertical mergers in the cement industry. *UCLA Law Review* 15 (June). 1153-1202.

Livesay, Harold C., and Porter, Patrick G. 1969. Vertical integration in American manufacturing, 1899-1948. *Journal of Economic History* 29 (September): 494-500.

MacAvoy, Paul W. 1971. The regulation-induced shortage of natural gas. *Journal of Law and Economics* 14 (April): 167-99.

McCarthy, J. L. 1964. The American copper industry: 1947-1955. *Yale Economic Essays* 4 (Spring): 65-130.

McGee, John S. 1958. Predatory price cutting: The Standard Oil (N.J.) case. *Journal of Law and Economics* 1 (October): 137-69.

McGee, John S., and Bassett, Lowell R. 1976. Vertical integration revisited. *Journal of Law and Economics* 19 (April): 17-38.

McKenzie, L. 1951. Ideal output and the interdependence of firms. *Economic Journal* 61 (December): 785-803.

McKie, James W. 1955. The decline of monopoly in the metal container industry. *American Economic Review* 45 (May): 499-508.

________. 1959. *Tin cans and tin plate*. Cambridge, Mass.: Harvard University Press.

McLean, John G., and Haigh, Robert W. 1954. *The growth of integrated oil companies*. Boston: Graduate School of Business Administration, Harvard University.

McNicol, David L. 1975. The two-price system in the copper industry. *Bell Journal of Economics and Management Science* 6 (Spring): 50-73.

Macdonald, Robert M. 1967. Collective bargaining in the postwar period. *Industrial and Labor Relations Review* 20 (July): 553-77.

Machlup, Fritz. 1955. Characteristics and types of price discrimination. In *Business concentration and price policy*, ed. NBFR Conference Report, pp. 397-435. Princeton: Princeton University Press.

Machlup, Fritz, and Tauber, Martha. 1960. Bilateral monopoly, successive monopoly, and vertical integration. *Economica* 27 (May): 101-19.

Maddala, G. S. 1965. Productivity and technological change in the bituminous coal industry, 1919-1954. *Journal of Political Economy* 73 (August): 352-65.

Magat, Wesley A. 1976. Regulation and the rate and direction of induced technical change. *Bell Journal of Economics* 7 (Autumn): 478-96.

Malmgren, H. B. 1961. Information, expectations and the theory of the firm. *Quarterly Journal of Economics* 75 (August): 399-421.

Mancke, Richard B. 1974. *The failure of U.S. energy policy*. New York: Columbia University Press.

________. 1976. *Squeaking by: U.S. energy policy since the embargo*. New York: Columbia University Press.

Mandelstramm, Allan B. 1965. The effects of unions on efficiency in the residential construction industry: A case study. *Industrial and Labor Relations Review* 18 (July): 503–21.

Manne, Henry G. 1965. Mergers and the market for corporate control. *Journal of Political Economy* 73 (April): 110–20.

Markovits, Richard S. 1967. Tie-ins, reciprocity, and the leverage theory. *Yale Law Journal* 76 (June): 1397–1473.

Martin, Donald L. 1972. Job property rights and job defections. *Journal of Law and Economics* 15 (October): 385–410.

________. 1973. Legal constraints and the choice of organizational form. *American Economic Review* 63 (May): 326–34.

________. 1976. *An economic theory of the trade union: A new approach.* unpublished manuscript.

Masson, Robert Tempest. 1971. Executive motivations, earnings and consequent equity performance. *Journal of Political Economy* 79 (November/December): 1293–301.

Masson, Robert T., and Allvine, Fred C. 1976. Strategies and structure: Majors, independents, and prices of gasoline in local markets. In *Essays on Industrial Organization in Honor of Joe S. Bain*, ed. Robert T. Masson and P. David Qualls, pp. 155–180. Cambridge, Mass.: Ballinger.

Maurice, S. Charles, and Ferguson, C. E. 1973. Factor demand elasticity under monopoly and monopsony. *Economica* 40 (May): 180–86.

Miller, Merton H., and Upton, Charles W. 1976. Leasing, buying, and the cost of capital services. *Journal of Finance* 31 (June): 761–86.

Miller, Richard A. 1963. Exclusive dealing in the petroleum industry: The refiner-lesee-dealer relationship. *Yale Economic Essays* 3 (Spring): 223–47.

Mills, Daniel Quinn, 1972. *Industrial relations and manpower in construction.* Cambridge, Mass.: MIT Press.

Mishan, E. J. 1968. What is producer's surplus? *American Economic Review* 58 (December): 1269–82.

Mitchell, Edward J. (ed.). 1976. *Vertical integration in the oil industry*, Washington, D.C.: American Enterprise Institute for Public Policy Research.

Morgan, James N. 1949. Bilateral monopoly and the competitive output. *Quarterly Journal of Economics* 63 (August): 371–91.

Myers, Robert J. 1967. The mine worker's welfare and retirement fund: Fifteen year's experience. *Industrial and Labor Relations Review* 20 (January): 265–74.

Neale, A. D. 1970. *The antitrust laws of the United States of America: A study of competition enforced by law.* 2nd ed. Cambridge, U.K.: Cambridge University Press.

Nelson, Steven Robert. 1970. *An economic analysis of antitrust policy in the automotive parts industry.* Unpublished Ph.D. dissertation, University of Wisconsin.

Nerlove, M. 1967. Recent empirical studies of the CES and related production functions. In *The theory and empirical analysis of production* (Vol. 31 of NBER Studies in Income and Wealth), ed. Murray Brown, pp. 101–21. New York: Columbia University Press.

Nutter, G. Warren. 1959. The limits of union power. In *The public stake in union power*, ed. Philip D. Bradley, pp. 284-300. Charlottesville: University of Virginia Press.

Oi, Walter Y., and Hurter, Arthur P., Jr. 1965. *Economics of private truck transportation*. Dubuque, Iowa: William C. Brown.

Okuguchi, Koji. 1975. The implications of regulation for induced technical change: Comment. *Bell Journal of Economics and Management Science* 6 (Autumn): 703-705.

Pashigian, Bedros Peter. 1961. *The distribution of automobiles: An economic analysis of the franchise system*. Englewood Cliffs, N.J.: Prentice-Hall.

Peck, Merton J. 1961. *Competition in the aluminum industry, 1945-1948*. Cambridge, Mass.: Harvard University Press.

Pen, J. 1959. *The wage rate under collective bargaining*. Cambridge, Mass.: Harvard University Press.

Penrose, Edith D. 1955. Limits to the growth and size of firms. *American Economic Review* 45 (May): 531-43.

________. 1959. *The theory of the growth of the firm*. New York: Wiley.

Perry, Martin K. 1975. *The theory of vertical integration by imperfectly competitive firms*. Memorandum No. 197, Center for Research in Economic Growth, Stanford University.

________. 1976. Imperfect competition and vertical integration: The monopsony case. Bell Laboratories Economics Discussion Paper No. 56.

________. 1977a. Vertical integration of successive monopolists: A comment. Bell Laboratories Economics Discussion Paper No. 79.

________. 1977b. Price discrimination and forward integration: Alcoa reexamined. Bell Laboratories Economics Discussion Paper No. 80.

Peterman, John L. 1975a. The Brown Shoe case. *Journal of Law and Economics* 18 (April): 81-146.

________. 1975b. The Federal Trade Commission v. Brown Shoe Company. *Journal of Law and Economics* 18 (October): 361-420.

Peterson, H. C. 1973. The effect of regulation on production costs and output prices in the private electric utility industry. Memorandum No. 151, Center for Research in Economic Growth, Stanford University.

Pigou, A. C. 1920. *The economics of welfare*. London: Macmillan.

Posner, Richard A. 1975. The social costs of monopoly and regulation. *Journal of Political Economy* 83 (August): 807-28.

Primeaux, Walter J. 1977. An assessment of X-efficiency gained through competition. *Review of Economics and Statistics* 59 (February): 105-107.

Rader, Trout. 1972. *Theory of microeconomics*. New York: Academic Press.

Reddy, Nallapu N. 1975. The demand for coal: A cross-sectional analysis of multi-fuel steam electric plants. *Industrial Organization Review* 3:37-42.

Rees, Albert. 1962. *The economics of trade unions*. Chicago: University of Chicago Press.

________. 1963. The effects of unions on resource allocation. *Journal of Law and Economics* (October): 69-78.

Rehmus, Charles M. 1971. Collective bargaining and technological change on American railroads. In *Collective bargaining and technological change in American transportation*, ed. Harold M. Levinson et al., pp. 85-242. Evanston, Ill.: The Transportation Center at Northwestern University.

Reynolds, Lloyd G. 1964. The impact of collective bargaining on the wage structure in the United States. In *The theory of wage determination*, ed. John T. Dunlop, pp. 194-221. New York: St. Martin's Press.

Rice, Robert. 1966. Skill, earnings, and the growth of wage supplements. *American Economic Review* 56 (May): 583-93.

Richardson, G. B. 1972. The organization of industry. *Economic Journal* 82 (September): 883-96.

Robinson, Joan. 1933. *The economics of imperfect competition.* London: Macmillan.

Ross, Arthur M. 1948; 1956. *Trade union wage policy.* Berkeley and Los Angeles: University of California Press.

Rusin, Michael, and Atwood, Jane. 1976. Quantitative definition and measurement of vertical integration. Research Study No. 002, American Petroleum Institute.

Samuelson, Paul Anthony. 1947. *Foundations of economic analysis.* Cambridge, Mass.: Harvard University Press.

Scherer, Frederick M. 1970. *Industrial market structure and economic performance.* Chicago: Rand McNally.

Scitovsky, Tibor. 1954. Two concepts of external economics. *Journal of Political Economy* 62 (April): 143-51.

Schmalensee, R. 1973. A note on the theory of vertical integration. *Journal of Political Economy* 81 (March/April): 442-49.

Shackle, G. L. S. 1964. The nature of the bargaining process. In *The theory of wage determination*, ed. John T. Dunlop, pp. 292-314. New York: St. Martin's Press.

Sheahan, John. 1956. Integration and exclusion in the telephone equipment industry. *Quarterly Journal of Economics* 70 (May): 249-69.

Shepherd, William G. 1972. The elements of market structure. *Review of Economics and Statistics* 54 (February): 25-37.

Shultz, G. P., and Myers, C. A. 1950. Union wage decisions and employment. *American Economic Review* 40 (June): 363-80.

Simler, Norman J. 1962. The economics of featherbedding. *Industrial and Labor Relations Review* 16 (October): 111-21.

Singer, Eugene M. 1968. *Antitrust economics: Selected legal cases and economic models.* Englewood Cliffs, N.J.: Prentice-Hall.

Smith, V. Kerry. 1974. The implications of regulation for induced technical change. *Bell Journal of Economics and Management Science* 5 (Autumn): 623-32.

__________. 1975. The implications of regulation for induced technical change: reply. *Bell Journal of Economics and Management Science* 6 (Autumn): 706-7.

Spann, Robert M. 1974. Rate of return regulation and efficiency in production: An empirical test of the Averch-Johnson thesis. *Bell Journal of Economics and Management Science* 5 (Spring): 38-52.

Spence, A. Michael. 1975. The economics of internal organization: An introduction. *Bell Journal of Economics* 6 (Spring): 163-72.

Stelzer, Irwin M. 1961. The cotton textile industry. In *The structure of American industry: Some case studies*, ed. Walter Adams, pp. 42-73. New York: The Macmillan Co., 1961. (Third Edition).

Stigler, George J. 1951. The division of labor is limited by the extent of the market. *Journal of Political Economy* 59 (June): 185-93.

________. 1963. United States versus Loew's, Inc.: A note on block-booking, In *1963: The Supereme Court Review*, ed. Philys B. Kurland, pp. 152-57. Chicago: University of Chicago Press.

Teece, David J. 1976. *Vertical integration and vertical divestiture in the U.S. oil industry: Economic analysis and policy implications.* Stanford: institute for Energy Studies, Stanford University.

Telser, Lester G. 1960. Why should manufacturers want fair trade? *Journal of Law and Economics* 3 (October): 86-105.

________. 1965. Abusive trade practices: An economic analysis. *Law and Contemporary Problems* 30 (Summer): 488-505.

Theil, H., and Tilanus, C. B. 1964. The demand for production factors and the price sensitivity of input-output predictions. *International Economic Review* 5 (September): 258-72.

Troxel, C. Emergy. 1966. Telephone regulation in Michigan. In *Utility regulation: New directions in theory and policy*, ed. William G. Shepherd and Thomas G. Gies, pp. 141-86. New York: Randon House.

Tullock, Gordon. 1967. The welfare costs of tariffs, monopolies, and theft. *Western Economic Journal* 5 (June): 224-32.

________. 1975. The transitional gains trap. *Bell Journal of Economics and Management Science* 6 (Autumn): 671-79.

Turnovsky, Stephen J. 1971. The theory of production under conditions of stochastic input supply. *Metroeconomica* 23 (January-April): 51-65.

Ulman, Lloyd. 1966. *The rise of the national trade union: The development and significance of its structure, governing institutions, and economic policies.* Cambridge, Mass.: Harvard University Press.

University of Chicago Law Review 19 (Spring 1952): 583-619. Comment, Vertical forestalling under the antitrust laws.

Vernon, J. M., and Graham, D. A. 1971. Profitability of monopolization by vertical integration. *Journal of Political Economy* 79 (July/August): 924-25.

Warren-Boulton, Frederick R. 1974a. Vertical integration in telecommunications. Paper presented at the Telecommunications Policy Research Conference, Airlie House, Va., April 1974.

________. 1974b. Vertical control with variable proportions. *Journal of Political Economy* 82 (July/August): 783-802.

________. 1977a. Vertical control by labor unions. *American Economic Review* 67 (June): 309-22.

________. 1977b. The effect of factor-saving technical change on factor usage. Mimeo.

Weidenbaum, Murray L. 1975. *Government-mandated price increases.* Washington, D.C.: American Enterprise Institute for Public Policy Research.

________. 1977. *Business, government, and the public.* Englewood Cliffs, N.J.: Prentice-Hall.

Weinstein, P. A. 1960. Featherbedding: A theoretical analysis. *Journal of Political Economy* 68 (August): 379-89.

Weiss, Leonard W. 1967. *Case studies in American industry.* New York: Wiley.

Weitzman, Martin L. 1974. Prices vs. quantities. *Review of Economic Studies* 41 (October): 477-91.

Whalen, T. J., Jr. 1969. Vertical mergers in the concrete industry. *Antitrust Law and Economics Review* 3 (Fall): 113-24.

Whinston, Andrew. 1964. Price guides in decentralized organizations. In *New Perspectives in Organization Research*, ed. W. W. Cooper, H. J. Leavitt, and M. W. Shelly II, pp. 405-48. New York: Wiley.

White, Lawrence J. 1971. *The automobile industry since 1945.* Cambridge, Mass.: Harvard University Press.

Whitney, Simon N. 1955. Vertical disintegration in the motion picture industry. *American Economic Review* 45 (May): 491-89.

Williamson, Oliver E. 1964. *The economics of discretionary behavior.* New York: Prentice-Hall.

________. 1967. Hierarchial control and optimum firm size. *Journal of Political Economy* 75 (April): 123-38.

________. 1968a. Wage rates as a barrier to entry: The Pennington case in perspective. *Quarterly Journal of Economics* 82 (February): 85-116.

________. 1968b. Economies as an antitrust defense: The welfare tradeoffs. *American Economic Review* 58 (March): 18-36.

________. 1970. *Corporate control and business behavior.* Englewood Cliffs, N.J.: Prentice-Hall.

________. 1971. The vertical integration of production: Market failure considerations. *American Economic Review* 61 (May): 112-23.

________. 1975. *Markets and hierarchies: Analysis and antitrust implications—A study in the economics of internal organization.* New York: Free Press.

________. 1976. The economics of internal organization: Exit and voice in relation to markets and hierarchies. *American Economic Review* 66 (May: 369:77.

Wolfe, J. N. 1961. Coordination assumptions and multiple equilibria. *Quarterly Journal of Economics* 75 (May): 262-77.

Wu, S. Y. 1964. The effect of vertical integration on price and output. *Western Economic Journal* 2 (Spring): 117-33.

Yale Law Journal 79 (November 1969): 86-101. The logic of foreclosure: Tie-in doctrine after Fortner versus U.S. Steel.

Zelenitz, Allan. 1975. The attempted promotion of competition in related goods markets: The Ford-Autolite divestiture case. Department of Economics Working Paper No. 26, University of Pittsburgh.

Author Index

Subject Index

Law Case Index